THE MENTAL ABC's OF PITCHING

THE MENTAL ABC's OF PITCHING
A Handbook for Performance Enhancement

H.A. DORFMAN

DIAMOND COMMUNICATIONS
An Imprint of the Rowman & Littlefield Publishing Group

Lanham • South Bend • New York • Oxford

THE MENTAL ABC'S OF PITCHING:
A Handbook for Performance Enhancement
Copyright © 2000 by H.A. Dorfman

Manufactured in the United States of America

**Published by Diamond Communications
An Imprint of the Rowman & Littlefield
Publishing Group**
**4501 Forbes Boulevard
Suite 200
Lanham, Maryland 20706**
Distributed by National Book Network

Library of Congress Cataloging-in-Publication Data

Dorfman, H.A. (Harvey A.), 1935-
   The mental ABC's of pitching : a handbook for performance
enhancement / H.A. Dorfman.
      p. cm.
   ISBN 1-888698-29-2
   1. Pitching (Baseball)--Psychological aspects--Handbooks, manuals,
etc. I. Title.
   GV871.D67 2000
   796.357'22--dc21   99-047262

TABLE OF CONTENTS

Dedicated to Karl Kuehl,
Who saw the trail, built the wagon,
And put me in the driver's seat.

INTRODUCTION

Not too long ago, I had a telephone conversation with 1990 Cy Young Award winner, Bob Welch. Bobby, who had been a devoted reader of *The Mental Game of Baseball*, ended our chat by saying, "You know, you ought to write a book just on the mental game of pitching. Pitching is what the game's all about. Pitching IS the game. You know that."

Well, yes, I do believe that—and, lo and behold, I found myself following his advice and writing that book. This book.

In *The Mental Game of Baseball*, Karl Kuehl and I attempted to help athletes, coaches, and fans understand the mental inhibitors to performance and to offer strategies for getting rid of those inhibitors—allowing the athlete's talent to fully express itself. Easier said than done. We knew that. The responsibility for application was, is, and always will be the athlete's—entirely.

The Mental Game of Baseball is a fully developed presentation (337 pages), with lengthy chapters on responsibility, dedication, mental discipline, and the like.

The Mental ABC's of Pitching is a handbook, so to speak, a more succinct A-to-Z reference guide to the problems every pitcher can face before, during, and after competition—and strategies for solving these problems. The book is meant to be a companion to *The Mental Game of Baseball*, not a replacement. Naturally, it is specific to pitching. The book is an alphabetical compendium of my 15 years of experience as a mental skills instructor/counselor with the Oakland A's, the Florida Marlins, and the Tampa Bay Devil Rays.

The book is not all-inclusive for two reasons. First, I did not think it necessary to discuss everything I know about pitching. Second, I do not know everything there is to know about pitching.

The topics listed are the ones that most frequently (always?) come up when talking with a player about his pitching. I would wish the book to be comprehensive, but I realize there will be some topics not treated, either by choice or by inadvertent omission. Most listings are clearly inter-related; sometimes they seem—and may well be—synonymous. I would hope to spare the reader tedious repetitions. Yet, the inter-relatedness should illustrate and emphasize the fact that effective pitching in competition results from the applications of a very basic core of mental principles. Pitching is not just the activity of physically throwing a ball. On the other hand, it isn't, and shouldn't be, complicated; people are complicated; baseball is not. This book speaks to that complexity and simplicity.

Some entries are quite brief, either because the topic needs no elaboration on the obvious, or because the topic overlaps with another entry in the book. Others, of course, require more expansive treatment.

These ABC's address the ways pitchers can inhibit and limit their effectiveness. More importantly, they reveal how these same pitchers, when allowing themselves to apply the appropriate mental skills to the simplicity of the game, can improve themselves and enhance their performance considerably.

The greatest percentage of my time has been spent working with pitchers. They are, after all, the sinecure on the baseball field, on an elevated stage of dirt, an island in a sea of grass (or turf); the only offensive player on the defensive field. Action begins when the pitcher delivers the ball. He is pro-active; the hitter re-active. At least, that's the way it SHOULD be. All too often, however, the pitcher forfeits that edge.

This "handbook" is meant to help the pitcher recognize, develop, and maintain the advantage that is built into the game for him. It is, in the end, the pitcher's responsibility to integrate these strategies and philosophies with behavior. Actions, we all know, speak louder than words. At the end of each entry is a most important section: "WHAT THE PITCHER SHOULD DO." These are the mental and physical keys that will allow and encourage appropriate actions to "speak" for the pitcher. They are mainly mental activities, of course, that lead to the penultimate physical one of executing the next pitch.

It might be useful to the reader to glance at the complete Table of Contents before beginning the book. This will allow for familiarity with terms being used in the "SHOULD DO" sections. Helpful cross-references will then be made with greater ease.

I hope readers, Bob Welch included, find these references and entries interesting and instructive

—*H.A. Dorfman*

"I may not hope from outward forms to win
The passion and life, whose fountains are within."

—Samuel Coleridge

"I have snatched my share of joys from the grudging hand of fate as I have jogged along, but never has life held for me anything quite so entrancing as baseball."

—Clarence Darrow

"A well-executed pitch is one of the most graphic images in sports…a joy to see. But it is more rewarding to be able to perform such artistry."

—Tom Seaver

■ ADJUSTMENTS

It seems appropriate that the first entry in this alphabetical book is ADJUSTMENTS, since conventional wisdom tells us that "baseball is a game of adjustments."

To make an adjustment is to make a change, an adaptation. In the context of the baseball definition, it presumes a thoughtful, rational assessment of A) what the pitcher was trying to do, B) what went wrong, C) what he must do to fix it.

A key word here is "rational." Too often, when something goes wrong for a pitcher, he reacts emotionally, not thoughtfully. I've witnessed a range of emotional reactions on pitching mounds—from temper tantrums to submission and surrender. No poise, no rationality—no adjustment.

An immediate and very brief emotional reaction is acceptable, on the condition that it purges the pitcher of his unhappiness and frustration, and it's an internal reaction (not observable by opponents and/or teammates). Only then is it possible for the pitcher to make an adjustment and get back to the business at hand—the next pitch.

Making adjustments in the dugout after an inning is better than making no adjustment at all. Making an adjustment before the next hitter is better still. Making an adjustment before the pitch is best.

To think a pitcher will never make a mistake is unrealistic. Kevin Brown was a self-proclaimed perfectionist, but he came to realize that he had never met a perfect pitcher (or person, for that matter). He conceded he was not going to be the first one in the world. By making the necessary adjustments, Kevin learned to light a candle, instead of cursing the darkness.

1

What the Pitcher Should Do...

- Be rational, rather than emotional.
- Step off the mound and gather himself and his thoughts.
- Think of what to do, rather than what is happening "to him."
- Know what he had been trying to do, what went wrong, and what adjustment he wants to make.
- Bring his thoughts to the next pitch.
- Get back on the rubber for pitch selection and location.
- Focus on the target.
- Exhale deeply.
- Be aggressive and under control—and attack the strike zone.

■ ADVERSITY

Adversity is, at the same time, a formidable test and a stern teacher. The confrontation with difficulty, problems, or failure introduces people to themselves. Henry Fielding wrote that "adversity is the trial of principle. Without it a man hardly knows whether he is honest or not." Whether he can pass the test and learn from the experience.

During the course of my daily talks with the team before stretching each spring training, I've invariably included the reminder, "If you want to know who I am, watch me when things aren't going my way." That's an indicator I always use when observing others, when observing pitchers during competition. Unfortunately, many fail the test.

Lucretius wrote, "Look at the man in the midst of doubt and danger...It is then that true utterances are wrung from [his] recesses...The mask is torn off; the reality remains."

Here's a recurring reality: A pitcher is sailing along with a two-run lead going into the sixth inning. He gets into some trouble; the score becomes tied. He's scuffling. He "needs an out." Two men on, two out. He makes a pitch and gets a groundball to short. The shortstop boots it.

I cannot count how many times I've seen the pitcher come unglued in this circumstance, or one similar to it. His responses to an adverse situation—the disappointment that comes from thinking he had closed out the inning, only to have an error committed behind him—takes him out of his game, away from his approach, into a fog of frustration or anger or self-pity. If I had a dollar for every pitcher who failed to finish that inning, I'd have a wallet thicker than this book.

The pitcher's behavior was revealing and unacceptable. His ego took over. His thoughts centered on himself—on what was happening to him—instead of on the situation and what he could make happen to improve or remedy it. Circumstance controlled him and he took on a victim's mentality, giving himself no chance to "get the job done." Typically—my wallet gets fatter—the pitcher would invoke, "Here we go again," instead of, "Here I go." Therein is the difference between being the hunter and being the prey.

Some of the indicators I've witnessed at such times were: immediate drop of velocity, over-throwing, terrible body language, complete loss of interest and energy—quitting. Courage and discipline were not in evidence.

It should be mentioned here that all of us, at one time or another, meet with adversity away from the field, as well. The serious illness of a family member, for example, can be a terrible burden and distraction. At the ballpark my advice to players in such cases has been simple and direct. First, it must be determined whether the player should be elsewhere. Is there something he can do to remedy the situation or solve the problem? If so, then I encourage him to stop agonizing about what to do and fulfill his responsibility. Do what needs to be done.

If there is nothing that can be done—no immediate control the player can exert over the adverse circumstance to improve it—I try to help that player concentrate on what he *should* be doing at the field. That is, functioning professionally and effectively during a complicated time. Easy to say, hard to do. How many times will the reader see these words on these pages? If he had a dollar for every time…

A pitcher may feel ill himself—or tired—before and during competition. The best competitors pitch effectively even when they are not at their physical best. Actually, the body most often will provide the pitcher what he asks for if he wants to "win the war." The body's sympathetic nervous system kicks in as compensation for the fatigue or illness. A "battler" will get an extra adrenal charge. Everyone who has ever competed can remember a day (days!) when, though he felt terrible, his performance was wonderful.

When facing adversity, a choice must be made. Will it be fight—or flight? "Tough" pitchers will last longer than tough times.

What the Pitcher Should Do…

- Recognize that he will inevitably be faced with adversity in his professional and/or personal life, rather than ignoring or denying that eventuality.
- Consider, philosophically, that an adverse circumstance is a challenge, rather than a threat.
- Be self-assertive, rather than self-pitying.
- Think of possible solutions, rather than the problem.
- During competition, think about what to do (see the target; execute the pitch), rather than give in to how he is feeling.
- Recognize what is happening; get off the mound; gather his thoughts; coach himself with positive self-talk—"C'mon, attack the strike zone," "Good low strike here," "Throw through the target," or whatever MANTRA the pitcher chooses. All this, rather than forfeiting his internal control to adverse external factors of the moment.

■ AGGRESSIVENESS

One of the synonyms for "aggressive," as noted in *The American Heritage Dictionary*, is "assertive." The term will serve those well who wish to understand what aggressiveness should mean to a pitcher.

In order to be assertive, a pitcher must put himself in an attack mode. He must attack the strike zone—and establish the count in his favor. Success for a pitcher, in his confrontation with the hitter, comes from adopting that philosophy and putting it into action.

By being aggressive in the strike zone, the pitcher increases the personal likelihood of success beyond the statistical one built into the game. The statistical history of the games indicates that in the on-going battle between pitchers and hitters, the hitters will "fail" more than seven times out of every 10 at-bats. The assertive pitcher—the one who throws strikes with his best stuff early in the count—improves that statistic for himself.

"Best stuff" should be applied to each pitcher as an individual. Jamie Moyer's best stuff may be best represented by a changeup, Roger Clemens' by a fastball, Kevin Brown's by a sinker, Pedro Martinez' by his entire repetoire. The test is not *what* the pitch is, but *how* it is thrown—with commitment, confidence, assertiveness. Just throwing hard does not make a pitcher aggressive. Being under control is required to locate pitches and to command the strike zone. Greg Maddux is far from over-powering, but he is considered to be a very aggressive pitcher. He attacks *and* commands.

To be aggressive on the mound is to be pro-active, rather than re-active. The hitter will recognize the difference quickly—perceiving the pitcher to be aggressive or passive—or, worse yet, submissive. If the pitcher's goal is to avoid contact of ball with bat, he'll end up pitching mostly in hitters' counts, throwing strikes only when he "has to," often guiding the ball over the plate, instead of letting loose with his good stuff. This is an all-too-frequent occurrence. A hitter loves it; his confidence grows. The pitcher has established himself as non-aggressive, to put it in most polite terms. He's forfeited his edge, to, again, say the least.

How many times have pitchers also been told they have fielders behind them to make plays? How often have they heard that their infielders are on their toes when pitchers are aggressive—and on their heels otherwise?

Aggressors have usually been victorious throughout history, because they intimidated through confrontation. If the pitcher forfeits the advantage built into the game for him, the hitter becomes the aggressor. The pitcher is the vanquished, not the victor.

I haven't met a pitcher who argued any of these points. Pitchers know. Intelligence and understanding are there. What is missing? Trust, courage, discipline—and, inevitably, assertiveness.

It *is* possible to be too aggressive. Remember, the Greeks said it 2,500 years ago: "Nothing in excess." Balance is required—control. Over-aggressive pitchers overthrow. They "try" to attack the strike zone, but strikes don't result; there is little or no command of the body—or the pitch.

A number of the many pitchers with whom I've discussed this problem have responded to my criticism with, "But I'm a COMPETITOR!" An ineffective one, I answer. It's one thing to want to win; it's another to know how to win. Over-throwing doesn't get the competitor what he most wants—success. [See COMPETITOR]

The pitcher who is too aggressive accelerates his thought process, which quickens his delivery and tempo, tightens his arm and grip on the ball. Command thereby suffers (the pitch is usually up—in or out of the strike zone), and velocity decreases. Poor control and less-than-good "stuff" both work against the "competitor's" aggressive intent. Too much becomes too little.

Years ago, I told a minor league pitcher in the Oakland organization that he pitched like a linebacker. "I AM a linebacker," he replied. I reminded him he was supposed to be a pitcher. He had, in fact, been a linebacker at the University of Arkansas, but he learned to harness the energy and competitive spirit he had brought to football and control his emotions on the pitching mound. He got to the big leagues and is now a minor league pitching coach. He advocates an aggressive, controlled approach, I'm certain.

Toronto Blue Jays pitcher David Wells is a good example of aggressiveness under control. He's extremely competitive and relentlessly challenges hitters with his fastball. He's aggressive in any count, yet rarely yields a base-on-balls. He knows how to harness his intense emotions. He wins.

In 1998, Wells' New York Yankees teammate, Hideki Irabu, was not showing the same aggressive approach. Yankees' pitching coach Mel Stottlemyre commented late in the season that Irabu "gets mad when he comes in here [the clubhouse], but I wish he'd just get more aggressive with strikes."

"Aggressiveness," I once told a Double-A pitcher, "isn't beating up the water cooler in the dugout, it's beating up the strike zone on the field." Like lrabu, he had it backwards.

A few words about pitching inside. Many pitchers are reluctant to do so. Some fear having their pitches hit; others fear hitting the batter. (Some both!)

Pitching coaches are in general agreement as to the importance of pitchers showing a willingness to pitch inside. Most outs are gotten on pitches away from hitters. But if the hitter is allowed to look for pitches on the outer half of the plate—and comfortably anticipate the location of the pitch there—and dive into it, the results are usually going to be to the hitter's liking.

A "purpose pitch" is one that delivers the message to the hitter: "you're getting hit if you don't move." The purpose is to create discomfort for the hitter. It is part of the pitcher's plan for pitching inside, and should not be an emotional reaction based on frustration or revenge.

Experience has led me to believe that a pitcher's reluctance to pitch inside is based on his poor mental preparation for doing so. The philosophy of pitching inside may be clear to him, but the approach is not. Because of this, the individual pitcher who makes the attempt usually executes the pitch poorly. The most frequent result is a hard-hit ball or a batter hit hard .

The pitcher who is afraid of making a bad pitch inside usually aims the ball. He steers it to the spot inside on the hitter. He is being very careful to get it exactly where he knows the hitter cannot hurt him, whether it's in off the plate or on the black. A "steered" ball is not thrown with conviction or with a pitcher's best stuff. Double jeopardy: a "steered" ball usually does not get to the intended spot. The result is poor; the pitcher decides, claims, believes he can't do it—and does not anymore. After a poor result, more than one pitcher has told me that "pitching inside isn't working for me." He is surely right. The fault, however, as Caesar was told, is not in the stars but in himself. And so I advise the pitcher.

Those pitchers who do not learn to pitch inside effectively suffer in other ways, as well. Their entire approach deteriorates. The hitters, comfortable in the knowledge that pitches will be away, away, away, have an easier time. They anticipate; they lean. I remember the words of Early Wynn, a tough competitor and efffective pitcher for the Cleveland Indians in the 1950s. "If my mother was diggin' in up there [in the batter's box], I'd drill her too." No tentativeness there. No comfort for hitters he faced.

The step from being tentative to being submissive is not a long one. Having taken this step, pitchers feel themselves far removed from the confidence they value and need. A person who is non-assertive needs to change his behavior before he can gain the feeling of confidence. A pitcher must learn to act aggressively, even though he is reluctant to do so. It does not happen over night; it is a challenging process. The more ingrained the bad habit, the more challenging it is to change it.

A pitcher's fear of hitting a batter holds an interesting irony, I think. So many hitters have told me of *their* fear of being hit by a pitched ball. After all, they will feel the physical pain. Shouldn't that create another advantage for a pitcher? In theory, yes. But once again, there is no advantage if it is given away. Why should so many pitchers fear hitting batters, since it is not the pitcher's physical pain? Well, psychological pain can also be great. Nice people do not want to hurt other people. But great competitors are not "nice people" on the field of competition. [See NICE GUYS] That is not to say a pitcher should want to hit a batter; it is to say that it is not the pitcher's problem if he does hit him. An aggressive pitcher will not allow it to be his problem. If it becomes one, he no longer will be an aggressive pitcher. If the mentality suffers, the pitch will suffer, as noted above.

This is what so often happens: the pitcher either steers the ball as far away from the hitter as possible—or he hits him. It will be determined by the pitcher's *eyes*—what he's directing them at. In the first case, the pitcher looks at the safest spot to assure he won't drill the batter. In the second case, he is so concerned with hitting the batter, he continues to focus his thoughts, and subsequently his eyes, on him. That's where the ball will go because of that focus. These are not my favorite scenarios for presentation to the reader, but they are real. One cannot combat an issue he is not aware of—or does not understand.

Finally, as Kevin Brown says—and now backs up with behavior: "You had better understand that you're going to make some bad pitches along the way. That's just the way it is. Bad pitches are going to happen. But—and this is the difference—if you make a pitch AGGRESSIVELY (his emphasis), you have a much better chance of getting away with it. However, if you make a pitch tentatively or cautiously, that's when you get nailed."

What the Pitcher Should Do...

- Continually remind himself that built into the game is the pitcher's statistical advantage over the hitter.
- Use the advantage by attacking the strike zone aggressively and immediately, in order to confront the hitter and get a further edge (psychologically and through the count).
- Be aggressive by pitching with his best stuff.
- Force contact, rather than "allowing" it, or avoiding it.
- Stay in control of thoughts and delivery, rather than being over-aggressive and out of control.
- Recognize when aggressiveness becomes extreme and make an adjustment by getting off the mound and coaching self calmly with positive, functional directions. Breathe deeply.
- Trust his aggressive approach knowing that the results will not always be favorable.
- Understand the importance of throwing inside and behave according and aggressively.
- Pitch inside with his best stuff, rather than guiding the ball.
- Focus with intensity on the target the catcher provides or the spot the pitcher wants to "hit," rather than looking at the batter.
- Let it fly, rather than dart-throwing the ball. If the batter is hit by the pitch, so be it. Stay with the aggressive plan.

■ ANALYSIS

The catch-phrases are clever and hold elements of truth:

1) "analysis equals paralysis"
2) "no brain, no pain"
3) "ignorance is bliss."

But rather than accept the phrases at face value, an athlete, or anyone else for that matter, should recognize what's misleading about them.

1) Too much analysis, the wrong kind of analysis, analysis at an inappropriate time *can* result in "paralysis." On the other hand, without analysis there can be no adjustment. (How about this cliché: "timing is everything"?) The major problem seems to be that intelligent, sensitive people often "look for trouble," and, having not found any, they invent it. These inventions can become a multitude of irrelevant and/or unlikely circumstances and consequences. Life and baseball then become complicated and difficult to manage. The most insignificant possibility is analyzed in the dim light of improbability. If this process goes on directly before or during athletic activity (pitching!), disfunction can result. Paralysis. The rational system (brain) is not the initiator of this problem; the emotional system (see "sensitive" above) is the culprit.

2) Though brains may register pain, they don't cause it. Every pitcher I've ever met has had a brain with enough capacity to allow its owner to function well. Poor function by the pitcher comes from poor use of that brain. Or no use at all. Also, I've seen players with the most limited intellectual ability feel the pain of frustration and failure. Pain is not exclusive to smart players. Actually, the bigger the brain, so to speak, the more able a player will be to understand and solve whatever issue is facing him. Yet, it's also true that the more fertile a player's mind is, the more capable he is of inventing scenarios that will cause "pain." And that's why the cliché of "no brain, no pain" is invoked by so many players. ("Just kidding," many players tell me when using the phrase while talking with me. But "many a true feeling is expressed in jest.") Those who hold this feeling thereby hold the brain responsible, instead of the self that uses it ineffectively.

3) People tend to value comfort greatly, bliss even more, because it is much more rare. Yet, the so-described bliss of ignorance—not knowing what's going on around or within you—has terminated more professional pitching careers than any other factor I can think of. Comfort, the diminutive brother of bliss, has kept more pitchers at a level of mediocrity than any other factor I know. Real bliss for a pitcher is being smart and using "smarts" to his advantage, not to his disadvantage. Most of the pitchers I've encountered have not been blissful, using either of these definitions. They tend to devalue their intelligence and analytical capabilities, because they have not adequately applied them before, during or after their performances. So they yearn for the bliss they say comes with being ignorant. I, myself, would rather take my chances with whatever intelligence I've been allowed, deal thoughtfully with whatever pain comes my way, and not create any for myself. (Or for others).

Catch phrases aside, let's treat the specific tendencies of over-analytical pitchers. First, I do not agree with their frequently expressed view that they "outsmart" themselves. My experience tells me that people—I know we're talking about pitchers here—who make that claim blame their intelligence. I attribute their behavior to self-doubt, uncertainty, and a lack of confidence in and commitment to whatever it is they're doing—such as delivering a pitch. A pitcher will formulate the proposition that he doesn't know enough—he has to analyze and assess—when he really just doesn't trust himself, or his talent, or the pitch selected to be thrown. And so on.

"I'm thinking too much." Or, "I'm out-thinking myself out there." These are the people who look at other pitchers who seem to be less intelligent ("no brain"), and wish they were like them. The "no brain guys," after all, don't appear to care about consequences. "Those guys are too dumb to worry about what can go wrong," I've been told more than a few times. It's a shallow point of view. It's also wrong.

Having analytical ability is an advantage, not a disadvantage. But pitchers too often "over-analyze" what might happen to them—the consequences—or what they shouldn't do, rather than what they should do. That is the textbook formula for developing negative thinking, cynicism, fear. Effective pitchers have better perspective. They are therefore able to convert rapid analysis into immediate plan. What *to do* next is their focus.

Analysis

Example: A pitcher senses he is dropping his arm during his delivery. That "analysis" should not be an extended, disorienting process during which the pitcher is distracted by his problem and the possible catastrophe that can result if he doesn't "get things together." (Meaning get his thoughts and himself together.)

"OK, I know what I'm doing." The problem is understood. This is the pivotal point in determining what kind of thinker—or non-thinker—the pitcher is. The immediate plan (made off the rubber) is simply to remind the muscles to "get the arm up." Done. That's an adjustment. On the other hand, agonizing over the past poor pitches and whatever might have resulted from them; feeling extended anger and frustration; thinking about where the arm is during the windup or stretch; focusing on the mechanic during the delivery—those are analyses that lead to failure.

The other most common example, based on what pitchers have told me over the years, has to do with pitch selection. Pitch commitment, I should say. Bruce Hurst confessed to it while he was pitching for the Boston Red Sox early in his career. He was in his delivery, his knee was cocked, and he was saying to himself, "I shouldn't be throwing a slider here." I've heard many variations on that theme over the years. Pitchers themselves attribute the problem to over-analysis—"thinking too much." My responses to them: "Trusting too little results in 'thinking too much.'" And, "Wrong thoughts; wrong time."

It's amusing to me that Greg Maddux has, over the past few years, continued to tell the media during interviews, "I'm not that smart." Yet, he is credited with being a very analytical pitcher. His "wisdom" is in knowing how to keep pitching simple while he's performing. (Socrates would be proud of him.) When asked about prospective Cy Young Awards, or getting into the World Series, or winning 20 games, or his earned-run average, Greg's response has been, "I just execute pitches." One at a time. That's his mantra; he won't be distracted from it. No analysis there.

But when he's not pitching, he does study, he does learn. He experiments in the bullpen during side work, and he is attentive to hitters during games when he's not pitching. So there is the formula: analysis when not competing, simplicity during competition. Every brain can then serve its master.

Analysis

What the Pitcher Should Do...

- Value his intelligence and understand that analysis is a process for becoming a more effective pitcher.
- Be a keen observer of the game and all its elements, including opposing hitters, noting their strengths, weakness, and tendencies.
- Analyze how others pitch to opposing hitters—which pitchers are more effective than others and why.
- Understand that extended analysis should not take place during competition. Recognize what is going wrong, step off the mound, coach self with brief and functional directives. On the rubber, get the sign, commit to the pitch, focus on target and execute the pitch.
- Continue to develop and reinforce that philosophy. If others (teammates, parents, coaches) are over-analyzing, the pitcher has the self-assurance to keep it simple for himself during competition.

■ ANGER

"Anger," my friend Frederick Buechner has written, "in many ways is a feast... The chief drawback is that what you are wolfing down is yourself. The skeleton at the feast is you."

People who are continually angry devour, at least, much of what is good about them. An angry pitcher loses his capacity to think—to rationally assess, understand and solve whatever needs solution before his next pitch. Anger brings on the loss of control and further results in disfunction. During competition, that is tantamount to becoming a "skeleton."

The angry pitcher's brain systematically sounds an alarm system for the automatic nervous system. Adrenaline pours into the bloodstream. Blood pressure increases, breathing become abnormal. The pitcher is ready for a "fight," rather than "flight." Yes, he's willing, but unfortunately, he's not able. An angry pitcher can't think, can't see the target, can't control his muscles. That makes it rather difficult to locate a pitch. He can't control a ball if he can't control his thoughts. He's not going to put up much of a fight.

And yet, I've had some pitchers tell me they like being angry. These fellows are most often sensitive, non-assertive, inhibited, and self-doubting, who finally explode, externally or internally, as a result of "the straw that breaks their back," as they've explained it to me. The anger frees them from their self-consciousness. From feeling, as they invariably do, that they are so terribly responsible for so many things. They like the freedom anger seems to provide. "I just don't care anymore," they've said. That's only natural, since they have been caring too much about too many of the wrong things. Those concerns "just don't matter," when they are angry. For them, the prospect of failure and always wanting to please others (what they "care" about) is washed away in a raging torrent of adrenaline. They pay a dear price, however. Because it rarely, if ever, works for them. And it can't be sustained if it does. [See AROUSAL]

Anger can work for a pitcher only if it is very brief in duration. It may "clean the blood," and then be used as an attention-getter for a wandering focus; it must subside before the pitcher gets back on the rubber. If anger continues, distraction from the task at hand continues. The pitcher will be preoccupied by whatever provoked the anger—usually frustrated expectations. Being mad is not being prepared. He must deal with his anger before he is able to deal with the immediate future: before the next pitch.

The pitcher will not be able to fix what has already happened, and if he doesn't fix himself, he can look forward to further problems. He'll be punished, not so much for his anger, as by it.

What the Pitcher Should Do...

- Understand his personality and emotional tendencies.
- Recognize the degree of anger he expresses, the timing of it, the causes of it.
- Understand that anger is a strong emotion that can pre-empt rational response and interfere with controlled thoughts, breathing, muscle movement, and vision.
- Having come to understand the importance of making adjustments as quickly as possible, recognize anger during competition, and separate himself from it quickly.
- With this recognition, learn to use anger, rather than allowing it to use him, by motivating himself to "pay attention to business."
- Then direct himself—off the mound—to calm down, breathe deeply, and get ready to focus on the execution of the next pitch. Only then should he allow himself to get back on the rubber.
- Once again, take the sign, breathe, focus on the target, and let go with his best stuff.

■ ANXIETY

Performance anxiety and fear are not synonymous. Performance anxiety most often produces negative anticipation; fear often results in a flight from participation or dysfunction during it. The important point to be made is that people have used the words without making any distinction as to behavior associated with them. In the context of performance, that difference should be established.

It is quite common for an athlete to be anxious prior to his performance. When I was playing ball in college, I was assured by a story I read about a lineman with the Kansas City Chiefs, whose anxiety before games had been with him since he played in junior high school. Before every game—through junior high, high school, college and professional football—his stomach churned to such an extreme extent that he was forced to throw up. Before *every game*. One Sunday, he did not, and could not, actually. He tried to force it; it didn't happen. He told the team trainer to get him to the hospital, where doctors discovered a significant intestinal problem. He knew something was wrong, he said, because he didn't have his "normal" pre-game feeling in his gut.

A brother-in-law of mine, a professional singer, told me he threw up before singing engagements that were particularly important to him. (This after I had revealed to him my own performance anxiety.)

The performances of the football player, the singer, and my own, for that matter, did not suffer from the anxiety. I cannot speak for them, but I believe mine improved because of it. And I've spoken with many athletes since who made the same claim: essentially, when they were not aroused enough to feel anxious, they did not play up to their expectations.

Performance anxiety is considered to be a heightened arousal—an exaggerated internal response. As noted, it happens prior to performance and can happen during it, as well. Usually before or in the midst of a particular situation the athlete (pitcher) perceives as important or threatening.

What happens? 1) The performer performs—there is no "flight"; 2) the anxiety subsides and then, most often, disappears as soon as the competition or the situation is *faced directly*, physically; 3) the initial heightened arousal is converted from anxiety to intensified focus, that is, from tension to attention. The performer, having placed such significance on the event, becomes more attentive in his approach. The key is to properly channel the stimulus, so that function is enhanced and dysfunction avoided. (Much like what must be done with anger.)

Pre-performance anxiety is not an anxiety disorder. It may bring "old age [on] too soon" (Ecclesiastes), and it may be an unpleasant feeling, but if understood and managed, it is rarely debilitating once performance begins.

[See FEAR]

What the Pitcher Should Do...

- Be aware of anticipatory feelings prior to the game, or the feelings produced by the advent of a critical situation within the game.
- If a feeling of pre-performance anxiety exists, distract himself from it by re-directing his focus during pre-game preparation. (Some pitchers put on earphones and listen to music {vocals are particularly helpful because language is provided as an alternate to the pitcher's thoughts; the pitcher should be attentive to the lyrics}. Others engage in conversation with teammates. This is done, not to distract the pitcher from an effective mental preparation, but rather to improve it. The activity addresses anxiety-producing thoughts; the pitcher is responsible for changing them. The timing and degree of activity is adjusted, through experimentation, according to the pitcher's individual needs.)
- As the final preparation, focus on his plan: what he wants to do vs. the opposition; reminders of his own mental "keys"; reminders of his mechanical keys (keeping it simple). (He is channeling mental energy, converting it from anxiety to intensity. The focus is on the game not himself and his feelings.)
- When the game begins, consider a feeling of anxiety to be just another distraction, and treat it as such. Get off the mound, coach himself, and be certain to employ self-talk, using action-oriented, positive language. In other words—what he wants to do.
- Usually, tempo suffers during times of negative anticipation. Recognize these moments and make the appropriate adjustment. He should gain control of his thoughts and his body. [See TEMPO]
- Understand that there is nothing wrong with having pre-performance anxiety. Many of the best athletes have it. But they control it, rather than having it control them. As noted, many use it as a tool for motivation for attentiveness. Be attentive to function, rather than feelings.

■ APPROACH

When talking with pitchers about their performance, I make certain to lead the discussion toward how the pitcher approaches his profession: his general preparation, that is, his daily regimen—eating, sleeping, conditioning habits—and his routine at the ballpark. We then move down to the bottom rung on the ladder of abstraction. We talk about the very specific matter of his approach on the mound during performance, his identifiable behaviors—internal and external—during competition. Essentially, it's the litmus test for a pitcher; his approach will determine how successful he will be.

One of the meanings of the word 'approach' is: "the method used in dealing with or accomplishing something." 'Method' is the key word here, indicating *how* one goes about trying to accomplish whatever it is he sets out to do. In the case of pitching, the accomplishment is in executing pitches successfully. Getting outs is about results, remember. Making good pitches is about behavior. THAT is what pitchers and I talk about; first making the distinction between approach and result, then addressing the "hows."

How to eat properly, how to regulate sleeping patterns, how to get in shape and stay in shape are usually very obvious to players. (Whether or not they apply what they know is another matter.) Less obvious, and more difficult to apply even when understood, is how to mentally prepare between appearances, during bullpen sessions and during games (as a non-participant)—and how to think and act *during* competition.

As a youngster in elementary school, I was taught in arithmetic lessons that large fractions are unwieldy and unmanageable. It is, I was told, too difficult to add, subtract, multiply, and divide them. For example, how, as a fourth-grader, could I be expected to divide 160/48000 by 8000/24000? I was not, and I could not. (We had no calculators then.) But I could manage 1/30 divided by 1/3. By reducing to *lowest terms*—by getting those fractions to be as simple as they could be—I could effectively deal with the example and get the answer: 1/10. (The "lowest common denominator" was the vehicle for approaching the addition and subtraction of the large fractions.)

Now, let me specifically and simply apply this lesson to a pitcher's approach—the way it's supposed to be applied by the pitcher himself. The lowest common denominator every pitcher shares is the delivery of the next pitch. What has happened and what might happen will vary with each pitcher and each circumstance. But the next pitch must be made. It is a universal truth within the game. That is how the game progresses. One manageable pitch at a time. That is the focus of the moment—for observers and participants. That is the action reduced to simplest term: the moment, the task at hand, that next pitch.

But does this moment exclusively hold the pitcher's attention? If not, the approach suffers. A pitcher cannot expect the result he desires. The more complicated and scattered his thoughts, the more unmanageable his task. His distractions will force him to "think big," rather than "think small." Focus on the target will not be intense. This one "small" deficit becomes the pitcher's biggest inhibitor to pitching effectively.

The pitchers I've been with over the years have revealed any number of different intrusive and distracting thoughts. It is the human predicament to have conflicting thoughts and impulses. "Isn't that normal?" I've been asked many times, after having admonished a pitcher for his poor approach on the mound. It is, yes, but to be "normal"—ordinary—should not be the goal of an elite athlete, particularly a professional. "Exceptional" is the goal; "normal" is the excuse.

"Keep it simple," I say constantly. It should be a pitcher's mantra, as it is Greg Maddux', for example. Big thoughts, many thoughts, conflicting thoughts all divide the pitcher's attention, thereby corrupting his approach. A task is not done well if not approached well. It is critical for pitchers to understand and embrace the simple approach noted below.

The approach leads to a result. A good approach has a much better chance of producing the desired result. However, that is not an inherent guarantee within the game of baseball. Results *cannot be controlled.* A pitcher may execute a fine pitch—in his and everyone else's judgment—but the hitter battles it. That right-handed hitter goes and gets the nasty slider low and away, stroking a line drive double into the right-center field gap. Good approach by the pitcher, undesirable result. He *can* control the approach. Always. He can't control what happens after the pitch has been delivered. Never. He executed the pitch; he should repeat his behavior, instead of concerning himself with what the hitter just did.

I tell every pitcher that he defines himself by the way the ball leaves his hand. That's what indicates the quality of his approach. His plan, his poise, his intensity, his aggressiveness, his focus. His breathing pattern, his tempo, his body language. That is *behavior.* That is approach.

Approach   19

(Directly related, and as important, is the pitcher's response, which will be addressed in the "R" ·section of the book.)

What the Pitcher Should Do...

- Understand that the manner in which he approaches his goals and tasks identifies him to his teammates, his opponents, and, if he is paying attention, to himself.
- Examine the quality and extent of his preparation leading up to performance—his habits regarding sleep, nutrition, workouts, and routines.
- Recognize his past behavioral tendencies during competition, especially in difficult times and situations.
- Recognize that his approach is comprised of thought and deed; it is entirely his responsibility and within his control. (Results are *not*.)
- Understand what an approach to pitching, during the game itself, actually means. [See above.]
- Be aware of thoughts and behaviors that are not conducive to peak performance and make the necessary adjustments as quickly as possible. [See ADJUSTMENTS]
- Remind himself to reduce pitching to its most manageable form— one pitch at a time.
- Follow a consistent procedure during his performance. For example, step on the rubber, take the sign, exhale deeply, begin the delivery, focus on the target and attack the strike zone. Any thoughts or feelings that intrude on that approach should be dealt with off the rubber. The more serious intrusions and distractions will require him to get off the mound to make the mental adjustment.
- Hold himself accountable for asserting the mental discipline of an incorruptible approach.

■ AROUSAL

Many players I've been associated with, when asked what "arousal" means, tell me "being psyched-up—let's go!" Others have related the term to anxiety: having heightened feelings (heart palpitations, sweaty palms, diarrhea), they say, stimulated by a negative anticipation of the performance ahead. According to those responses, a pitcher, then, may be "worked up" for better or for worse. And so it is.

Studies have shown that athletes typically experience physical symptoms before competition in which they invest meaning. The best competitors I know invest the meaning of "challenge" to each pitching performance. Bruce Bochy managed Kevin Brown in San Diego during the 1998 season and was impressed by the challenge Kevin saw before each performance—"the fire and intensity that he [Brown] brings to every game he pitches," Bochy said. Some pitchers view competition as a "threat." There are those who invest minimal meaning to each game, and still others whose assessment is "reliably unpredictable," to borrow the words of novelist Brooks Hansen.

Each pitcher's arousal level is influenced by his interpretation of the event or situation he is to face. It is also influenced by the degree of trust he has in himself. The elite pitcher knows himself; he manages whatever physical indicators exist prior to his performance. He knows whether he has too much energy ("I'm hyper."—"I'm out of control.") or too little ("I can't get up for this."—"I can't get my mind on business.")

When a pitcher and I talk about finding an appropriate arousal level, we first examine the type of personality he has. For example, some people are introverted, others extroverted. Some are hyperactive, others "laid back."

We then consider the differences in types of activity and the particular arousal level for each. Remember the linebacker referred to earlier? When playing football, his high-energy, high arousal served him because that gross motor activity involved strength, stamina, physical contact, and bursts of speed. Pitching requires fine muscle movements, precision and control, balance, and intense concentration on a small field of attention (the target). During competition, a pitcher is more likely to require "calming" mechanisms (as would a golfer) than those requiring more "power" (as would a weightlifter).

And personality? Many sports psychologists believe that individuals have distinctive biological differences affecting arousal. An extrovert tends to produce a slower and less pronounced stimulus than does an introvert. For the extrovert, there is a need for more intense input. The introvert, often the "more sensitive" person spoken of earlier in the book, tends to produce a stronger sensory signal for himself, and so requires less input to become aroused.

Many pitchers (many *people*) see the opposite as being true, because of a pitcher's outward appearance. They don't see inside the pitcher, however. They see fire in a Kevin Brown's eye, perhaps, but not in Jamie Moyer's. They've seen it in Dennis Eckersley but not in Bob Tewksbury. But all of these pitchers have a competitive approach. And they have all developed their own methods for optimal arousal, based on how they are predisposed to feel before performance. The fact is, is a high-energy personality needs a greater in-put to generate his greater need for excitement, more fuel to keep that motor running. He has a higher threshold for arousal and uses external sources of stimulation (a "big" game). Introverts don't require those outside signals. They tend to have more developed fine motor skills. They are usually "control (command) guys," not power pitchers.

Most important is the ability of a pitcher to properly adjust and channel whatever level of arousal he's feeling. To "psyche up" or "psyche down," according to need. The metaphor I use is the flame of a kerosene lamp. "If it flickers, it will be of no use," I tell the pitchers. "At the other extreme, you don't want to burn the house down! Heat and light, that's what we want. Heat and light. The same with arousal."

What the Pitcher Should Do...

- Understand his individual predisposition toward anticipated competition.
- Determine the level of arousal he has had when his performances have been positive, as well as the level when they have not been satisfactory.
- Recognize the possibility that he may need to heighten his pre-game arousal—turn the flame up. If so, he should concentrate his thoughts on his game strategy and visualize past performances when he has dominated, in order to get adrenaline flowing early.
- Recognize the possibility that he may need to lower his arousal—turn the flame down. If so, he should sit in a quiet place, breathe

deeply in a consistent pattern, relax his muscles and employ self-talk in a calming and low-key manner.

- During the game, if necessary, get off the mound and make the same adjustments, though for shorter duration. An example of self-talk to heighten arousal: "Let's go! Get focused; attack the strike zone!" To lower arousal: "Be easy now. On the target; good, low strike here."

■ ATTITUDE
[See APPENDIX A]

Viktor Frankl, in his profound book, *Man's Search for Meaning*, speaks of our ability to be self-determining. "Man does not simply exist," Frankl writes, "but always decides what his existence will be... [E]very human being has the freedom to change at any instant... The last of the human freedoms is to choose one's attitude in any given set of circumstances, to choose one's own way."

In other words, we are not bound to be tomorrow what we have been today; we are not bound to act tomorrow as we have acted today. We have the freedom to make a choice about our attitude.

Players I've come across who were considered to have bad attitudes are, as their teammates so directly put it, "clueless" about all this. The players with good attitudes act like "free" people, and they are healthier and happier—and greatly valued by people in the organization they're with. And they play to their peak far more consistently than "bad apples." They *always* contribute to the team—by their example alone.

The major point, for me, is that they are free. Players with poor attitudes are unhappy—and victims of themselves, though they are quick to blame circumstance or other people when confronted about unacceptable behavior. They have forfeited their freedom. They wait for the world to make them happy. It does not happen often, and when it does, it doesn't last very long.

To ask why people have bad attitudes is to open the subject beyond what is necessary here. As it is to ask why people have good attitudes. What is clear to me is that all the players I've met understand the difference. I would further say that *almost* all appreciate the benefits of having a healthy attitude. Some just do not have the personal strength and self-discipline to work on changing. They are victims, then, of their bad habits also.

In *The Mental Game of Baseball*, Karl Kuehl and I spoke about attitude as it related to cooperation, openness to learning, selflessness, responsibility and their opposite "bad attitudes." We spoke of the effect an attitude has on all dimensions of a player's performance—and his life. Whether it be in calm or troubled waters, the relationship between the sailor's attitude and his voyage should be clear. A troubled sailor makes for a troubling voyage.

A pitcher doesn't have to be a troublemaker on a team to qualify as having a bad attitude. He is a troublemaker for himself. Negative expectations burden him and inhibit his performance. His perspective on his performance, and on life in general, is clouded to such an extent that he cannot make necessary changes. He just bemoans his fate and/or disparages himself. His self-talk works against him. And on it goes.

One pre-eminent pitcher in the big leagues had been accused of having a less-than-desirable attitude. It annoyed others, at worst, and it frustrated him, at best. He wasn't entirely who he was perceived to be, and he didn't entirely like who he perceived himself to be. When he was asked what his association with me was like, he responded simply by saying, "He holds a [expletive deleted] mirror up in front of your face and forces you to look in it."

Then what? The pitcher has the *choice* of being honest about what he sees, and the *freedom* to change what he sees and does not like. Some encouragement may have been helpful; personal commitment and determination on the pitcher's part was responsible for the change.

The best attitudes exist in pitchers who understand themselves and the game of baseball. These pitchers are selfless, rather than selfish. They do not pitch for their statistics; the team's success concerns them more. They understand the difference between approach and result, so they are focused on their own behavior, instead of what "happens to them." It is amazing to me, though it shouldn't be, to observe the upbeat attitude of a pitcher who has that perspective. His performance generally reflects it. The people who play behind him feel it. Their performance generally reflects it.

A few words about the term "attitude" as used by those who say a pitcher "has an attitude" when he competes. The extensional meaning in that context defines the pitcher as tough-minded, aggressive, and insensitive to irrelevant environmental conditions—conditions which would distract someone without the "attitude." Exemplars: Todd Stottlemyre, Tim Belcher, Pat Hentgen. Years ago, when I first saw Bob Gibson pitching for the St. Louis Cardinals, I was struck by his relentlessness. Another outstanding attitude. Such pitchers give no quarter; they are "pit bulls" who will have to be dragged off the mound. Theirs is an "attitude" that gets respect in their dugout and in the one across the field.

Our attitude is the state of mind with which we approach our surroundings, our performance, our teammates, our opponents, and our lives.

What the Pitcher Should Do...

■ Make himself aware of his existing attitudes through honest evaluation.

■ Make the effort to understand why and how these attitudes were developed.

■ Appreciate the freedom of choice he has to change an attitude, rather than feeling he is destined to stay the same because of genes or circumstance.

■ Recognize what attitude changes, if any, he would like to make.

■ Exert the consistent energy to forming and reforming desired attitudes through self-awareness and persistence.

■ Understand the many choices of attitudes that exist. Choices between attitudes of being:

> Pessimistic or optimistic
> Cooperative or uncooperative
> Open-minded or close-minded
> Responsible or irresponsible
> Selfless or selfish
> Committed or indifferent
> Realistic or unrealistic
> A problem solver or a problem causer
> Relentless or yielding—And so on.

■ BALANCE

Baseball provides many lessons for players—lessons that are too often lost because they become clichés. A cliché is timeworn and familiar. But it is *true*, and that is why it has endured—to become a cliché. What happens to the truth is that it's heard so much that the familiarity, though not necessarily breeding contempt, does breed inattentiveness. It encourages people to take its meaning for granted.

"Keep on an even keel" is one example. Many players don't know what a "keel" is. Most don't know what it means in its original context. They *do* say, when I ask them, that it means, "keep your highs low and your lows high." A mixed metaphor, for sure, but they're on a ballfield, not in an English class. The general idea is understood.

Specifically, "an even keel" is supposed to present an image of "steadiness." The "highs and lows" address an appropriate range of emotions, similar to the example of the flame discussed previously. In this case, it is not so much about arousal as it is about the extremes of elation and depression.

The term "balance" is my choice when discussing the idea with pitchers. The image is a balance beam. The trick in competition, and in life, is to stay on the balance beam. "You can fall off to either side," I say. "One by being too aggressive, the other by being too cautious/submissive."

A pitcher will have a tendency to fall off a particular side. I tell the pitcher that my preference is for him to be too aggressive, rather than passive. An overly aggressive pitcher will scramble right back up on the beam to try his balance again. The fellow who falls off because he's too cautious is often reluctant to get back on the beam. Neither extreme will serve the pitcher well.

An analogy I often use is a racecar and its driver. The car has an accelerator and a brake. The use of the accelerator will allow the driver to win the race; the use of the brake will ensure that he finishes. Speed is aggressiveness; brake is control of the car—no walls being hit. The proper balance—"moderation," the Greeks called it, gives us all a chance in our races.

Another example pitchers can understand easily is the read-out from an EKG. If the pitcher is having his heart checked, and the graphic shows his beat to be irregular to the extremes—jumping from too high to too low—the physician will be very concerned by these extremes. If, on the other hand, the line is straight across the paper, the pitcher is dead. Health is the consistent up and down within a narrow range. The highs, low; the lows, high.

To have balance, as a pitcher, is to not be swayed by events, surroundings, or emotions. It is to perform—"walk on the beam"—with a command of attitude, with understanding of purpose, with a trust in his ability and a relaxed focus on his task. It is to maintain balance through a consistent perspective about pitching, about the situation, and about himself.

King Harald the Ruthless (1015-1066) paid his highest compliment to a particularly valued person by describing him as unaffected by sudden events. "Whether it was danger or relief or whatever peril loomed, he was never in higher or lower spirits, never slept less or more, and never ate and drank save according to custom," said the admiring King. A 900-year-old balance beam.

Here's a favorite excerpt from *The Way of Life According to Lao Tzu*:

Not to have edges that catch
But to remain untangled,
Unblinded,
Unconfused,
Is to find balance,
And he who holds balance beyond sway of love or hate,
Beyond reach of profit or loss,
Beyond care of praise or blame,
Has attained the highest post in the world.

What the Pitcher Should Do...

- Understand that properly balanced behavior, rather than extreme behavior, is conducive to peak performance.
- Recognize the individual predisposition for immoderate behavior, that is, "Am I too aggressive or too passive?" (The answer will be obvious, if the question need be asked in the first place.)
- Apply the appropriate techniques and strategies, as presented in ADVERSITY, ADJUSTMENTS, AROUSAL, *et. al.*
- Using the example of Lao Tzu, perhaps, maintain an awareness of how the pitcher reacts to different situations and people.
- Develop a personal definition of balance—or "credo"—to use as a model for application on the mound and in life.

■ BEHAVIOR

"Behavior" is the pay-off word. Everything already read in this book leads to behavior. Everything that remains to be read leads to behavior. Good behavior provides a good payoff; poor behavior yields no payoff. Executing a pitch is behavior; battling is behavior; throwing a fit is behavior; caving in is behavior. The most important thing a pitcher can do is behave appropriately. Having done so, he can take whatever happens like a man. He can come to terms with results, because he has come to terms with himself. He did as much as he could do. That is all anyone can ever ask of him. That's all he should ever ask of himself.

It is a lot to ask. Nevertheless, behaving well as a performer and as a person is the entire responsibility he has. Preparation, approach, adjustments—behaviors all. They stem from thoughts, attitudes, and beliefs (the next topic to be discussed). Too often, they stem from feelings. The pitcher who operates out of his feelings—who concerns himself with his feelings—is the pitcher with whom I spend the most time. He is the pitcher who invariably will get little or no "payoff," until he learns to perform in spite of feelings that are troubling to him. If his behavior is driven by these feelings, I tell him, he can expect more "trouble."

The pitcher must train himself to act out what he knows instead of what he feels. If he acts bravely and wisely, I suggest to him, his feelings will change. The habit of behaving appropriately will be established. Habit is powerful. He must, as Lawrence Durrell has written, "begin by pretending, in order to end by realizing." (Remember the song from *The King and I*—"I Whistle A Happy Tune?"—"Whenever I feel afraid, I hold myself erect ...for when I fool the people I fear, I fool myself as well...") I try to assure the pitcher that if he fools himself for a short while, he will become what he acts out for a long while. "The parody of goodness," Durrell added, "can make you really good."

Angels pitcher Tim Belcher, in a recent interview, commented on my propensity for saying to pitchers, himself included, "I don't care about your feelings—I care about your actions." In other words, their behavior. My recommendation is that, at the end of a performance, a pitcher should evaluate himself according to that behavior—grade himself out. [See APPENDIX B] The more he addresses behavior, the more apt he is to be successful. Pitchers who have used APPENDIX B regularly have found this to be true—not because of the sheet, but because of their heightened aware-ness of their actions. They shift their concern from outside distractions, feelings, "pressures," and concentrate instead on behaviors that will help "get the job done." Done well.

What the Pitcher Should Do...

- Understand that behavior is driven by thought and feelings.
- Recognize the particular driving force within the pitcher before, during, and after competition.
- During performance, be certain that the rational is in charge, rather than the emotional. That is, focusing on what to do, rather than on how he feels. If necessary, make the appropriate adjustment. [See ADJUSTMENTS]
- Discipline himself to act out enhancing behavior, despite inhibiting feelings.
- Through repetition, integrate what he knows, rather than what he feels, into behavior.
- Hold himself accountable for behavior by grading himself after each performance, using APPENDIX B.
- Pursue his own understanding of excellence, rather than others' expectations for him.

■ BELIEF

One man with a belief is worth 99 with an opinion. Though everyone in the game of baseball has an opinion, the opinions of others should be of no concern to the pitcher. What *should* matter to him is what he thinks of himself and what he knows about pitching: his belief system. If he doesn't have one, he'd better develop it.

"Man is what he believes," Chekhov wrote. If every pitcher (player, person) believed what others have said about him, he would then be defined by those others, rather than by himself. It is an all-too-common tendency—a "normal" human tendency. People are often inclined to live from the outside in, rather than from the inside out. They respond to others' possible perceptions of them, rather than developing themselves into self-assertive, confident individuals. [See CONFIDENCE]

It is impossible for a pitcher to be confident in competition if he is concerned with others' evaluation of him. He will act out of that concern ("worry" is the word I usually hear). He will be terribly distracted by it. As a result, aggressiveness suffers, focus suffers, objective self-evaluation suffers. The pitcher suffers.

Dave Stewart did his share of suffering. In 1984, he had a 7-14 record with the Texas Rangers. In 1985, he was 0-6 with Texas and Philadelphia. He had a much-publicized off-field incident. The Phillies released him in May 1986. The Japanese team that had an interest in Stewart told him to stay home. He was not coveted by Major League organizations.

Dave Stewart's belief in himself as a man and as a talent never wavered. He won the Rangers' 'Good Guy Award' for 1985. Lesser men would not have shown up at the award ceremony to accept the honor, in light of public knowledge of the off-field humiliation. Stew showed up. He addressed what surely was an uncomfortable audience, and put them at ease immediately. "Sometimes," he began, "good people do bad things...."

Dave Stewart could still believe in himself, while not believing in a singularly weak behavior of his. He could also make the distinction between belief in his talent and recognition of conditions within himself and outside himself that resulted in his not winning a Major League game for almost two years.

Coming to an environment where his belief system was reinforced, rather than challenged, he became the outstanding pitcher and community exemplar he had always known he could be. (Twenty or more victories in four consecutive seasons with the Oakland Athletics—1987-1990.)

I remember well a wager I made with one of Oakland's minor league instructors. This individual had been on the Texas coaching staff in '84 and '85. He offered the wager against my spring training optimism regarding Dave Stewart's performance for the upcoming season, 1987. "A steak dinner on me at any restaurant you choose if he is anything better than a .500 pitcher," he said. "If not, you buy." I took the bet.

We ate at Ruth's Chris in Scottsdale, Arizona, in June. My colleague had conceded. Stew's record was 9-1 at the time.

All environmental factors do not support our belief system. The challenge is to rise above a poor or challenging environment. It is another very difficult task on the road to self-fulfillment as an athlete and as a human.

During an Oakland Athletics' seminar on leadership training, I had the opportunity to "set up" one of our staff members—to challenge his belief system as an experiment. Of course, I felt he would be a good sport about it, and he was.

The situation was set up so as to have three others, two coaches and a manager, in on the experiment. They knew what was going on. I stood at a writing board in front of the entire minor league staff. They were seated in rows of chairs, and the men involved in the "experiment" were in the front row. On the board I wrote the number 2; under it I put another 2, with a + sign to left of it. I drew a line under the numbers. So it was a simple arithmetic example: two plus two.

The "set-up" staff member was the fourth to be called on. The first coach, having been asked for the answer to the example, said, "Five." The next person, a manager, said, "Five." The third "plant" answered, "Five."

Now it was the victim's turn. Without hesitation, he responded, "Five." The room was in an uproar. The victim was, despite initial embarrassment, mostly angry with himself for selling out his belief. It can happen that easily. I then tried to explain the process of having that belief—the "absolute" knowledge that the answer is four—eroded.

The first person says "five" and the victim says to himself something like, "Is this guy wacky?" The second response of "five" makes the victim look at the example on the board with more "concentration," asking himself something like, "What's going on here? What am I missing?" The third "five" leads to panic, the victim knowing he has to speak in a moment. That fear of being wrong leads to a collapse of his belief system.

It is a valuable lesson about how vulnerable people can be to forces that may reveal a self they don't want others to see. They become blind as to what they want to be, seeing instead what others might think them to be.

To understand the results a placebo, a sugar pill, can get is to understand the power of belief. Many medical studies support this view. Psychoneuroimmunology addresses the theory, validated by research, that the body manufactures disease fighting cells if the patient, a person discovered to have cancer, for example, is upbeat, aggressive, and an active participant in his own healing process. This patient, who believes in himself and in life, is not a "victim." He is a battler, a winner. And it usually is revealed by pathology, during his immune system's battle with the disease. His "stats" for survival are by far superior to those of someone who believes in the disease more than in himself and his approach for combating it.

What the Pitcher Should Do...

- Understand the power of belief. He is what he believes. [See CONFIDENCE]
- Understand that every person is vulnerable to forces, outside himself and within himself, forces that challenge his beliefs and are capable of eroding them.
- Recognize that his own belief in himself and in his talent is prerequisite for becoming an elite pitcher.
- Believe also in his knowledge of what it takes to be successful, as gained from direct and vicarious experience.
- Remember that this faith and knowledge is of little value unless "it informs every action" (de Duras) he takes.
- In competition, use his beliefs as an instrument to focus on the task at hand, rather than on doubts that inevitably arise.
- Review the process of making that adjustment, if necessary.

Belief

■ BIG INNING
(Preventing It)

Almost always on the agenda for spring training pitchers' meetings is the topic, "stopping the big inning." Pitching coaches place great emphasis on trying to develop in pitchers the ability to extricate themselves from potentially disastrous innings—innings in which the opposing team scores many runs.

All manner of contributions may be heard during those discussions—from both coaches and players. Each contributor is trying to "find a way" to accomplish the task of "stopping the bleeding."

Pitchers frequently offer their personal bad experiences from these innings—their thoughts and feelings as the disasters developed. I have heard, "Before I knew what was happening, I'd let five runs five in." The words should be a terribly significant revelation to those who hear them—or read them. Many of those in the room where they were spoken, nodded their collective heads. One pitcher said what others were thinking, "Been there, done that."

Actually, nothing was done *by* the pitcher. "Before he knew what had happened," indicates that. He "was done" by the inning, so to speak. If awareness is prerequisite to making an adjustment, not knowing what is happening makes adjustments impossible. And that is essentially the nature of the "disaster" the pitchers spoke of. They felt helpless; they didn't have a chance to recognize what they'd been trying to do, what had gone awry, and how they were going to fix it. The inning, as I indicated, had "happened" to them; they themselves were not capable of making anything happen.

So the first order of business for "stopping the big inning" is for the pitcher to stop himself. To gather himself [See GATHERING]—get off the mound, collect his thoughts, recognize the situation and have a plan before toeing the rubber again. By doing this, the pitcher assures himself of "knowing what's happening." He then has a chance of doing something about it.

Pitchers do not "stop the bleeding" if, as noted, they do not stop themselves. The tendency of pitchers in trouble is to speed up [See TEMPO] They want to get out of the inning quickly, get off the mound, get into the dugout—now! The greater a pitcher's sense of urgency, the more he rushes his mind and muscles. Self-control leaves him. The inning "wins"; the pitcher loses.

Other pitchers who "tell on themselves" in the meetings speak of their internal reactions when they find themselves looking at runners on every base, with no outs having been recorded. They talk of being "overwhelmed" by the situation, at worst, and "very pressured," at best. What to do now? They didn't know. Runs will almost surely score. The focus is on forces outside themselves—on runners and runs, rather than execution of a pitch. No solution there.

Still other pitchers have the perception that a "big inning" means having had two runs scored. I recall a minor leaguer pitching for Oakland's Madison, Wisconsin, farm team years ago. He became so angry after two runs had scored, he threw his next pitch over the stands behind home plate—out of the ballpark.

I was witness to this adventure, amusing in an obvious way, but not so to the pitcher. After the inning, in the dugout, I waited a few moments and then went over to the young man. We had words. Actually, I had words. When I finally gave him an opportunity to speak, he explained the "terrible" results of the inning: two runs. I'd like to believe his viewpoint has changed. Certainly his behavior has. (He's still pitching, recovered from arm surgery, and will be in a major league spring training camp this year.)

After all the confessions at the pitchers' meetings, after all the perceptions and definitions, the question of how to get out of the "big inning" is addressed directly. At that time, pitchers are asked to volunteer their more positive approaches. The first response from a pitcher is a view held that, in a bases-loaded, no-out situation, if only two runs score, "I'm golden." A different pitcher says he will concede the run from third base. And on it goes. But this discussion or dispute is philosophical, not practical. What should the pitcher *do*?

Before I address that question in a meeting—and it is the essential question—I issue a warning. "Anytime," I begin, "*Anytime* the focus is put on the definition of an inning, the perception of it, the concern for runners and runs, the idea of making special a particular situation (the "big inning"—a negative, at that), something very important—most important— will be pre-empted: the pitcher's focus on executing the next pitch.

"And *that* is what will give you a chance to avoid 'big innings.' We get outs by paying attention to the task in front of us, not the runners behind us."

Calling attention to special situations [See SHUT-DOWN INNING] is an attempt to forewarn pitchers of pitfalls. But being forewarned is not entirely being forearmed. The warnings make distinctions between "big innings," big games, small games, tie games...and such, in order to illustrate the variety of problems pitchers may face. But the "last word" on the subject(s) is, "There may be any number of problems; there is only one solution: Think small; execute the next pitch. You can manage that."

Reducing to lowest terms.

What the Pitcher Should Do...

- Understand that preventing a "big inning" is a legitimate and significant philosophical concern.
- Understand further that, though the prospect of a "big inning" exists, the reality, the prevention of it, or the stopping of it depends—to a great extent—upon the nature of his thoughts and behavior.
- Recognize his own tendencies of thought and behavior anticipating the adversity, during and/or after it.
- Understand that "big inning" is too large a thought to manage during competition.
- Be aware of the tendency of people—pitchers included—to speed up their thoughts and actions during perceived crisis.
- Remember, if this is the case, to break rapid tempo by stepping off the mound, gathering thoughts, breathing deeply, and focusing on task—pitch execution.
- At meetings and on the mound, know the difference between a broad focus and a narrow, concentrated one.

■ BODY LANGUAGE

A pitcher should ask himself this question, "Do I want to be perceived as a focused and relentless competitor?" If the answer is affirmative (if it is not, why is he reading this book?), then he must know how to look the part before he can play it. A pitcher who gives off signals of vulnerability will not act out appropriate behavior. Furthermore, opponents and teammates will recognize these signals. The actual perception of the pitcher will fall far short of the one he values and desires.

Wearing one's heart on his sleeve is dangerous in competition, if it is not the "heart of a lion." More appropriately, the heart of a warrior. I speak here of body language, a language understood by anyone who is paying attention. Why would any pitcher want to project, through his posture and movement, the language of frustration, uncontrolled anger, self-pity, fear, or complacency? He would not, I believe. That the pitcher may be speaking through his body in any of these ways is an indication that he has been distracted and disturbed. He cannot effectively compete. He's not fit for combat.

It is hard for many to believe that the pitcher, himself, is most often not aware of the signals he is giving off. But consider this: if he's distracted from attention to task because of his frame of mind, then he is focused on the major concern of the moment. It follows that, as absorbed as he is, he is inattentive to all else—including his appearance.

It is natural enough for people to want things to go their way. It is just as natural for them to be affected when they do not get what they want. The test of each individual is how he responds to such a circumstance. He can rise above his disappointment, or he can sink below it. A pitcher's body language indicates whether he is in the process of elevating himself or burying himself. [See RESPONSE]

The nature and degree of disappointment will vary, but the appearance of a pitcher during competition should not vary, for consistent behavior leads to consistent performance. Poor body language leads to poor performance. It is *already* poor behavior—and not consistent with the pitcher's physical actions when things are going well for him. [See CONSISTENCY]

A few years ago, while seated in the Florida Marlins' dugout for the opening spring training game, I was chatting with one of our pitchers. The opposing pitcher had taken his last warm-up pitches, and we turned our attention to the game. Matters began to go poorly for the pitcher, a veteran starter with more than 1,200 big league innings under his belt. He began to be visibly affected. His arm angle was different for each pitch; his release point inconsistent. Balls were going in the dirt, wide to each side. He lost control of his delivery; he had lost control of himself. He had taken on what Shakespeare called "an antic disposition." Balls that were in the strike zone were hit hard, mainly because he was steering the ball, not pitching it.

"Look at that," said the pitcher next to me. "He should know better. He'll never get out of this inning." He didn't. I'm sure he knew better after he was out of the game. That is not the ideal pitchers should seek, however. The fact that it was a spring training game—the opener, at that—does not relieve a pitcher from responsibility for his behavior. It's his body he is getting in shape. His mind and psyche play the game of life all year.

A number of years ago, a young pitcher came up from the minor leagues to pitch for the Oakland Athletics during the second half of the season. He pitched aggressively and effectively as a reliever; his rookie season statistics pleased him. He had a 1.93 era, a strikeout-to-walk ratio of almost two to one. He gave up only 45 hits in 72 innings pitched. The next season, however, he seemed a changed pitcher. He was tentative, behind in the count quite often, and the batters had much better swings at his pitches—and better results—than they had the previous season.

His body language told the story. The year before, I had referred to him as "a stalker" during our conversations. His posture was firm and strong looking. His manner said to the catcher, "Hurry up and give me the ball; let's go." He looked as if wanted to get back on the rubber and attack—again and again. And he had done just that, the way all aggressive competitors so.

But now, his performance was a different story; his body told a different story. And watching him was like watching a different pitcher. He clearly was not a "stalker." Instead, he appeared to be the one being stalked. He looked as if he didn't want to throw the next pitch; his tempo was excruciatingly slow. As he seemed to want to avoid the next delivery, he also tried to avoid contact. He "picked," was behind in the count regularly, and the quality of his pitches diminished. The hitters took advantage of it.

All this was rather evident to the pitcher. What wasn't, I felt, was how he looked out on the mound—the indicator of every bad thought and feeling he was internalizing. I asked him if he had tapes from the previous season; he did. We took a few recent tapes from the current season and went to his apartment. The format was to view them without comment. Just watch. He was astounded. He was disgusted with his current body language—the signals he was giving off. "This is what my teammates see?" he asked rhetorically. "This is what opposing hitters see," I added.

We then discussed the importance of a pitcher's appearance to a hitter. That hitter has perceptions of the pitcher, to a great extent based on what he sees. One of my goals, I told the young man, will be to intimidate the hitter in any way possible. The first way is to show myself on the mound as a relentless and aggressive competitor. If I look vulnerable, I am allowing the hitter to be comfortable facing me. More confident. It can be a subtle difference in the batter's mind, perhaps at a lower level of consciousness. But it will be there. As a pitcher, a tough competitor, I will not allow him to see me suffer. If I'm in command of the game, it's easy to act out superiority. But if I'm struggling, it's more difficult—and more important. By expressing negative thoughts and emotions through body language, I'd hurt myself. Not only couldn't I make an adjustment, but I'd be forfeiting my advantage to the hitter.

"This is exactly the garbage I've been bringing out there," said the pitcher.

The reason his behavior had changed from his rookie season, and the process he went through to address his issues, are irrelevant here. It *is* important to reiterate that the display of negative emotions while performing is not the behavior of effective competitors. Whether the body speaks in assertive or submissive language, it is speaking. And speaking is behaving.

What the Pitcher Should Do...

- Understand that his posture and gestures constitute what is called "body language."
- Understand, as well, that it is the tendency of people to express their internal thoughts and feelings through body language.
- Pay attention to his own body language during pitching performances, through the use of tapes or by having others observe and report.
- Recognize that tough-minded competitors show themselves to be that, in part, through their physical presence during competition.
- Establish the habit of acting out, through body language, who he

wants to be, rather than who he does not want to be, knowing that acting the warrior will help him to be the warrior.

■ Know that when faced with difficulty, an aggressive internal adjustment—off the mound—should include the physical posture he presents to the hitter, and to the world.

■ BREATHING

"Breathe or die," I warn pitchers. They don't need the literal warning. It is simply a verbal key, reminding a pitcher to pay attention to the "when" of breathing and the "where." The pitchers know how, and they know why. Yet some tend to forget everything they know in the heat of battle. It only seems to happen during periods of tension—when the relaxation technique is most required.

Anyone who has ever been to a movie thriller has had a chance to understand the relationship between tension and inhibited breathing patterns. For example, during a Stephen King film, an ax is held high, the killer poised to strike. Down comes the ax; off comes the head... The scene ends abruptly. Cut away to a pastoral scene now, quiet, peaceful. An audible gasp by the audience. People had been holding their collective breath. The cutaway relieved the tension; they could breathe again.

I have seen pitchers hyperventilate during competition, the result of racing thoughts and a general disorientation. The hyperventilation (shortness of breath) has mental causes and physiological effects. Muscles tense up; the arm does not have a fluid function. The delivery breaks down: coordination, range of motion, balance, timing, power, and accuracy are adversely affected. All this is triggered first by what the mind has focused on (danger) and, then, the unsatisfactory ratio of carbon dioxide to oxygen in the bloodstream.

To use the race car metaphor once again, carbon dioxide acts as a brake; oxygen acts as an accelerator. Carbon dioxide slams down on muscles; oxygen propels them smoothly. When exhaling deeply, pitchers release carbon dioxide from their blood stream and allow oxygen to take over.

The last act of downhill Olympic skiers, before they push off for their run, is to exhale deeply. Most basketball players do the same, before taking a foul shot.

Pitchers often forget. They breathe, for certain. But during crisis, many think about "the falling ax," and their breathing either becomes shallow or it stops. The skiers and foul shooters are not in the midst of action. Their breathing precedes it. And that, too, should be the case with pitchers. Breathing should be part of their preparation on the mound—on the rubber—before each pitch. As with every other good habit, the more consistent the breathing pattern, the more consistent the total approach.

How, specifically, can breathing help a pitcher's approach? First, it relieves muscular tension and enables the pitcher to maintain his typical physical/mechanical behaviors. Second, it will aid the pitcher in calming himself. In slowing himself down. The tendency of a pitcher in trouble is to rush—to speed up his tempo and his delivery. He will jump out. He usually will not come through with his arm, and his release point will be too high. As will the pitch. Power, as mentioned above, will be lost. But the major loss will be his ability to slow down his thoughts. How many times can such a pitcher be seen letting out a gasp when the catcher is *returning* the ball? Many times. He has no chance of making appropriate adjustments because his mind is racing. He has forgotten to breathe, and he will forget to get off the mound to fix himself.

It is easiest to create a pattern, a habit, of breathing if it is practiced. And it is easy to practice. It can be done in a pitcher's room and should be done during his side work in the bullpen. Working out of a stretch is conducive to developing a natural, deep exhalation. As the pitcher brings his arms down slowly in the stretch, he can slowly let air out from his mouth. It is a naturally coordinated procedure. Working out of the windup, a pitcher can look in to the catcher, take his sign, exhale slowly and then begin his delivery.

Effective breathing is not gasping. It is not necessarily a discernible action. It should be a regular one. A number of pitchers have involved themselves in martial arts training, the better to regulate and develop effective breathing patterns. Dave Stewart was a prime example. Reliever Robb Nen is one of the most consistent and regulated "breathers" among pitchers. (As a closer, he always works out of a stretch.) It is the first aspect of his approach he checks, when he's not satisfied with a performance during which might have rushed himself.

Each year, it seems, more pitchers learn to incorporate patterned breathing into their approach. It becomes obvious to them that random breathing is not as helpful to them as regulated breathing. Or no breathing at all.

What the Pitcher Should Do…

- Understand that breathing patterns—or no pattern, at all—have physiological effects on him during performance.
- Recognize what these effects are.
- Realize that breathing will involuntarily change during times of crisis and/or tension.

- Practice creating a consistent pattern of breathing before delivering each pitch, in order to relax his muscles and himself.
- Stand in front of a mirror in his room to see what seems to be best for him, and to feel what seems to be most natural.
- Experiment in the bullpen, until he is satisfied with his technique.
- Use it before every delivery, in order to integrate it fully into his approach.
- Check himself regularly, when making adjustments during the game and when reviewing behavior after the game. [See APPENDIX B]

■ CATCHERS

One goal a pitcher should consider is to have a catcher who is capable of being the pitcher's doppelganger—his alter ego on the field. The example most often referred to is the Steve Carlton-Tim McCarver relationship. Such a snug fit is the exception in a peg-to-hole metaphor. Unfortunately, there seem to be more round peg-square hole relationships. The former, an ideal fit, is often unattainable; the latter, a non-fit, is unacceptable.

At spring training camps of teams I've been with, catchers' meetings have been held more regularly than pitchers' meetings. The subject at pitchers' meetings is usually "pitching." The subject at catchers' meetings is usually "pitchers." Catchers and coaches discuss their tendencies, their strengths and weaknesses, and the individual needs of pitchers in specific situations. The discussions have one purpose: to inform the catchers, in order for them to be as helpful as possible during a pitcher's performance.

When I was a young boy, my father, a horseplayer, categorized racehorses into three classes. The first, he said, a jockey can just "hand ride. That horse will take care of business on his own." The second type required the jockey to "show him the whip" at regular intervals "to keep the horse's mind on his business." The third, he said, "the jockey's got to beat the hell out of." He added, "Much like people."

But not exactly. Some pitchers—people, after all—need a more sophisticated style of coaxing, need more encouragement, need a better plan when they are in trouble, a slowing of tempo, and so on. Catchers are not jockeys. They deal with people whose thought processes are more complex than those of horses, though their behavior sometimes challenges that notion.

Catchers should want to know how to help pitchers enhance their performances, because, in part, those performances reflect on the catcher. And pitchers should want catchers to know.

In 1988, Terry Steinbach was still learning about catching. He had been a converted third baseman and had caught for only two years before getting to the major leagues. Bob Welch was a veteran pitcher. Bob was a fierce competitor, who would "go harder" when adverse situations developed. [See TEMPO] It didn't work when the approach went out of control. Terry was concerned about it; he had felt responsible to help, but Bob's tendency continued. We got together and discussed the issue—and a discovery was made. Terry, a fierce competitor himself, would recognize the adverse situations and "encourage" Bob by shaking his fist at him. "C'mon, let's go." Accompanied by a fierce look.

In retrospect, Terry recognized that "it only made Welchy more fired up, which wasn't what he needed." And so, the catcher's tactic when he saw Bob on the brink was to put palm and glove facing the ground and give a slow-down, be easy signal. This they discussed beforehand, so the problem was clear to both, as was the "solution." It was effective.

After that, Terry wanted to review the tendencies of "his" pitchers every spring training, at a regular lunch meeting we had at Coco's, on Scottsdale Road. Because of his understanding of pitchers and his intelligence, Terry Steinbach's reputation for "handling" pitchers equaled (surpassed?) his reputation as a hitter.

If a pitcher understands the importance of working effectively with his catcher, he can save much valuable time by initiating and developing a good relationship with him.

What the Pitcher Should Do…

- Understand the importance of having a good working relationship with his catcher.
- Work at developing that relationship.
- Share with the catcher the pitcher's preferences, behavioral tendencies, mechanical cues and all else he wishes the catcher to know, thus enabling him to recognize signs of need and be able to address them.

- Inform the catcher of the specific "keys" and "cues" the pitcher uses for himself, so the catcher can provide them when necessary.
- Establish a "total" plan with the catcher before performance, regarding pitching strategies and behavioral patterns (e.g., tempo, body language).
- Remind the catcher of the verbal approach (e.g., tonality) that works best for the pitcher during the catcher's visits to the mound.
- Confer with catcher in between innings. Make the conference brief and to whatever point either player wants to make.
- Support the catcher with "professional" responses.
- Be honest, despite possible conflict of opinions.
- Take responsibility, rather than blaming the catcher for whatever is displeasing the pitcher.
- If a less-than-desirable relationship exists, think of ways to improve it—or rise above it.

■ CHARACTER

I am compelled to write more than the "few words" originally intended about this abstract term. The word is used and heard frequently by and from many people involved with sport. The term "character" is used regularly in and around professional baseball environments.

Not only do the people using the term often fail to agree on its definition (and who can blame them?), they differ in the value they give to "character," as it relates to their players—particularly major leaguers. This is discernable not so much by how they speak, as by how they act. To be candid, baseball people do not differ in their desire to *win*, they differ in the "price" they are willing to pay in order to have a chance to win. For some, therefore, a player's "character" has value relative to his talent. Others note that there is no value in a player who has character and little else. It is a valid argument. Once again, the problem is how to strike a proper balance. And what *is* a proper balance? I am thankful that these are not issues to deal with on these pages.

As to why *I* believe "character" matters, first, I would quote Goethe, "If you would create something, you must be something." The creation is only as good as the creator. The best pitchers I have talked with have had the most "character." It is no random truth. Their achievements have been the result of talent, to be sure. But their mental attitude, which is a major ingredient of "character," is an important part of their superiority.

Second, Lincoln spoke of "character" being like a tree, and reputation—the judgment of others—like a shadow. The shadow is what is thought of it—the tree is "the real thing." Players often tell teammates to "get real," but not everyone knows how to be "real."

Third, though not in order of importance, I share the view of the philosopher Heraclitus, who felt that "character" is "a man's fate." A pitcher is a man first. He is many other things to many other people, before he gets down to a lower rung on that ladder of abstraction—where he is identified as a pitcher. When statistics, expectations, and evaluations are put aside, he is ultimately defined to himself by his "character." That is his fate, whether he understands it or not. His "character" is his substance; his reputation is the symbol—in baseball, his "label." He should want to take control of defining himself—first and foremost *for himself*.

A good number of thoughtful and interested pitchers, having read about and heard the topic "character" being discussed—and having a respect for the game they play—expressed the idea to me that "baseball develops character." My own view, I told them, is that "baseball helps reveal character." A discussion usually ensued. "People develop their character," I offered as explanation. "Or don't develop it. Circumstances reveal it, in either case. How a person reacts to situations and circumstance reveals the person." Thomas Hardy wrote of "the influence of character upon circumstance." We spoke of character as a determinant of what happens to a man. His fate.

And so it went; the talk expanded (particularly when Al Leiter, intellectually curious by nature, was a participant) to the idea that, while temperament may be inborn, "character" is acquired. That's the major point I always wish to make to players. And that time and effort are required for its acquisition. "Character building begins in infancy and continues to death," Anna Roosevelt wrote. It is a life-long process, and the building site is wherever the person brings himself. Even to playing fields, where what is done every day, as Vince Lombardi told his teams, helps define who they will be the rest of their lives.

The Greek word "character" means *impression*. Pitchers should learn to regard Lincoln's words and make the distinction between who they are and who they appear to be. Though the difference may seem obvious, less so is the *connection*. This connection is "impressed" on his being—all through his life—by everything in his environment: family members, friends, teammates, newspapers, television, money, fame, statistics, music, social contexts, and more. Everything.

The impression is being made regularly—constantly. Put simply, people may be shaped; "character" must be formed. To the extent that each individual makes selections of what he defines as "right" and appropriate, and to the extent that he acts upon these selections, he develops his own "character." He is his own man, free of "impressions" that do not last, free of perceptions that do not matter.

A topic soon to be treated in this book is CONFIDENCE. Can a pitcher be confident if he believes he is defined by others? By statistics? Rhetorical questions. When a pitcher acts out of what he *knows* is "right," he is building his self-confidence through the process of developing his "character."

One of my lines to pitchers is, "Character is what you do when no one is watching." If someone knows an action or activity to be "right," he shouldn't need supervision to give his full mental and physical energy to it. It's much easier to behave well when being watched, whether by judgmental peers or by evaluating staff members. (It's a rare horse that can just be hand-ridden by the jockey. A special horse—one with "character.")

So people may act many ways in many places for many different reasons. The cynical but humorous writer, Ambrose Bierce, fully understood human tendencies. He commented with irony, "In every human heart are a tiger, a pig, an ass and a nightingale. Diversity of character is due to their unequal activity." The choice, he implied, is ours to make. Yet, people often choose to keep too great a distance between who they are and who they wish to be. It is not so much a choice to maintain that distance as a hesitancy to approach the task. Narrowing the gap is, after all, a very challenging task. It takes some "character" to develop more "character."

What the Pitcher Should Do...

- Understand that he gives impressions of his "character" through every singular act, on and off the baseball field.
- Examine his behavior and consider whether it is representative of who (how) he would like to be as a person and as a competitor.
- Understand that he defines himself not only by what he will do—but also by what he will fail to do.
- Recognize that the pitcher portrays his "character" by how he approaches his task and, even more so, how he responds to resultant circumstances. He reveals it by how he responds to failure—and how he responds to success. [See RESPONSE]
- Realize that "character" is related to attitude, and that his interpretation of his world ("boring" drills included) emanates from his attitude.
- Understand that what is impressed on him from the external world is the world's; what he projects to the world is his.
- Understand that when baseball people use the term "make-up" in judging him, they are, in their way, referring to his "character."
- Believe that, whatever importance his "character" may hold for others, it is most important to him. It is, after all, self-defining.
- Include in his commitment to his improvement as an athlete, the on-going development of his "character."

■ CLOSERS

In 1983, Ozzie Smith and I had a conversation, during which he mentioned his early days in the major leagues. In that time before he had established himself as a pre-eminent shortstop, Smith was used in the late innings of close games as a defensive replacement.

Said Smith, "A player put into the game for defensive reasons is *expected* [his emphasis] to make every play. If you don't, you've failed. It was a no-win situation."

The same expectation must be faced by a closer. And the ball is in his hands—as is the game itself—with every pitch.

The closer's role is to protect his team's lead in the late innings, the ninth inning. His performance is compressed into the action of pitching to a few batters—or one batter perhaps. He is expected to get the last out in order to preserve the victory—to "save" it. If he does not, he fails.

Herein rests one of the distinctions the closer must make for himself, if he is to be well suited for the role. Though he may fail to achieve his goal on a given day, *he* is not the failure. One interpretation speaks to task; the other personalizes the failure. Responsible people feel the great responsibility of having a game turned over to him, after his team has worked hard to keep or take a lead. How the pitcher responds to that challenge (threat?) determines his mettle as a closer.

"It's all about how you handle the mental side," Dennis Eckersley has often explained. "You've got to be as positive as you can, because a lot of negatives will happen to you [over time]."

Robb Nen calls the responsibility "a mental strain." Churchill called it "the price of greatness." But blown saves and bad outings erode today whatever claim to greatness was gained yesterday. "Those games make you feel like you've let people down," Nen said. "But you know you've got to go back out there tomorrow, so you'd better be ready and confident you'll get it done next time. You can't take the failure personally. That's not easy to do sometimes."

But that is exactly what needs to be done by a closer, or he will not remain one for long.

The theme in BIG INNING relates to the pitcher's perception of the irrelevance of runners on base. A closer would have had to develop this point of view early. Runners on base, runners in scoring position, the winning run, at that those situations are the rule, not the exception for a closer.

Before facing these situations, the closer, during his walk from the bullpen to the mound, should narrow his thoughts. "Get an out," should be part of the "reducing" thought process. Once he gets to the mound, "Make a pitch," becomes his focus. On the rubber: selection, location, target—aggressiveness under control. A mature, consistent, uncomplicated approach.

Over time, Yankees closer, Mariano Rivera has come to that approach. In the spring of 1999, catcher Joe Girardi said of Rivera, "He's more mature … He understands more about how to close, about the mentality."

The understanding that he cannot and will not succeed all the time is one that must be clear in a closer's mind, if he is to remain rational and functional. At the same time, he cannot use this truth as an excuse before he "goes into battle." That viewpoint at that time will usually lead to problems. The thoughts are not part of a preparation for success, but, rather, an explanation of failure. And failure will be the likely result. As has been discussed earlier, balance is required, and the beam can be narrow sometimes.

What the Pitcher Should Do…

- Understand that the mental requirements for a closer are distinctly unique, because of the circumstances he faces on a regular basis.
- Understand that these requirements include the psychological response a closer has to others' expectations of his success.
- Welcome the responsibility.
- Recognize the inevitability and impact of failures in the role.
- Address failure by defining it in situational terms, rather than personal ones. In other words, be certain perspective is clear.
- Manage responses by using positive self-talk to anticipate the next opportunity.
- Develop a routine for pre-performance time during a game, making sure arousal level is kept down until the late innings. For example, stay in the dugout during the game, to keep the preparation environment (bullpen) separated from thoughts and senses. Talk about matters of the game, rather than thinking about his own impending performance. Incorporate whatever works for him into a consistent routine.

- Know the game situation and have a plan before leaving the bullpen.
- Use appropriate task-oriented self-coaching language on the trip from the bullpen to the mound. ("Get an out." "Be aggressive.")
- Have appropriate task-oriented focus when on the rubber. (Selection, location, target, etc.)
- Attack.

■ COACHING SELF

I tell major league players, "The most important coach you'll have from now on is you." Surely the players have learned and will continue to learn from others, but unless the information is properly integrated into behavior, it will be of no value during performance. And coaching behavior is, for the most part, what I am alluding to when I speak of self-coaching. Self-coaching *during* performance.

It has been said that we are all brilliant in retrospect. Also, that best laid plans often go awry. But past and future are not the concern of those who coach themselves effectively. The present, the moment, the task at hand—this is the appropriate concern. What the pitcher does to help himself—or hinder himself—will be the precursor of success or failure. (Recall the pitcher with the "antic disposition," who didn't make it out of the first inning of a spring training game.)

Much of what has already been said in this book speaks to a pitcher's need to coach himself during competition. Making adjustments, behaving properly and coping with adversity all require the pitcher to direct himself or redirect himself. Doing this is an internal process. No one except the pitcher knows what he is thinking and feeling. (Sometimes even he doesn't know!) [See GATHERING] Pitching coaches can only respond to the observable behavior of a pitcher. The cause of much of it is not revealed to him. He can only guess, and such guesses can be risky for the coach—and the pitcher. So it is imperative for pitchers to be aware of their thoughts, feelings, and needs as they compete. Only then can they help themselves by being good coaches. By knowing what to do, when to do it, how to do it.

Pitchers tend to be hard on themselves. The language they use when talking inside their heads—on or behind the mound—is often nasty. The tone of their collective inner voice can be harsh and overly critical—emanating from a disgusted attitude. That kind of talk is neither positive nor encouraging. It certainly is not conducive to building confidence. [See SELF-TALK]

I'll often ask a pitcher what he says to himself when he's dissatisfied or unhappy with what he's doing on the mound. I ask what happens as a result. Those who are poor at self-coaching—and I've found them to be a vast majority—tell me of their self-flagellation. Here is a typical conversation:

"I beat myself up."

"Does it work?"

"No."

"If I were the pitching coach, and I came out to the mound and said to you what you've said to yourself, what would you think of my coaching?'

"I'd think it was horsebleep."

"The how would you judge your own coaching technique?"

"Horsebleep."

"Then what are you going to do about it?"

I'll end the report there, though that's just the *beginning* of the talk.

A good coach has to "know what's going on," and he has to know how to respond to what's going on. [See RESPONSE] Effective pitchers have that understanding of game situations. The pitcher must also understand his thoughts and feelings, as they affect his behavior. As only he can know them. In effect, he is both a pitcher and a coach.

The difficulty in knowing when and how to differentiate is understandable. Simply put, when on the rubber, he is a pitcher; when off the rubber, he can be a coach—if a coach is needed. Naturally, when matters are going well—everything flowing smoothly—he should "go with the flow," just as the pitching coach should "let it flow" without interference.

The only thoughts a pitcher should have on the rubber should relate to pitch selection, location, and focus on the target. He should have already coached himself to be aggressive and be under control. He should already have given himself mechanical "cues" he might have needed. This he did behind the rubber or off the mound, depending on how much time he required to gather himself and coach himself. He has told himself what to do and how to do it—off the rubber. The quality of the next pitch he throws is greatly determined by the quality of his self-coaching.

Many pitchers admit to being much better coaches of others than they are of themselves. Their awareness of the difference is helpful. They recognize the fact that they know what to say and how to say it, albeit to others. "I'm smart for others and stupid for myself," one pitcher told me recently. "It's hard to see the picture, when you're inside the frame," I answered. "And when you're in the heat of battle, you're inside the frame."

That is why it is so important to get off the rubber and/or off the mound and become a coach, instead of a pitcher. By first "getting out of the frame."

What the Pitcher Should Do...

- Understand that only he is capable of knowing what he is thinking and feeling, so only he is capable of addressing these matters as a coach, during performance.
- Be aware of what is happening in the game and within himself.
- Know that, while on the rubber, he is the pitcher, not the coach. (Selection, location, target.)
- When necessary, coach himself first by staying off the rubber, getting behind the mound, perhaps turning his back to homeplate and rubbing the ball while employing positive self-talk. Use tonality that is appropriate to the need. That is, if the pitcher is being complacent or tentative, use strong directives with an aggressive tone, in order to heighten arousal and intensify focus. If arousal is too high and/or tempo too fast, the pitcher should employ calming language and tonality.
- Use positive, functional, task-oriented directives before getting back on the rubber.
- In between innings, according to need, quickly review his mental approach during the previous inning. Prepare himself by bringing to mind the mental adjustments desired when he goes back out for the next inning.

■ COMPETITOR

Pitchers who express admiration for other pitchers tend to identify their most admirable trait as being "a tough competitor." Though I share the object of their admiration, I believe the term they use to characterize it to be a redundancy. To my mind, a pitcher who is not mentally "tough," is not an effective competitor at all. That toughness (my own working definition is "mental discipline") is prerequisite.

It seems that many people hold an image of a tough competitor to be a pitcher, for example, with fire flaming from his nostrils. He scowls, he snatches, he swears, he sweats. Sort of an unpleasant dragon in a china shop. More assassin, perhaps, than linebacker. The term "killer instinct" is frequently used, and aptly so. That instinct is admirable and necessary, if one is to be a tough competitor. But a "calculated cool" must accompany the instinct if the job is to be "executed," so to speak. I would not send a dragon or a linebacker to do the job.

Philip Roth, in a short story entitled "Defender of the Faith," wrote of a soldier learning to have an "infantryman's heart." That is what an effective competitor must have. Think of these possibilities: infantryman A runs from the battle (quitting); infantryman B freezes during it (panic); infantryman C rapidly unloads all his ammunition, firing his weapon aggressively but aimlessly, hitting no one (loss of control and focus); infantryman D sets up properly (courage), aims carefully (focus), fires with deliberation (poise), hits his target (execution—indeed).

I want infantryman D on my side—on a battlefield—and on a playing field. *He* is the true competitor, the balanced performer, the guy with mental toughness, who faces fire and takes care of his task, rather than fearing consequences. He's got the "infantryman's heart."

The image of Greg Maddux during competition comes to mind. Prepared, controlled, focused. A pit-bull, not a raging bull. The term dogged perseverance seems to be similarly applicable. No giving in, no grandiose gesturing, Maddux executes pitches with the consistent intensity, irrespective of score or circumstance. That his agenda, at least.

Yet the best competitors can "lose" their approach from time to time. It does not take them long to get it back, and they "come at you," as pitchers are wont to say, with renewed determination. Kevin Brown told the media in 1998 that he was still learning to guard against such a loss of perspective.

Pitching for San Diego that season, he had a no-hitter for seven innings against the Dodgers then gave up a number of "choppers, hardly a clean hit"—and lost the game, 4-2. "If you're a competitor, that can really bother you, and it bothered me," Brown said. "But you have to learn not to dwell on the past. I had to focus on the next game, the next day. It's not easy, but it's essential."

The point has been made in earlier pages: a pitcher's appearance is not the determining factor in judging his competitive efficacy. His behavior defines him. Stomping and ranting is usually just posturing—behaviors of an actor, not a competitor. How the pitcher "goes after it" gives meaning to the man.

Many pitchers have "competitive spirits." Of course, they all want to win, to succeed. Who doesn't? Spirit alone, however, does not suffice. A will—and a "way" must accompany it.

One of the measures of a pitcher's competitive tendency is not how he pitches with his "best stuff," but by how he pitches when his stuff has deserted him. Ineffective or poor competitors panic, try to do too much (overkill) or give in to "one of those days" (surrender). A true competitor recognizes the need to compensate for lack of "stuff" with intelligence and persistence. Courage is required, as well, and it is a competitor's instinct to stick to his battle plan, rather than succumbing to disorientation or losing his spirit (heart and soul). The true competitor holds himself even more accountable to employ all his mental resources on those days when his physical skills seem to be unavailable. *Seem* to be.

Quite often I have witnessed pitchers, in the course of the battle, "find their stuff." The phrase they use is significant. Pitchers who "found it" were not searching for it. As they focused on task, and kept themselves and their team in the game, the "stuff reappeared." I often use a particular metaphor for explaining this to young pitchers. I will ask the question, "How do you catch a bird?" I answer the question for them. "Not by doing this," I say, as I snatch at the air with my hand. I open my hand and hold it still with my palm up. "This is how you 'catch' it; open your hand and trust it will fly in." The same theory applies to stuff. The bird will not always alight there, but a grabbing, flailing hand surely will never catch it.

Pitchers who have the courage to battle with limited resources and trust themselves give their muscles time to get their "rhythm" (a term often used by pitchers) because of their indomitable spirit—and will—and approach.

Along this line of thought is the evaluation of "stuff" a pitcher makes when warming up in the bullpen. So many pitchers, especially young ones, use that evaluation as a forecast of what they will take into the game. Yet so many pitchers will say there seems to be no correlation between bullpen "stuff" and game effectiveness. Information gained in the bullpen can be useful, predicting the future is not. So long as the pitcher knows how to behave, and his impression of his bullpen "stuff" does not alter that behavior, he'll be fine. The information relating to what pitch seems to be working well on that day and what pitch does not may help the pitcher when he enters the game. But very often the information is limited only to what is going on in the bullpen. When game "stuff" is executed, it may change. The point to be made is that a pitcher's predicting his physical efficacy—for better or for worse—too often leads to the corruption of mental efficacy. It is to be avoided.

A notion some pitchers have expressed to me is that to be a fierce competitor one must be an arrogant, ignorant, and obnoxious person. As stated, this view is most widely held by intelligent, sensitive, often deferential people [See NICE GUYS] Intelligence is an *asset* "between the lines"; sensitivity and deference are not. A fierce competitor's concern is knowing how to go about his task and battling to give his team and himself a chance to win. He has no other concern; he is insensitive and unyielding. He is not a terrible person. "Nice guys" might identify him as such, because they feel they themselves are not capable of competing fiercely, and use personality as an excuse.

Rick Honeycutt, to use a favorite person of mine, is a "gentleman," a "nice guy"—*off the field*. He pitched for 20 years in the big leagues, not because people liked him, but because he was given the ball often and competed always. He reminded me of an old English sea captain Thomas Fuller wrote of. Fuller noted that Captain Somers, a veteran "of many Atlantic voyages" in the late 1500s, was "a lamb on the land, a lion on the sea." Rick Honeycutt and other gentlemen still pitching are sensitive, caring people who become fierce competitors on the mound. They know how to win battles.

One of the wonderful aspects of sport is that warrior metaphors—battles and infantrymen and sea captains—can be used when speaking of great competitors, pitchers who "take no prisoners," but cause no fatalities. Because intense competition, in the words of William James, is just "the moral equivalent of war."

What the Pitcher Should Do...

- Understand that behavior, rather than appearance, is the determining factor in becoming an effective competitor.
- Understand that the mentally tough competitor responds to fear, frustration, or inadequacy by being able to direct and maintain his thoughts and focus on what he can *control*—his behavior.
- Remember that the intensity of a competitor is directed to executing the next pitch, rather than thinking about outcome.
- Remember that aggressive behavior must be controlled. A proper balance must be struck.
- Develop a consistent, persistent approach, one not related to score, circumstance or "meaning" given to the game. In every outing, "run through the finish line." Battle to the end of his performance.
- Be unyielding, even when he does not have his "best stuff."
- Develop his concentration skill to a level at which he can be oblivious to irrelevant external cues and aware of relevant internal cues.
- Understand that the hitter is an irrelevant, external cue. Focus on the target.
- Remind himself of the difference between being a gentleman off the field and being a fierce competitor on it.

■ CONCENTRATION
[See APPENDIX A]

Concentration is prepotent. Whatever troubles a person might have, if he also has a highly developed ability to concentrate, he will be able to focus intently on whatever task is before him. Prepotent, his concentration will be more powerful than any possible distraction.

That is the ideal. Rarely do people have such a highly developed prepotency. As important as concentration is in athletics, it is surprising to find how small is the percentage of athletes who actively work on improving theirs. A player can learn how to pay attention to his task. It is a skill and should be *practiced regularly*, in order to bring it to a high level of development and maintenance.

Distinctive differences exist among pitchers, in both their natural capacity to concentrate and to address the appropriate "object" of their concentration—what they are paying attention to. For example, one pitcher, let us say Jamie Moyer, is a calm, apparently low-key personality. Another, let us use Kevin Brown as an example, is a more "high-key" type. When I have asked other pitchers to conjecture on the effectiveness of concentration of those two, responses would tend to name Kevin Brown, because he appears to be more intense. His external manner, his type of personality, would lead people to that conclusion. In contrast, observers would see Jamie Moyer as a more "mellow" type. If they missed the point, it is because I asked the question in a somewhat vague and misleading way.

The real question to be asked about *all* pitchers should refer to selective attention—identifying not only the intensity of their concentration, but also the quality of it. This quality is measured by evaluating their ability to focus on the specific needs and tasks of the moment, and also by determining the length of time that focus can be sustained. It should be obvious that the most effective performances will result from a pitcher's ability to identify the appropriate object of his attention, focus with intensity, and sustain that level and direction of that focus.

So, getting back to Moyer and Brown, the answer to who is concentrating more effectively can only be found in the pitcher's hidden agenda: who is thinking about what he is supposed to be thinking, who is seeing clearly what he is supposed to be seeing, as noted above. External demeanor is not the entire or accurate measure of what is going on internally.

Unless, of course, the observer sees body language that indicates a "hurricane in the head"—the performer losing control of himself.

I have referred to Jamie Moyer and Kevin Brown for a reason. First, they are different personality types. Second, they developed their concentration efficacy based on different needs. That is a major point I wish to make here: a pitcher must recognize the flaws or weaknesses in his concentration skills, and then he must know what to do to address them. And he must have the will to do so.

Before getting to the specifics of that practice, a reminder about distractions. Pitchers, when asked, provide me with a catalogue of distractions. One "appears" most frequently—by far. Since it has been discussed in earlier pages, I will identify it but not elaborate.

The most common distraction relates to self-consciousness. The pitcher pays more attention to himself, his desires, his doubts, his fears, his image, the consequences of his actions, and whatever other needs he might be addressing, than he does to his task. In order to effectively compete, the pitcher must learn to redirect his thoughts and move his attention to his responsibility. This ability will combat anxiety and other distractions. The stronger the concentration skills become, the more the distractions diminish in strength. At the highest level, the skill, as noted, becomes prepotent.

Concentration requires self-discipline; practice requires self-discipline. A typical form of practice for pitchers is "PFP"—pitchers' fielding practice. During spring training, instructional league and regular intervals throughout the professional season, PFP is used as a standard, essential drill. The routine includes practicing all the fielding plays a pitcher will be called on to make during a game. Practiced over and over—and over again.

The pitchers' bodies are out there on the field, but where are their minds? A short period of observation is all that is necessary to determine that. Each individual reveals himself as he goes about his business—and it *is* his business.

Pitchers have complained to me that these drills are "boring." A drill is a drill, I tell them. Their perception defines it; their attitude paints their perception. The question is, what's the purpose of the drill? Does it have value? In theory, yes. But the pitcher's behavior will define the actual value for him. The drill will be as effective as the pitcher. He'll get out of it no more than he puts into it. If he is "boring," so too will the activity be "boring."

Tom Seaver said that he appreciated anything that helped him reach his goal of being a successful pitcher. When pitchers acknowledge the theoretical value of a drill but devalue the activity itself, they speak volumes about themselves, not about PFP. They reveal their perspective and their self-discipline. Or lack of it. Concentration is connected in the eyes and mind to both perspective and self-discipline. Bad memory is rooted in bad attention. That includes muscle memory. The pitchers who regularly "make the plays" during the game, regularly attend to them during practice.

PFP can be a great opportunity for a pitcher to work on his concentration skills, as well as on the plays he is supposed to make. By holding himself accountable for sustaining his intense focus during the activity, and by monitoring himself, he can enhance his ability to have selective attention and increase the span of his attention.

Sidework in the bullpen is another activity that a pitcher can use to help develop better concentration skills. Whatever the purpose of the work, a conscientious pitcher addresses it with intensity. If there is no specific mechanic to be worked on in the bullpen, the pitcher should be certain to maintain a disciplined focus on the target. Everything done should have a purpose, and, in the absence of any other, concentration alone is ample purpose. Concentration is not just looking at a target, but seeing it. (Recall the Rapp anecdote: he had no recollection of seeing the target, though he was "looking at it.")

Just one final clarification. I use the words "concentration" and "focus" as synonyms. *The American Heritage Dictionary* says that to concentrate is "to pay close attention"; to focus is "to concentrate on." "Focus" has become the more popular term with ballplayers. But when San Francisco pitcher Shawn Estes said in September 1998, "My focus is just not there," he was saying that his concentration was poor. "It's not as easy as I thought it'd be," Estes added. Definitions are easier to come by than skills.

What the Pitcher Should Do...

- Recognize the prepotent power concentration has over distracting thoughts.
- Understand that concentration is a skill that can be developed and improved through specific activities and a disciplined approach.
- Apply this understanding to every practice activity on the field.

- Apply this understanding by practicing his concentration, using the exercises suggested below or any other that the pitcher knows or learns elsewhere.
- Draw a grid with 100 small squares. Make a number of photocopies. Fill in one grid randomly with the numbers 00 through 99 (use 01,02, etc., so every number is double-digit.) Use a pencil or pen and go through the grid by crossing out the numbers in numerical succession. [A favorite drill of Jamie Moyer.] Time the activity from start to completion. If one number is illusive, stay with the activity, fighting frustration with refocused concentration. Work the grid activity regularly. Change the number placement on grid (using the blank copies) to avoid memorization. When skill increases noticeably, put on the radio or CD player. Have instrumental music at first; progress to music with lyrics, preferably from songs familiar to the pitcher. Continue the progression by increasing the volume. Create whatever variations the pitcher can think of.
- Tie a heavy key or a finger ring to a piece of string nine or 10 inches in length. The weight of the object hanging on the string should pull the string taut. The pitcher should lean his elbow on a table, keeping his (pitching) arm firm and stable as he holds the string in a relaxed manner between his thumb and forefinger. His hand and forearm should be at a 45-degree angle to the surface of the table. In this relaxed manner, attention should be concentrated on the object at the end of the string. Focus intensely on the ring (or key), "seeing" it revolve in a clockwise orbit or circle through this concentration. The pitcher should just relax and be easy with his hand. Soon, he will feel the object move in the pattern of his concentration, with no apparent movement of his hand and/or arm. He can then understand how muscles are capable of responding to concentrated thought. (Appropriate thoughts will help produce appropriate muscle activity, as inappropriate thoughts will have the opposite effect.)
- Sit in his room and look at a picture or poster on the wall. Now *see* the picture. See it entirely. Next, he should narrow his focus. Concentrate on a particular image. If it is a flower, for example, *see* the flower. Then a petal. Then the tip of that petal. Sustain concentration, noting how his mind wandered, when and how long before he

returned attention to the end of the petal. (Can PFP be as "boring"? No physical activity here, aside from the eyes. But the mental discipline of sustaining concentration is the activity's purpose.)

- At the ballpark, use the same exercise, attending to outfield signs.
- Visualize performance while doing distance running. Maintain concentration on a particular sequence of behavior during the performance.
- Be an observer. Notice everything. See everything. Be active during a game, while not performing, by being attentive to details within the game.
- Understand that the mental discipline and energy devoted to all such "ordeals" (PFP included) will help to bring the pitcher's concentration skills to a higher level of development.

■ CONFIDENCE
[See APPENDIX A]

"Confidence," wrote Cicero, "is that feeling by which the mind embarks in great and honorable courses with a sure hope and trust in itself." It's difficult to imagine pitchers, or anyone else, for that matter, having a consistently "sure . . .trust." Circumstance will challenge a person's confidence daily, particularly an athlete's. Yet confidence, players tell me, is the most significant influence on their success. Pitchers say they "know" they will do well when their prevailing feeling is one of confidence, rather than doubt.

Doubts come with being human. A "confident pitcher" will still have his share of occasional doubts. That is not all bad; doubts are a countervailing force against complacency. Fred Buechner has written, "At least doubts prove that we are in touch with reality, with the things that threaten faith, as well as with the things that nourish it."

Being grounded in reality can serve as more than insurance against complacency. It can also—and I am constantly speaking to them about this "reality"—assure pitchers that failures on the baseball field are not as catastrophic as they may be inclined to feel, when they perceive that "the sky is falling." [See FEELINGS] [See PERCEPTIONS] And I assure pitchers that fluctuations in confidence level do not make pitchers dysfunctional. Trust the talent, have a plan, function. Confidence will heighten. The process itself can be helpful. "Suffering is good for you," my father advised me, when I was a complaining young boy.

Newspaper sports pages are textbooks, I tell players. "Read them. Just about every day a ballplayer is talking about confidence. It comes and goes for most. That's the first thing to realize." I then recall with them ideas related to confidence. Some are already discussed on these pages, such as ADVERSITY and ATTITUDES, BALANCE and BEHAVIOR, for example. The relationship between the rational and the emotional is reiterated. How we think vs. how we feel—to be specifically treated on pages to follow.

Now, to the sports pages—to random clippings from the 1998 season. Item: Los Angeles "occasional" closer, Antonio Osuna, after two saves in consecutive appearances in June said, "At the start of the season, I did lose my confidence, but I've been pitching well lately, and it's back to normal."

So performance got "back to normal" *despite* lack of confidence. No catastrophe there. He must have done something right.

National League Rookie of the Year, Kerry Wood, spoke about the 20-strikeout one-hitter he pitched against Houston on May 6. "It helped me finally realize that I was capable of pitching at that level," said the Cubs' right-hander. "*Finally.*" Four prior starts had been "rocky." He must have done something right against Houston.

Lefthander Al Leiter, pitching for the Mets in '98, had this to say in August of that season: "Three years ago, if I had runners on second and third with nobody out, they're both scoring." [See BIG INNING—again] "Just through lack of confidence," Leiter said. "And that's just the difference between having a good year and a bad year." The confidence came from *somewhere*!

I find a clipping from 1984, one yellowed with age. White Sox pitcher Britt Burns, more recently a staff colleague of mine with the Florida Marlins, spoke these words at that time: "After pitching some good games and losing, you go out and are a little apprehensive." Confidence eroded, even after pitching "good games."

In 1985, Cardinals pitcher Ken Dayley had this to say: "I think struggling made me stronger. Pitching is 80% mental, and confidence is an awful lot of that mental part... I just needed a little boost."

Finally, a "Peanuts" strip I must share. Four frames. In frame one, Charlie Brown says to Lucy, "You never have any self-doubt, do you?" "Me?" asks Lucy in the second frame. She laughs raucously in frame three: "HA HA HA HA!!" In the last frame, Charlie Brown, looking like he feels, says, "No, I guess not." Whatever the truth may be, Lucy *acts* as if she's confident.

A pitcher must remember that an appropriate approach will "get the job done." And that concentration can be prepotent. He must remember that a *feeling* of confidence is still a feeling. So much the better if he has a good feeling, but good behavior is the payoff.

The major problem with loss of confidence is that a pitcher will tend to perform out of that feeling, that loss, and forget what he knows about his approach. The degree to which he believes in his talent and in his ability to be effective will affect his efforts to produce a positive outcome. A confident pitcher will exert greater effort to attack challenges. On the other hand, a pitcher who lacks confidence will tend to greet the first sign of adversity with the "here-we-go again" syndrome. Lack of confidence is lethal when it changes a pitcher's approach and response. Succumbing to self-doubt is not an option for a pitcher who aspires to being an elite performer. Fighting through self-doubt is pre-requisite. [See COMPETITOR]

The challenge, then, for a pitcher "invaded" by self-doubts (and he is often responsible for having "opened the gates" to them) is to discipline his mind to focus on task, irrespective of turmoil in his heart. Discipline may not make the heart grow fonder, but it will surely make it grow stronger. Most important is that the pitcher revert to his plan of attack. [See APPROACH] The pitcher's sense of being prepared [See PREPARATION] is a seed for his confidence and self-trust, which grows as he nurtures it with appropriate and consistent behavior. [See CONSISTENCY] Further fed by the knowledge that he is capable of struggling through difficult times.

People differ in their degree of self-confidence. So much of what they feel about themselves is based on what they heard about themselves while growing up. The expectation people have is that precocious young athletes hear messages that build their confidence. Not so. Parents may have their own agendas and may have their own problems. Abused children have their confidence destroyed at an early age. I've dealt with a number of major and minor league players who were abused by an alcoholic parent. A young person's outstanding physical talent may vault him into professional baseball, but he brings a bruised psyche with him. Self-doubt is always there, until he addresses his issues and becomes the man he knows he can be, instead of remaining the child he has always felt himself to be. It is an arduous process, starting with pain, ending with pleasure. And self-confidence.

Often, parents and coaches seem to be supportive of the young player. But their expectation is for the youngster to be perfect. [See PERFECTION] The young player sees that he is unable to meet such an expectation. He believes he is doomed. With the help of those who hold such expectations for him, he considers anything less than perfect to be failure. Such a perception is not conducive to building confidence.

Recently, a pitcher sat with me in the room where I write these words. He spoke of his difficulties developing a positive belief system—confidence—because all he ever heard as a boy was criticism. "If I would have struck out 26 kids, I'd be jumped on [by a parent] and asked what happened with the kid who hit the ball." The exaggeration is clear, but so is the theme. "It seems like my whole life has been justifying my past and worrying about my future." And ignoring the present, he might have added.

I hear many such stories, with a variety of particulars, but similarity of theme—parents living vicariously through their children. Damage can be done. The child must explain every mistake he makes; the boy does that and also learns to twist the truth; the man does both and also makes excuses. For such a person—such a pitcher—converting self-doubt into self-trust becomes a long and arduous process.

The healthiest person is susceptible to external "impressions" that change his level of confidence. Recall the anecdote in BELIEF—2+2=5. I have done the following experiment in a college psychology class: An individual is sent to read a notice aloud to two groups of students in two different rooms. In the first room, he reads with energy and enthusiasm—confidence. He considers himself to be superior to this group; he is older, and they are remedial students. He then goes to the room where senior, older, students work in a physics lab. They are the intellectual elite of the college. His words to them are barely audible and rushed. He cannot wait to get out of that room, and he doesn't wait long.

It is tough on those who live from the outside in, rather than from the inside out. Confidence can disappear quickly. Think about social settings people are in. When they feel confident, they are comfortable, chatty, glad to be there. When they lack confidence because of the particular environment they are in, they are ill at ease, quiet, searching, perhaps, for someone who they think looks more vulnerable than they feel, and they look forward to leaving. Some would not even attend.

A final "type" of confidence problem for pitchers. Professional athletes have, as noted, been precocious, in terms of talent, from an early age. They dominated the opposing hitters, and, as they progressed in age, they saw their future as a professional. After having become a professional, they saw—at some time—the "playing field level." The players they dominated were not good enough to be pros. The competition became more talented. Where the opposing lineup might have included a couple of hitters worthy of respect, lineups became more imposing. The good hitters, like good pitchers, advanced.

But good pitchers get good hitters out most of the time. Somehow, pitchers lose that truth. They can find it only by looking within. Yet, pitchers often pay an inordinate amount of attention to hitters. They can "learn" to give "too much respect to opposing hitters." These words have been spoken by many, many pitchers, in their owning up to why they lose their confidence. They think about what hitters might do to them, rather than what they are going to do to the hitters. The confident pitcher knows that if he executes pitches, he will get hitters out. To think otherwise is to interfere with the ability to maximize that effort.

What the Pitcher Should Do…

- Understand that confidence is not a constant.
- Realize that self-doubt is to be expected but not encouraged.
- Focus on task during performance, rather than feelings.
- Be the pitcher he wants to be, rather than the one he is expected to be.
- Be accountable for behavior, rather than outcome.
- Know that life-threatening, catastrophic consequences will not result from a poor pitching performance.
- Understand that failing at a task is not synonymous with being a failure as a pitcher.
- Know that he has done everything possible to prepare for performance, and that he is ready to do what he has done successfully many times before.
- Take responsibility for his own goals and actions, rather than being influenced by others and feel the need to apologize or make excuses for mistakes. Let his behavior speak for him.
- Take risks, rather than be careful.
- Be rational; examine any fears that might erode confidence and identify them as irrational—emotional.
- Be prepared. Have a plan, an approach that is aggressive and clear. Be confident in this preparation and focus on the behaviors within it.
- During competition, remember to coach himself regularly, using positive, task-oriented self-talk.
- Focus on what he wants to do, rather what the hitter might or might not do.
- During periods of diminished confidence, remember to trust his talent and know that "this too shall pass."

■ CONSISTENCY

Change is inevitable. The ability to change indicates an open mind. [See LEARNING] But when speaking of a behavioral approach to pitching, an established and appropriate approach, a pitcher will value consistency. He values it because he has defined and established his pitching approach; he has reached an understanding of what it takes to be an outstanding competitor, and so on. He learns more about the game and himself as he continues to pitch. And he adjusts—changes—accordingly. But as he goes about pitching, he trusts his behavioral plan—and sticks to it. His consistency is an indicator of his mental discipline.

"Consistent behavior leads to consistent performance," I tell pitchers. To stay with what a pitcher knows will work for him is to be rational, rather than emotional. It is a sign of trust, which requires courage. It is a focus on what to do, rather than how one feels. Consistency reinforces what the pitcher knows is appropriate, and this behavior becomes a habit. [See HABITS] By re-enacting these habits on a consistent basis, pitchers, to use one major leaguer's wry statement to me, "have a hard time doing the wrong thing." And his behaviors are pro-active, rather than re-active.

The consistency of performance will indeed be greatly determined by the consistency of a pitcher's state of mind—his thoughts and the resultant habituated actions. In competition, the pitcher strives to be unwavering, indiscriminate, methodical (meaning having a method and sticking to it), reliable…He practices with the same consistent intensity and focus. He always applies his mental energy to his purpose: to being a "winner." As Vince Lombardi reminded his players, "Winning is not a sometimes thing." The striving for excellence must be consistent, the execution must be consistent, and then only can the performance be consistent—a "winning" performance. [See WINNING]

Bobby Cox had this to say about Greg Maddux in 1995: "After watching him for two and a half years, you come to appreciate the consistency in performances, the consistency in his work between games, the consistency in his thought processes, the consistency in the excellence of his innings, his games. It is amazing, just amazing to watch. It just never varies." Years later, it still hadn't.

Greg Maddux continues being spoken of as an exemplar, deservedly so. Readers are well aware of his achievements and approach by now. But how about Bruce Walton? "Who?" you ask.

Bruce Walton is currently a minor league pitching instructor for the Toronto Blue Jays. He was selected by the Oakland Athletics' organization in the 16th round of the 1985 free-agent draft, and pitched in the minor leagues for Oakland from '85 to '92. Every spring, to my best recollection, he was a candidate for release. One or more minor league staff members always spoke up for keeping him, and so he was retained. Every year he had to fight his way onto a roster, and every year he did his job. He was unflappable and consistent. He loved the game and he loved pitching. Moreover, he was dependable, reliable. He took the ball as a starter, a middle reliever, a closer. "Whatever," he said. "I'm just happy to get the ball." He got the ball consistently, and he threw it with consistency.

In 1991, he was rewarded for that behavior—and by that behavior; he was called up to the major league team. Here was a pitcher with limited talent, that fact agreed upon by staff and by Bruce himself. But his approach never varied. He competed as if he were a "prospect," which no one considered him to be. He always pitched aggressively, and pitched ahead in the count as a result. His composure was remarkable. His achievement worthy of his make-up.

I recall this event: Oakland's Triple-A team, Tacoma, had a very bad flight time after a get-away game. The team was flying to Las Vegas; the pitching staff had been 'used up,' shot; a daytime doubleheader was to be played after the late-night/early-morning arrival. Walton was asked if he could start the first game. "Give us five innings, if you can," the manager coaxed. (Walton had been relieving.) Of course, he consented—and pitched a seven-inning shutout. His value to the organization was not based on talent; it was based on a trust of how he would behave on the mound when he took the ball, irrespective of the game's circumstance—or his own. Bruce Walton was dependable, consistent.

His pitching career ended after the 1994 season. His winning percentage as a major leaguer is 1.000—2-0.

What the Pitcher Should Do...

■ Realize that consistent performance is the result of consistent behavior, and that consistent behavior requires a consistent pattern of thought.

■ Understand that consistency is developed through mental discipline—repeatedly doing the "right thing," irrespective of circumstance or consequence.

■ Reiterate on a regular basis his "plan" (i.e., approach, behaviors, techniques, keys, etc.)

■ Hold himself accountable for the consistent implementation of this "plan" on the practice field and on the playing field.

■ Evaluate the consistency of his behavior on a daily basis—his work habits and game habits.

■ Be aware of the factors that tend to "throw him off the beam" and work rationally so as to be able to quickly "climb back on."

■ Remember that consistency also results from an unwavering trust in his own appropriate thoughts and behaviors, as they are reinforced through repetition and reinforcement. And that inconsistent views expressed by media, fans, opponents, *et. al.*, are irrelevant.

■ CONTACT

Many pitchers try to avoid contact of the ball with the hitters' bat. They do so either by trying to strike everyone out, thereby overthrowing, or by "picking"—"nibbling"—pitching out of the strike zone, where the hitter is unlikely to reach the ball. Neither of these two approaches is ever successful over time. (I am tempted to say *anytime*, but will restrain myself from throwing around absolutes.)

What little can be said about this topic is nevertheless essential. First, it should be noted that successful pitchers do not *avoid* contact; neither do they *allow* contact. Successful pitchers *force* contact. They want the hitters to put the ball into play, and they make the hitters do so. The sooner, the better.

Effective pitchers recognize and trust the probability of outcome being in their favor when a hitter makes contact. Statistics have taught him that. And they know from experience that when they attack the strike zone, when they act aggressively and confidently, they will most often have a positive outcome from a ball put into play.

Intelligence tells the pitcher this. Courage reminds him of it, when his left brain deserts him. With this appropriate mental message, the pitcher's talent will best be able to express itself. He will be in the "attack mode" when his message to the batter is, "Here, hit it."

The pitcher who values contact, shows that he values the defensive teammates behind him. His fielders reciprocate that feeling; defensive players love pitchers who force contact. Infielders particularly are quick to admit they are "into the game more," when hitters are swinging their bats. The defense is on its toes, rather than its heels, as it is when pitchers are trying to avoid contact.

The irony in a pitcher's reluctance for, or fear of, contact is that his behavior plays into his fear. He is feeding the monster he fears, rather than starving it. By avoiding contact, or by squeezing the ball and overthrowing, the pitcher invariably falls behind in the count. [See COUNT] When he feels he *must* throw a strike [See STRIKES], he does so in the hitter's count, *and* he usually steers or aims the ball. This is done with considerably less than his "best stuff." When the pitch is then hit hard, his fear or reluctance is validated. The monster has been fed.

The hitter has not been first cause in this event, though the pitcher's perspective often makes him see it that way. First cause must be traced to the pitcher's thought pattern and the resultant behavior. Responsibility rests there, and the pitcher must re-examine his thinking and his approach—and adjust them.

Part of this re-examination, particularly for starting pitchers, should include the recognition that "going after hitters" will reduce the pitch count. By forcing contact, pitchers will be able to stay in games longer, thereby allowing themselves to compete more effectively and help the entire staff to be better rested. They also will better preserve their own arm strength by reducing the number of pitches thrown.

When I have shagged in the outfield with pitchers during batting practice, I've spent considerable time watching what hitters are doing. Many hitters are outstanding "five o'clock hitters." But at 5:40 P.M. many seem to become less effective. That is the time coaches are apt to say, "This last round is for basehits." Approaches change, hands and muscles tighten. The hitters "have fun" as they "try" to get basehits. (A result goal.) The proportion of basehits to attempts is low.

If a hitter is at all susceptible to *that* kind of stimulus as an influence on his approach, what might happen during a game? The question is addressed to whomever I'm standing with in the outfield, as we watch balls popped up or pulled on the ground during this "round for hits." The pitcher knows the answer, and he also knows his "stuff" is superior, by far, to that of the coach throwing batting practice.

What the Pitcher Should Do...

- Review the statistical history of pitcher-hitter confrontation.
- Remember that aggressiveness is a desired aspect of an effective pitching approach, and that it implies "going after hitters."
- Understand that an aggressive and competitive pitcher does not want to avoid having the batter make contact, nor does he want to allow contact. Rather, he *makes* the batter have contact by attacking the strike zone early and often during the at-bat.
- Identify himself with the aggressive action of forcing contact, thereby defining the hitter's behavior as a reaction to his own.
- Understand that establishing the above behaviors is establishing one aspect of a pitcher's "dominance" over hitters.

- Value groundball outs more than strikeouts, as a general philosophy.
- Minimize the number of pitches thrown during each appearance by aggressively forcing contact early in the at-bat.
- Understand the related value of throwing fewer pitches, in terms of benefits to the defense, the rest of the pitching staff, and for his own arm strength and health.

■ CONTROL

The term "control" is misunderstood by many pitchers. The initial response when defining the word reveals an individual's belief that someone "under control" does not have strong emotions. This violates a pitcher's sense of competitive spirit. That is why I always remind such an individual that "aggressiveness under control" should be a competitor's mantra. The accelerator and the brake. Without the accelerator, the race cannot be won; without the brake, the race cannot be completed. The aggressive, competitive spirit is a great asset to a pitcher. But it must be accompanied by an ability to control strong emotions.

Control is also required of pitchers who tend to falter in competitive settings by having distracting thoughts related to failure. Doom and gloom. Their self-control must address the issue of passivity—not challenging hitters and/or not focusing on the task at hand. As noted in BALANCE, a pitcher can fall off the balance beam to one of two sides—being too aggressive or being too passive. In either case, falling off the beam implies a loss of control.

The popular "serenity prayer" addresses an essential point about control. In it, the speaker asks for help in order to understand and dismiss what cannot be controlled, strength to deal with what can be controlled and the wisdom to know the difference between the two. That wisdom, a prerequisite, can be hard to come by. It requires an introspection and awareness that is often obscured by the emotions of the moment. During competition, unharnessed emotions will send all the wrong messages to the pitcher's muscles. The pitcher must either be in control of his muscles or regain that control. Without it, he cannot compete effectively.

Part of a pitcher's understanding of how to better be in control of himself comes from making a distinction between "control" and "influence." Pitchers have told me they have lost control—of thoughts, muscles and the strike zone—to circumstance and surroundings in a game. But they do not lose control *to* them. They were influenced by events and environment; they lost control *because* of them. But they also lost control because they allowed their response to these factors to affect them in a way that forfeited control. The final responsibility was—and remains—theirs.

It should be made clear, therefore, that a pitcher "in control" is a pitcher in control of himself. It may appear that he is in control "of the situation," as a pitchers have said to me when things were going their way. But a pitcher cannot control a "situation" or results. An opposing player's actions are involved; the direction in which a ball is hit is involved; an umpire's questionable judgment can be made. Wind, rain—all uncontrollable. The pitcher can, however, control his own thoughts, his own body, his focus—the ball as it leaves his hand. His self-control *influences* outcome in his favor, in the long run, despite the workings of factors beyond his control.

Let me now identify a sampling of factors that can affect a pitcher's sense of control. The following list will serve that purpose:

- Anxiety related to results
- Pitching for statistics
- Men on base
- Giving hitters too much credit (fear of contact)
- Expectations of others
- Feeling a lack of preparation
- Perception of a threatening situation (big game, big inning)
- Sense of not having "best stuff"
- Disappointment (after a big hit or an error)
- Having a few bad outings
- Trying to please the manager or coach
- Trying too hard
- Frustration over last pitch

Just a sampling. The pitcher will either try to do too much (overthrow) or lose aggressiveness (try to avoid contact). He will have been influenced by any of the above factors, and as a result his thought pattern changes. He is distracted from his task, and in that way loses control of his approach, because of his attention to matters he cannot control.

The most common loss of control at the big league level is a pitch-to-pitch unhappiness, annoyance—frustration. Unless an adjustment is made before the next pitch, command and control will be lost. Brilliance in retrospect is not good enough for those who aspire to be excellent. The adjustment—off the mound—can just be a simple reminder to re-focus. "I've brainwashed myself to remember that you can't control your last pitch," said Kevin Brown. "It's already been thrown. So get over it. All you can control is the next pitch you're going to throw."

Greg Maddux learned long ago to distinguish between what he could and could not control. "I can control the pitches I make, how I handle my mechanics, how I control my frame of mind. [It] benefited me most... when I realized that I can't control what happens outside of my pitching," he explained.

In 1995, Philadelphia outfielder, Ryan Thompson, said of Maddux, "He's so good he's funny. It's like he's controlled by somebody." Funny to say, the somebody is *himself.*

Francis Bacon wrote, "The instruments of the mind...are as important as the instruments in the hand." A pitcher who controls his mind, will control the ball.

What the Pitcher Should Do...

- Understand there are matters he can control and those he cannot.
- Know the distractions which typically intrude on his thoughts before or after competition.
- Work at rationally diminishing and/or eliminating these uncontrollable elements.
- Be attentive always to the nature of thoughts that exist during competition—and control them so as to assure appropriate focus.
- Make necessary adjustments when there is a sense of loss of control by re-directing focus to task, getting off the mound and coaching self.
- Recognize that concentration, arousal, breathing, and all other behaviors are entirely within his control.
- Fortify himself regularly by reiterating his approach, with the goal being to have a mind impenetrable to distractions during competition.
- Should adverse circumstances develop during competition, remember to focus on what is most important and most controllable—the next pitch to be delivered.

■ COUNT

"...[C]ommon sense and statistics concur: Get ahead in the count," Tom Seaver has suggested. The thought is shared by anyone who discusses the game of baseball from a pitcher's point of view. "A no-brainer," as pitchers say. The statistics Seaver referred to came from thousands of pitching counts examined by a computer programmer. The three major league organizations I have worked for kept their own breakdown of averages when hitters put the ball into play on particular counts. Though their numbers vary somewhat, their theme is identical: "the game is the count." Bob Welch used that phrase often. It is an accurate one, I believe.

The numbers indicate that batters hit less than .200 when they are behind in the count, and that they hit over .300 on 2-0 counts, over .320 on 3-1 counts. The statistics have indicated that batters at the bottom of the order hit for higher average when hitting 1-0 in the count than the third or fourth hitters in the lineup, when these hitters are hitting 0-1. Another compelling statistic supports the cliché of most baseball broadcasters: the leadoff batter who walks scores almost 80 percent of the time. More statistics can be cited (there are *always* more statistics), but the point, I hope, has been made. Those who pitch ahead in the count will dramatically increase their chances for success.

Let us examine the count from the hitter's point of view. This I have learned: batters do not like hitting while behind in the count. As a result of having this attitude, many hitters put the ball into play on the first pitch. They are often called "aggressive hitters." But I consider many of them to be "anxious hitters." They have a particular aversion to hitting with two strikes, so they make certain not to get to two strikes. The stats on first-pitch batted balls are, as usual, in the pitcher's favor—by far.

With the count at 0-2 or 1-2, the hitter has a discomfort and uncertainty about what pitch the pitcher might throw. Having created that advantage by being aggressive, the pitcher should further that advantage by attacking the hitter in his vulnerability. The further into the count the pitcher gets by throwing pitches for balls, the more he loses his advantage of count. Hitters become more comfortable as they consider the pitcher to have fewer options of pitch selection.

Dennis Eckersley and Bob Tewksbury are retired. I will miss seeing them pitch. The two were exemplars, insofar as establishing a favorable pitcher's count is concerned. It is unsettling to many hitters to know they will surely be behind in the count. Many tend to change their approach from being aggressive to being defensive. Eck and Tewks could do that to hitters. David Wells has also been noted as a good example of a pitcher who seems to have the count in his favor at all times. Hitters know that and respond accordingly. A pitcher should, therefore, be determined to put hitters in the disadvantaged position of being behind in the count. To do otherwise would be, as Seaver would remind him, to fly in the face of common sense and statistics.

What the Pitcher Should Do...

- Be aware of the statistics that confirm the advantage of pitching ahead in the count.
- Understand that part of that advantage is based on hitters' discomfort, uncertainty and frustration in continually being in pitchers' counts.
- Recognize that pitching ahead in the count is a further statistical advantage, in that the averages which typically are in a pitcher's favor become more so.
- Define as a goal the ability to establish the count in his favor on a regular basis—by being aggressive and confident in the strategy.
- Recognize that many hitters who know a pitcher is regularly ahead in the count tend to become defensive, meaning anxious and unselective.
- Determine to get ahead in the count—and *stay* ahead.
- Attack the strike zone. [See STRIKES]

■ COURAGE

One of my pat introductions to a pitcher I'm meeting for the first time goes like this: "If I tell you that you'll be successful if you give me two things—intelligence and courage—and you tell me that you can only give me one of them, which do you think I'd ask for?"

The answer is too often, "Intelligence." Those who so reply, I advise that throwing a baseball aggressively does not take all that much intelligence. I find that for many, it does take a greater degree of courage than they seem to have. It is, perhaps, understandable. But it is not acceptable, if excellence as a pitcher is his goal.

I further explain that whatever "smarts" a pitcher may have is negated by his lack of courage. If a pitcher acts out his fears, he forfeits his intelligence, since he behaves emotionally, rather than rationally. He loses a doubleheader.

The Latin *cor* means "heart." To have courage is to have "heart"; that term is heard often enough around ballparks. To many, it implies fearlessness. But that is not the point of courage. To have courage is to act bravely *in spite* of the existence of fear. Dennis Eckersley has exemplified courage for as long as I have known him. Here is a pitcher—a man—who fought and won the battle against alcoholism, and who announced to the world that he was terrified of failure—of public embarrassment and humiliation should he perform poorly. The strategy was clear to him. Essentially, he said to himself, 'If I don't want to fail, then rather than acting out what I *feel*, I will act out what I *know* will help me to succeed." And he did; he was a consistently aggressive as a pitcher. And courage was evident in that consistency, which he expressed irrespective of circumstance. As a recovered alcoholic, Eck recognized that it is himself a person abandons when he acts out of his fears. [See FEAR]

Courage is facing fear and "spitting in its eye." Trying to avoid danger, as so many pitchers do by trying to avoid contact, is not an effective strategy. Nor does it bring safety. Rather, as has been said earlier, it almost guarantees failure. The advantage a pitcher has over the hitter is lost. The feeling of vulnerability is reinforced by the lack of courageous behavior. Dennis Eckersley's behavior pre-empted his feelings. As a result, fear dissipated; courage prevailed.

Courage allows the pitcher to express all his other qualities; acting out of fear suppresses them. Stifles them. Challenging fear elevates behavior and elevates the man. It even seems to elevate the pitching mound.

To not have fear is to not require courage. Remember earlier the words of some pitchers: "No brain, no pain." The implication is that one is blessed who doesn't know enough to be afraid. Yet some people would wonder at a discussion of pitchers—professional pitchers, at that—being fearful about playing a game. But all people have fears, whether hidden or exposed—whether an athlete or an accountant. Since one's emotional system is the source of one's fears, the environment and activity is less significant than the personality and perception of the fearful person. Baseball may just be a "game" to a spectator, but it can be quite a bit more to a participant.

Courage is more than acting against fears. For a pitcher, courage is required to act against fatigue. Performance that reflects a "feeling" the pitcher has of being tired also reflects a "giving in." If "fatigue makes cowards of us all," as Vince Lombardi suggested, it behooves a pitcher to be in shape. But well-conditioned pitchers may still work hard enough to become tired. A courageous pitcher does not let a decrease in his level of physical energy diminish the level of his mental energy. Tired muscles should not be allowed to surrender because they are being "led" by a tired mind. "Sucking it up," as pitchers say, is an expression of courage. Satchel Paige used to brag that the more tired he became, the more effective he became. Self-indoctrination such as that makes bravery easier to come by.

As discussed in an earlier section, battling through adversity also requires courage. "Losing one's heart" is really "giving one's heart away." Not an act of courage. Having everything seemingly going wrong during a performance tests a pitcher's mettle. Umpires' calls, errors behind him, lack of "good stuff," general bad luck—all can be included in the test. The strong of heart fight through it. They pass the test. [See RESPONSE]

Whatever the circumstances may be that might "threaten" a pitcher, [See PERSPECTIVE] whether it be starting a "big game," facing an imposing hitter, coming into the game in a crucial situation, the resolution to stay with his aggressive approach and the courage to act it out will make a "winner" of the pitcher, irrespective of the results.

All the qualities of a pitcher are better able to express themselves when courage clears the way. Talent armed with bravery becomes a formidable combination, as I tell those pitchers I meet for the first time.

Unfortunately, I have seen too many pitchers disappear from professional baseball because they could not so arm themselves. The words of Sydney Smith apply exactly, "A great deal of talent is lost in this world for want of a little courage."

What the Pitcher Should Do...

- Realize that courage, by definition, allows for the existence of fear.
- Understand that a pitcher's attempt to avoid "danger" is focused on fear or caution and will most likely produce whatever he is trying to avoid.
- Recognize that a fear has an emotional basis, whereas a plan of attack has a rational one.
- Integrate a rational, aggressive plan—approach—into behavior and fear is pre-empted by the courageous act.
- Know that behavior is entirely within his control, and that courageous behavior is a "winner's" behavior.
- Identify the situations or circumstances that challenge his courage, so, forewarned, he is forearmed—and better able to face up to these fears or worries.
- Understand that courage allows talent to express itself.

■ DEDICATION
[See APPENDIX A]

Although every pitcher proclaims that he wants to succeed (I've never had one ask me to help him fail), not everyone wants to do what it takes to reach that goal. Yet, if the truth be told, and it is my intention to do so, 95 percent of the pitchers I have been around over the past 15 years—at the major and minor league levels—have conscientiously dedicated themselves to their profession. That vast majority wants to do "whatever it takes." It is another matter "to know what it takes," but I'll defer that point for a moment.

There are lapses in commitment, to be sure. Part of the human condition. An example is the laxity too often displayed in PFP, as discussed earlier. Pitchers may "skate" on conditioning more on occasion—their running or lifting program. More than occasional is their straying from a proper diet. All part of being human, but that is not an appropriate rationalization. [See EXCUSES]

Anyone who dedicates himself to excellence in his field must make sacrifices. In making them, he elevates himself to a level of extraordinary behavior, separating himself from the ordinary. He asks more of himself, within reason, rather than allowing less of himself. He shuns instant gratification, the pleasure of mass man. Instead, the exceptional man opts for behaviors with a long-term payoff. A payoff that moves him toward his long-term goal through short-term focus on daily achievement. Such acts require and further develop trust, courage, discipline, intelligence, responsibility, focus, and such. The process is not an unappealing one for the truly dedicated pitcher. As Tom Seaver discovered quite a few years ago, whatever enhanced his ability to do well became a joy to do.

The daily pursuit of excellence indicates a commitment to personal and professional growth, which, in turn, helps build and reinforce self-confidence. If it were easy, everyone would do it. It isn't; they don't.

The pitcher who wishes to be an exceptional performer must learn to be an exceptional "behaver." First, as suggested above, he must know "what it takes." In addition to knowing what will help him enhance and maximize his performance, he must have the desire to do whatever he has determined to be required. And he should enjoy the doing—the process—as well as the payoff.

This attitude does not come naturally for most. But attitudes are choices, and any pitcher who aspires to excellence makes "unnatural" good choices that, over time, become "second nature." Good habits are as hard to break as bad ones. [See HABITS]

Years ago, catcher Rich Gedman told me of Roger Clemens' dedication to his physical conditioning. Clemens seems to be as good as he ever has been, and it is more than 10 years since Gedman shared his thought with me. That would be the mid-'80s. In 1997 and 1998 Clemens won his fourth and fifth Cy Young Award.

While Clemens and all those who work so diligently on their physical conditioning are to be admired, it "takes" mental conditioning, as well, to become a peak performer. The ordeal involved in this process is a hidden one; the person on the outside cannot admire a pitcher's mental preparation the way he can the physical. He cannot judge it—until it's time for competition. And though the observer cannot see inside a pitcher's head, he can see the expression of the pitcher's thoughts and feelings—his preparation or lack of it—through the pitcher's behavior on the mound. How he competes, how he makes adjustments, how he approaches the hitters, how he responds to adversity—how he executes his pitches.

And *that* is a big part of "what it takes." Physical preparation *and* mental preparation are the ingredients for success. After his trade to the Yankees in February 1999, an executive of the team who traded Clemens and who traded for him called Clemens "a warrior." The Toronto and New York general managers alluded to both of the aforementioned ingredients. [See WARRIOR]

Pitchers who are diligent in their running program, who work on their lifting program regularly and appropriately, and whose sleeping and dietary habits are impeccable, are indeed preparing for excellence. However, the mental and the physical must complement each other. Extra running in the outfield the day after a poor pitching performance, and I have witnessed this form of self-flagellation numerous times, will not help a pitcher to learn how to get ahead in the count, or replace negative thoughts with positive ones during competition. Perhaps a pitcher is not aware of his actual needs. That is one problem that is easier to solve than a pitcher's flight from doing what he knows he needs to do. I have had to address this issue with a significant number of pitchers over the years. Their reactions in words have often been much like their reactions in deed (the extra running). It is a form of denial, as Byatt says, a "shrink[ing of] reality to a single pattern." Run more, lift more, run more, lift more—understand less.

Extra physical work neither compensates for nor corrects an unacceptable mental approach. For many, running is an easier task than: A) confronting his mental/behavioral inadequacies; B) having the self-discipline to make his "psyche sweat," by working on the improvement of the mental part of his game. Unless a pitcher addresses A and B, he cannot consider himself to be "dedicated" to maximizing his ability to perform. This book addresses the issues and strategies of the mental game of pitching; a pitcher's total dedication is measured, after all is said, by what is done.

What the Pitcher Should Do...

- Learn *"what* it takes" to succeed, so he can *do* "what it takes."
- Understand that any dedication to success includes the sacrificing of instant gratification for long-term achievement.
- Develop an attitude that reflects an appreciation of whatever process helps him develop into a more effective pitcher.
- Understand that physical conditioning is one factor of that development and mental conditioning is another—and that they are not mutually exclusive.
- Be aware of a possible tendency to react to an ineffective performance by "working harder" at physical conditioning, though the cause of the ineffectiveness has been his mental approach.
- Identify the elements of the "mental game" and dedicate himself to their development and improvement as regularly as he does to physical enhancement. [See TABLE OF CONTENTS!]

- Understand his own strengths and weaknesses, i.e., the specific skills he needs to work on.
- Be determined to hold himself accountable on a daily basis for improvement of these mental skills. [See GOALS]

■ DISCIPLINE

The longest chapter in *The Mental Game of Baseball* is the one that treats the topic of mental discipline. *The American Heritage Dictionary* defines discipline as "training that is expected to produce a specified character or pattern of behavior, especially that which is expected to produce moral or mental improvement."

Mental discipline is the umbrella that covers just about everything else concerned with "the mental game." A pitcher can develop the ability to effectively and consistently direct his mind through this discipline. Courage in battle takes discipline; concentration takes discipline; preparation, self-coaching, consistency, the breaking of bad habits through the development of good ones are all under the umbrella. Or, to use some players' more palatable metaphor, mental discipline is "the whole enchilada." A pitcher who hopes to perform at his highest level of physical ability must develop an insistent discipline of the mind.

A more common term used in the game of baseball is "mental toughness." It is an adequate term, if it is properly defined. But my concern has always been that it can be misunderstood, because, to many people, the word "toughness" implies an aggressive action exclusively, without the suggestion of self-control. The "tough" fighter in the boxing ring, who fearlessly flails away at his opponent, can console himself only with his fearlessness—physical toughness—after he gets up off his rear end. "Mental toughness" requires aggressiveness and *control*. "Physical toughness" alone does not adequately define "mental toughness."

After the defining of terms, I find it easier to use "mental discipline" when addressing pitchers. They then understand that what is under the umbrella requires discipline: patterned thinking, controlled focus, controlled behavior, consistent preparation, and persistent expression of will. That serves me better than just telling them to "be tough," though after the enactment of these behaviors, they certainly get my respect for being just that.

In June 1998, en route to the Chicago Bulls second "three-peat" of the decade, Michael Jordan noted that fans and critics had expressed concern about the Bulls' "physical tiredness" during the finals against Utah. "You don't become champions five times without having some type of mental advantage. Right now, we are mentally strong enough to defend what we have...The mental side counts for something." It counted for plenty. It helped them become champions for the sixth time, though Jordan felt the

Bulls "…may not be as gifted [as Utah.]" The discipline was in playing with focus on function, rather than on fatigue or the perceived "physical gifts" of the opposition. After all was said and *done*, that was playing "tough."

The expression of mental discipline requires great energy and dedication. The process is an exhausting one for those who have not previously held themselves accountable for such consistently controlled and determined behavior.

In the late 1980s, the Oakland organization had a Triple-A pitcher named Rick Rodriguez. (He is a minor league pitching coach these days.) During his performances, Rick had a tendency of using much of his energy by reacting excessively when he was unhappy or frustrated by circumstance, or when he was angry with himself. He would stomp around the mound, kick the dirt, and talk internal trash. Of course, his attention would be misdirected.

He decided to work at changing that pattern of behavior, on keeping his mind focused on task through self-discipline. The first step toward that goal—his awareness—had already been taken. Next, he needed a strategy—the "what to do." When he sensed himself "losing it," as he would say, he separated himself from the rubber and/or the mound. He changed his environment, so to speak. He calmed himself, coached himself, established a regulated breathing pattern and directed his energies toward the execution of a pitch. He also controlled his responses to pitches and results. [See RESPONSES]

The first time he integrated his strategy into behavior (which is the last step in the process) was during a game played against the San Francisco Giants Triple-A team at Phoenix Municipal Stadium. Rodriguez was in trouble in every inning, it seemed. This, itself, was not a particularly unusual circumstance. What was unusual was the fact that he got out of every inning unscathed. Baserunners did not score. In the past, he had been distracted—"annoyed"—by having runners on base. That day he focused on the next pitch. On what he would do, rather than what had just happened. No emotional outbursts.

Rick Rodriguez was taken out of the game after seven innings with a 2-1 lead. After a time, I left the dugout and went up the ramp into the clubhouse, where I found him sitting in front of his locker with head in hands.

"Nice going," I said. "Are you OK?"

"I'm wiped out," he replied. "Mentally."

What Dante called *"tutta spenta"*—entirely extinguished—and Rodriguez looked it. "That was bleeping hard work," he continued. A pause. Then, "That kind of game—in the past—I don't make it out of the third [inning]." Energy well spent. Harnessed, directed. He had gotten out of jams each inning through the ordeal of self-discipline. He had "hung tough," if you will.

It was a difficult task but, as Rick remarked the following day, "Worth it."

After having played his final hole in the Andersen Consulting Match-Play Tournament in February 1999, Tiger Woods spoke of being "mentally fried." Said Woods, "I know what I have to do, so I focus on that. But as soon as it is over, then you feel it." Those who work on it, feel it.

The process Rick Rodriguez and others have gone through is 1) the identification of the issue; 2) the formulation of a strategy; 3) the enactment of that strategy. The 'problems' and strategies are presented within the covers of this book. These strategies may be considered the "umbrella" of self-discipline. The pitcher is responsible for keeping that umbrella open, holding it high, and staying under it.

To have the ability to effectively address every topic in this book is to have optimal mental discipline. Self-discipline is a form of freedom. Freedom from laziness and lethargy, freedom from the expectations and demands of others, freedom from weakness and fear—and doubt. Self-discipline allows a pitcher to feel his individuality, his inner strength, his talent. He is master of, rather than slave to, his thoughts and emotions. A pitcher with great mental discipline is usually a pitcher with great confidence. And as Al Leiter expressed and hundreds of others have understood, confidence, or lack of it, ".. is the difference between having a good year and a bad year."

What the Pitcher Should Do...

- Understand that by developing effective mental discipline he is learning to control the emotions, thoughts, and behaviors that would, if uncontrolled, be distractions during performance.
- Recognize that mental discipline addresses whatever distractions or behavioral tendencies may adversely affect him before, during, or after competition.

- Know that this identification is prerequisite for the process of self-improvement, and includes eating habits, sleeping patterns, and conditioning.

- Be aware also of the more subtle "weaknesses" that inhibit performance, such as lax practice habits, being less attentive when his team is far ahead or far behind in score, not being mentally prepared for a game which seemingly has less or little importance.

- Understand that the process of developing mental discipline is an on-going and demanding ordeal, requiring mental energy and stamina, as well as the expression of will power. [See WILL]

- Set as a goal the mastery of individual mental skills he wishes to work on daily [See GOALS], knowing that a goal is a promise, but self-discipline is keeping it.

■ EMOTIONS

I refer again to pitcher Tim Belcher's reference to an "attitude" of mine: "… Like Harv always says, 'I don't care about your feelings, I care about your actions.'"

Perhaps I don't let on that I care about players' feelings, though I do. The problem is that they do not need any additional caring from me; they already care *too much* about players' feelings. The trigger to these feelings is the emotional system, and as I "always say" to pitchers, "Work out of your rational system, your brain, not your emotional system. You will dissolve reason by arousing passion." And many do. They operate out of what I call their "screaming (emotional) needs."

François Mitterand has spoken of examining "a situation with as little emotion and as much logic and intelligence as you can bring to it, which you cannot bring to it if your heart is breaking." Or your knees are shaking. A pitcher facing a situation to which he gives importance, whether he perceives it to be a threat or a challenge, will be required to master his emotions, if he is not to have them master him.

As has been stated earlier, no apology is ever needed for a pitcher *having* the feelings. We all have them. As Diane Ackerman has written, "It is both our panic and our privilege to be mortal and sense-full." But though a pitcher's emotions may be "normal," his behavior as a competitor should be exceptional. Being normal, again using the players' vernacular, "doesn't get it done." [See CONTROL]

The ideal is to have what one feels be the same as what he knows. In such cases, the pitcher's preparation and talent makes him confident, and that confidence allows him to behave accordingly. A "feeling" based on rationality, rather than emotionality propels him upward. When the stars of rationality and emotionality are aligned, the heavens in his head are without turmoil. "You can hope for it kid," my father would say, "but don't expect it." Work for it, I would say.

The experience of emotion involves the combining of information from three sources. A pitcher's brain gets feedback from internal organs, and body parts triggered by the sympathetic nervous system produce a state of arousal that is not clearly determined. The emotion experienced by the pitcher will be determined by the interpretation he gives to his aroused state. [See AROUSAL] If he interprets "threat," he will feel the related emotions; if he interprets "challenge," he will feel emotions produced from that interpretation. If he is bored, a corresponding state of arousal will be delivered to his consciousness.

The feedback a pitcher gets from three sources will result from his conscious experience of emotion. The sources are: 1) his memory of past experiences, good or bad, and his assessment of the current situation (whether or not he has done well under similar circumstances or in a like environment); 2) information from external sources colliding with his sensory system (hostile fans or the league's leading hitter at bat); 3) messages to the brain from his organs and muscles (sweaty palms, tight muscles, dry mouth, etc.).

The messages the brain gets from these sources are many and varied. So are the resultant emotions. Emotions such as: self-doubt, tension, fear, embarrassment, confusion, self-consciousness, guilt, susceptibility to intimidation, panic, frustration, anger, and more. My message to pitchers is simply, "Know your enemies. Only then can you learn to combat them."

I do not dwell on these feelings—on the emotional system—when I speak with pitchers. Certainly, I recognize when performances are being driven by disruptive feelings—when pitchers are stuck in what Robertson Davies called "the gumbo of their emotions." But my responsibility is to help them learn how to get "unstuck." And so, after understanding what emotions have been controlling the pitcher, and the reasons why, the compelling subject becomes *appropriate behavior*—and the ways to produce it. The agenda of this book is to take the reader through the same process. Once again, a pitcher must be aware of the issue or problem, he then (with or without assistance) develops a strategy, and he integrates it into behavior. Only the first of that triumvirate deals with the emotions. The payoff comes from steps two and three. Step three is his responsibility entirely.

A pitcher's performance declines when it is driven by any of the emotions mentioned above. These emotions can sneak into the pitcher's system in the most subtle of ways. A dramatic circumstance is not necessary to trigger trouble. The negative process can begin when he wakes up in the morning and has the feeling; "This is not going to be one of my days." It is not uncommon. His prophecy will be fulfilled. The way a pitcher interprets his warm-up in the bullpen also has been the cause of a detrimental negative emotion. These are but two examples to reinforce the point. The enemy can be camouflaged.

How to fight back? With awareness. With an intelligence that will help to control the emotions by preempting them with positive, functional thoughts. And/or with courage, which will help give the pitcher an opportunity to work through the emotions. The learned habits based on rationality and inner strength make a pitcher much less vulnerable to the disruptive forces of his emotions. But the habits must become strong, because the emotions produced in a highly competitive setting are formidable. Firm and constant governance is required.

What the Pitcher Should Do...

- Remember that behavior, rather than feelings, is what matters in competition.
- Understand the way in which the conscious experience of emotions is produced.
- Recognize that the many emotions which can intrude on his performance are normal and universal, but that extraordinary behavior is required of elite athletes.
- Understand that he can perform well despite intrusive emotions, if he controls them with thoughts related to function. Recognize, as well, that he can fight through them by applying mental discipline.
- Coach himself to get off the rubber and/or the mound to gather himself, breathe deeply, and to redirect his thoughts to task—focusing on the next pitch.

■ EXCUSES

Many years ago, as a boy, I came home after having played a baseball game at Frankie Frisch Field in the Bronx. The team I played for was the 52nd Precinct in the Police Athletic League, New York's beloved "PAL." I had not pitched badly, but when questioned about "how the game went" by my father, I managed to come up with some excuse for one of the many imperfections in my performance. He responded by calling me "Alibi Ike." I hadn't ever heard the name, but did not confess my ignorance. After asking around, I was informed of the source by one of my friends. Alibi Ike was a character in a short story by Ring Lardner.

I found a collection of Lardner stories in the school library. "Alibi Ike" was written in 1915. It was a baseball story, and Ike was, naturally, the main character in the story. He was a talented baseball player who nevertheless felt compelled to make excuses. Many of them. A teammate named Carey described Ike as the most prolific excuse-maker he, Carey, had ever met, though "prolific" was not Carey's term.

He explained, "I've known lots o' guys that had an alibi for every mistake they made; I've heard pitchers say that the ball slipped when somebody cracked one off'n them; I've heard infielders complain of a sore arm after heavin' one in the stand, and I've saw outfielders tooken sick with a dizzy spell when they've misjudged a fly ball." But Alibi Ike "got the world beat."

Ike explained *everything* he did, the good and the bad. He was an apologist and a bore. His personal weakness was apparent to his teammates, if not to him. A mistake could be explained, and a good performance could be improved upon "if only." No act of his spoke for itself.

Needless to say, I was not flattered by my father's reference after having read the story, and I vowed not to make that kind of presentation again. I have since heard how obvious excuses sound to the listener. And I grew to understand how harmful they could be to the maker.

Excuses can be a double-edged sword. The main purpose for their use is to deflect criticism. By doing that, the excuse-maker keeps himself from learning to correct whatever mistake he has made. There is a point on that sword, as well: the point of irresponsibility. By not taking responsibility for his actions, he is illustrating a lack of courage and lack of confidence in himself. That is a painful slicing and sticking oneself.

Voltaire said that to understand a man makes it impossible to hate him. One can hate an excuse, but should understand the excuse-maker. Especially if it is the pitcher himself making the excuses. In the understanding is the opportunity to fix the problem. The excessive excuse-maker was probably the object of frequent, and very often painful, criticism as a youth. Either he felt a need to defend himself continuously—or he didn't dare to, fearing further "abuse" from the severe critic. Whatever the case, he dragged the need from childhood into adulthood. [See FEAR OF FAILURE]

To oversimplify, as time passed, this youth perceived everybody to be a potential critic. He tended to over-explain every action that might seem to be questionable. The explanations took on the form of apologies, which, as presented by him, became excuses in fancy attire. His days can now be very difficult, often filled what might be called a subtle, constant "psychological toothache." Sometimes not so subtle.

An excuse engenders weakness, rather than courage. The courage of honest introspection is a required first step toward the changing of negative, ingrained habits. As has been said quite often, awareness is the first step to change. If no one else tells a person about his tendency, the person is left with himself as his sole resource. If the reader, as a pitcher particularly, suspects such tendencies in himself, he should re-read this material and then look within.

It should be noted that the people who are hearing the excuses, the excuse-maker's audience, hear them as a confession of guilt, not innocence, as was the original intention. The only person being deceived is the excuse-maker, because he has trained himself to believe his excuses, a form of denial, and/or because he wrongly believes he is deceiving his audience. In either case, he does harm to himself. He hears denial; the audience hears admission. In the world of baseball, teammates lose respect for the pitcher who makes excuses. The pitcher, himself, has little chance to build self-respect through such behavior. The most compassionate verdict would be "guilty with an explanation." But still "guilty."

Finally, I will present a list of excuses I have heard over time from professional pitchers. It is my hope that the discussion of excuses that precedes the list has revealed my serious concern for the issue and the players who have tried to deal with it. I make mention of this only because a self-actualized reader may think the subject to be problematic. Others may feel the presentation to be made with an amused, critical tone. Neither is true.

The list of excuses includes the following:

- A bad mound
- A bad catcher
- A bad defense
- A bad arm, undetected by medical staff
- Bad luck
- Bad seams on the baseball
- Too long a period of time between pitching appearances
- Too short a period of time between pitching appearances
- Bad concentration, attributed to the perception that the pitcher is only used "to mop up games"
- Distractions related to:
  contractual situations
  trade rumors (often only heard by the pitcher himself)
  rumors of demotion in level
  rumors of promotion
  unidentified "personal problems"
  a pitching coach's poor opinion of his ability
  a manager's poor opinion of his ability
  a minor league director's poor opinion of his ability

Though I feel the list to be excessive as I write it, I also know it is incomplete. The point, I hope, has been made. [See RESPONSIBILITY]

The pitcher must first slay his demons, before he can slay dragons. Excuses die, achievement endures.

What the Pitcher Should Do...

- ■ Understand the source of excuses.
- ■ Be sensitive to any tendency he may have to make excuses.
- ■ Recognize the damage done by excuses, including the inability to learn and make corrections because the mistake is denied.
- ■ Understand the source of his own behavior, but not so as to use *that* as an excuse.
- ■ Be introspective and identify the qualities that have enabled him to reach the level he has, as a person and as an athlete.

- Build a positive self-image by taking responsibility for his thoughts and actions, rather than by trying to excuse them.
- Understand that mistakes are surely not goals, but they are opportunities for growth, if followed by learning, rather than by an excuse or excessive explanation.
- Understand that mistakes are important, because they illustrate the pitcher's areas of need for improvement. Correction, not excessive criticism—whether it comes from a parent, a teammate or a coach—should be the focus. [See LEARNING]
- Realize that courage and conviction are required to change a negative habit, particularly if experience has taught him to have the automatic response of excuse making.
- Know that, through his determination to change his bad habit, he can learn to like himself more, even as he is not necessarily liking some of his behaviors.
- Remember that all change is process.
- Pay attention to his "progress" on a daily basis.
- Know the very best strategy for controlling excuses is to keep quiet and allow the deed to represent itself—for better or for worse. And know that in either case, he is on the path to self-respect, though it may be difficult for him to believe at the beginning of the journey.

■ EXECUTION

The execution of pitches, one at a time, is the singular task that moves a baseball game from its opening to its close. All that appears in this book is aimed at and reduced to the execution of each pitch as it is delivered.

Unfortunately, all the complexities that are part of the human condition, all the complications pitchers bring to the game of baseball, too often engender the execution of a pitch. In order for that pitch to be well executed, the depth, fullness, and complexity that is part of being human must be replaced by the limited, narrow focus, and simplicity of thought required to be a pitcher. An effective pitcher, that is.

A character in an Iain Pears novel talks of someone who puts "so much effort...into squeezing in knowledge that there isn't room left over for common sense." Many pitchers are guilty of just that. They try to squeeze information into their heads about their mechanics, about the hitter, about irrelevant circumstances and consequences and leave no room for the common sense of focusing on the target and delivering the baseball aggressively.

Such pitchers fail to "keep it simple, stupid." The simplicity of "selection, location and target" is a required component of a well-executed pitch. Also, a pitcher's trust in his talent and preparation allow him to be relaxed, aggressive, and under control. Anything else gets in the way of effective execution.

I tell pitchers that they are defined by "how the baseball leaves their hand." By this I mean that the pitcher has control over his approach (and response), but not over the result—what happens to the ball once it leaves his hand. He is entirely responsible for how the pitch is executed, but not for how the batter behaves. If he gets an out on a poorly thrown pitch, he may be happy with his good fortune, but he should not be satisfied because of the result. His execution was not acceptable, and that is how he is measured—or should be.

Conversely, if he makes a great pitch and the hitter manages a "lucky hit" or battles the pitch and gets on base, the pitcher surely has his momentary unhappiness about the result, but he did what he wanted to with the pitch; he executed it well. He had better understand that. [See RESPONSE] As he is competing, the execution is all that that should matter—because it is what he can control.

Ron Darling pitched with the Oakland Athletics during part of my tenure with the organization. A very intelligent Ivy League college graduate, Darling had a tendency to "think too much" about the wrong things. His manager felt that, on the mound, Darling did not use "common sense." The penetrating thought required to arrive at a complicated answer is not the stuff of effective execution of a pitch. Darling, and the many others whose "profound" but distracting thoughts inhibited their performance, would have been better served by applying the wisdom of Occam's Razor, which suggested that "...the simplest explanation of a phenomenon is usually the most trustworthy."

On July 18, 1998, Al Leiter returned to the mound for the New York Mets, after having partially torn a tendon in his left knee on June 26. He pitched six scoreless innings, giving up two singles. "It was fun," Leiter said after the game. "It's such simple stuff. Move the ball around. Change speeds. Locate the ball...Get ahead of hitters." Execute, pitch by pitch, in other words. It is better to "understand" a little than misunderstand a lot.

Tampa Bay pitcher Wilson Alvarez struggled through the 1998 season. In the latter part of the season, after having had downtime because of an arm injury, Alvarez ran off five consecutive good performances. He explained to the media, "I'm just trying to be aggressive and not trying to throw the perfect pitch. I'm just letting it go and seeing what happens because I've got eight guys in the field who can make the out for me." A simple—and appropriate—assessment of his execution. He said nothing about hitters. An effective pitcher does not out-smart the opposition, he out-executes them. [See HITTERS]

I spoke in earlier pages about natural instincts and acquired instincts. In order to be a successful pitcher, one is not required to have a genetic predisposition for understanding how to execute a pitch effectively. The understanding and the skill can be developed. [See LEARNING] When interviewed a few years ago, Greg Maddux told the interviewer that he would not have had such success in his career if he hadn't started to learn to change his focus while with the Chicago Cubs early in his career. He learned the value of focusing on execution.

"I was worrying so much about winning and losing, or getting an out, or giving up a hit, that it was affecting the way I was pitching," Maddux explained. "It was interfering with my ability to make good pitches," he said. Thinking exclusively about execution, Maddux went on, "...made a lot of sense to me, so I tried to do it. It's easier said than done because you play this game to win. But at the same time you have to forget about that and concentrate on what it takes to win. For me, it's making good pitches."

A few years ago, when I was working for the Florida organization, the Marlins played a game against Atlanta at Joe Robbie Field, as it was then named. Maddux pitched that particular night. He left the game with a 2-1 lead after having pitched seven innings. The reliever gave up the tying run, so Maddux did not get a "W." The Braves eventually won, 3-2.

After the game, I met Maddux in the player's parking lot. I thought I'd "test" him. I asked him ambiguously," "So, how was it out there tonight?" Would he complain about not getting a win, about meager run support? His answer was, not surprisingly, exemplary. He looked at me with a knowing smirk and replied, "Fifty out of seventy-three." All that needed to be said on the subject. He had thrown seventy-three pitches and had executed fifty to his satisfaction. No results, no explanations. Maddux evaluates his performance by assessing the ratio between intent and action, pitch by pitch, as he competes with himself first, in order to effectively compete with the hitter. He works toward pitching what writer Richard J. Brenner called "that perfect Platonic game." That is the theoretically "simple" bottom line for every pitcher. [See SIMPLICITY]

Poet Gary Snyder might describe the simplicity of executing pitch after pitch as "relentless clarity at the heart of work."

What the Pitcher Should Do...

- Recognize that he has complete responsibility for and control of the execution of a pitch.
- Know that the individual pitch is the immediate task at hand and should therefore be his immediate and exclusive concern and focus.
- Understand that he, with all the inherent complications of being human, must bring simplicity and singular focus to the game.
- Recognize that this is done by being attentive to the effective execution of each pitch—that the next pitch is the most important pitch he will throw. Then the next one after that, and so on. One at a time.
- Remember that selection, location, and target are the keys for focusing on execution. And that an aggressive, controlled delivery is the other element of the proper execution of a pitch.
- Include as a major component in any evaluation of performance the relationship between the number of pitches thrown and the number effectively executed.

■ FEAR OF FAILURE

Many years ago, I walked up a dirt road in Vermont, holding the hand of a son who was about to wait for a school bus for the first time. He would board the bus that would take him to his first kindergarten experience. As we got to the top of the hill, where we were to wait, I sensed an edginess in him. He was anticipating what was to come, of course. I thought I'd short-circuit any possible anxiety. "This is exciting," I said enthusiastically. "Melissa (his older sister) is excited; Mom is excited; I'm excited!"

His reply was matter-of-fact. "*You're* excited; "*I'm* nervous."

Indeed, there is a difference.

Nervousness is an excited state grounded in worry, which, in turn, can create a feeling of anxiety strong enough to affect behavior. [See ANXIETY] If not adequately addressed, a performance anxiety can grow into a pervasive fear. In baseball, that fear is usually a fear of failure. Two factors determine the extent to which the fear will adversely affect performance: the magnitude of the fear and the individual's coping mechanisms, or absence of them.

Fears are acquired through direct and vicarious experience. Difficult and troubling situations can have dramatic effects on people, whether they personally go through them or witness others going through them. The more dramatic the situation, the more likely the person experiencing it is to acquire a related feeling of fear. From that point, the fear may be maintained and intensified through traumatic memory and a self-defeating anticipation of meeting the situation again.

A pitcher with such a negative expectation is not likely to cope with a performance he sees as threatening, rather than challenging. His preoccupation is with his feelings regarding danger. He is distracted by these feelings and therefore unable to focus on task. He expects to perform poorly and he does.

A pitcher who knows or believes he is able to cope with (i.e., control) threatening events diminishes his fear of them. He gives himself a chance to perform well. Of course, the ideal is for a pitcher to see any situation as a challenge—a joy! That pitcher knows he has nothing to fear. He expects to do well, and he usually does.

Well then, what *does* a pitcher have to fear? Getting back to Dennis Eckersley's pronounced fears, I can list embarrassment and humiliation at the top. I have experienced pitchers who fear disapproval of a loved one; others fear disappointing people—parents, teammates. They have a distorted view of their responsibility, just as the more dramatic fears illustrate a distorted view of the individual himself and his world. All these narrow fears are spokes of a wheel, which has "failure" as its hub. The important understanding is that these fears are real to these people. Very real. Someone who has not felt anything closely approximating such intense feelings cannot empathize—nor even understand, perhaps.

The performance of a pitcher with fear is adversely affected by more than the mental distraction itself. The body produces an alarm reaction, produced by a number of stressors. The sympathetic nervous system readies the pitcher for "fight or flight." In the first case, the "fighting" will be uncontrolled—panicky and desperate, and ineffective, needless to say. In the second case, the pitcher will "cave in." [See PRESSURE] In either case, the pitcher's respiration and heart rates will increase, too much adrenalin will surge through him, his muscles will tense, breathing will shorten, his sugar level rise, blood will move away from the skin surface, so he will lose his "feel" of the ball. So much for the bad news.

The good news is that I have seen a good number of pitchers overcome their fears, and a greater number learn to cope with them so they would not interfere with performance. The very exceptional, Dennis Eckersley, for example, harnessed their fears and used them to motivate themselves to succeed.

All three processes require what is called "intellectualization." The first step is "catastrophizing." A player and I would explore the worst possible scenario, the most dramatically "terrible" thing that could happen in his career. The core of his fear. The intent is to reduce the arousal caused by the perceived threat by distancing the player from the discomfort, through the use of his intelligence, rather than his emotions—the prevailing emotion being fear. The great golfer, Jack Nicklaus, used the technique successfully. A pitcher who uses the technique learns that fears tell lies. They suggest to the pitcher that situations he will face are more difficult to deal with than they actually are.

Iris Murdoch wrote, "Demons and viruses live in every human organism, but in some happy lives never become active." But it is possible to deactivate the active ones. When someone intellectually examines his fears or concerns, he diminishes the impact the emotion can have on his system. For a pitcher to be perform successfully, a "locus of control" must be developed. Essentially, that was what Walt Weiss did. I encouraged him to live "from the inside out, rather than from the outside in." People with internal control are able to cope with fears because they come to understand the fears are their response to—their interpretation of—external events or situations. They are not inherent in the "outside world."

Catastrophizing allows them to further understand what Shakespeare expressed centuries ago: "Present fears are less than horrible imaginings." What a pitcher invents in his imagination creates more fear than any actual "threatening" situation may cause. Rational thinking helps combat all this. It is a reality check. "How likely to happen is the abysmal failure you fear?" I have asked countless times. On a scale of one to ten, ten be the most likely, pitchers' responses *very* rarely are above six. "Then you have an excellent opportunity to take control," I suggest.

Working toward internal control encourages a person to recognize his own responsibility. The world at large (baseball in particular) is not waiting to attack or threaten him. He has something to say about the situation and about the fear itself. Taking responsibility is admitting to his fear what poet Joy Harjo expressed so well: "You have choked me, but I gave you the leash."

"Think about what you want to do, not what might happen to you," I advise the pitcher. I tell him the brain can process threatening impulses quicker than it can develop helpful thoughts, so he must learn to give himself time—time to assure thoughtful, rather than emotional responses being brought to the next pitch. [See GATHERING] By being pro-active through thought, he will help himself to eliminate reactive emotional responses. "Emotions feed the monster," I tell him. "Thought starves it."

Phillies pitching prospect Ryan Brannan was said to be on a "fast track to the big leagues" in 1997. Somehow he was derailed. When Brannan returned to the Double-A Reading team in 1998, manager Al LeBouf, according to the media, "saw an entirely different pitcher." Said LeBouf, "Last year when he walked to the mound, he just knew he was going to get people out. This year he looked scared and confused. Well, maybe confused isn't the right word. But timid."

The feeling and the accompanying behavior are *very* common in young pitchers, especially those who experience failure for the first time. Brannan had not fared well at the Triple-A level the previous year. He was, said a *Baseball America* article written by Paul Hagen, "...getting knocked around on a regular basis for the first time in his career." That will do it. I've seen it happen many times.

"I think a lot of athletes are really fearful of failure," pitcher David Cone has said. "I used to have some fear..."

Most performers walk a plank between a great desire for recognition and appreciation—and a fear of what they believe to be the humiliation and embarrassment that come with failure. They have great responsibility within the game being played; they are "center stage" on an elevated stage, at that. A dirt mound—an island—in the midst of a sea of green. All eyes are on them before each pitch, all action starts with them; all responsibility, they feel, ends with them. Vulnerability hovers; fear lurks.

I use the plank referred to above as a metaphor when talking with pitchers about fear. The pitcher and I will imagine a four-foot-wide plank going across the length of the floor of the room we are in. "Watch me," I say, as I skip or pirouette across the "plank," looking at the pitcher as I do so, in a confident and unconcerned manner. "But put this plank across the Grand Canyon..." I do not have to complete my thought. The pitcher understands. "Fear and dysfunction sets in," I say. "I focus on consequences, on making one false step. But why should I make a false step, when I can negotiate this plank so easily? Not because I'm unable to do it, but because fear causes a lack of confidence in my ability to do so, and I freeze up. I cannot allow "future" to enter my head; I focus on the present—the next step I will take."

In such a situation I could develop what Ambrose Bierce called "a sense of the total depravity of the immediate future." I could become an entirely different "walker," as Ryan Brannan became "an entirely different pitcher." But it would all depend on my ability to cope, to concentrate on task, albeit not as naturally relaxed as I had been. But perhaps I am able to "unnaturally" coach myself across the plank with positive, functional directives. With controlled thoughts and breathing. "Easy? Of course not," I admit to the pitcher. "But I refuse to believe that pitching poorly is comparable to falling into the Grand Canyon." Thus far, they have all agreed. Subtle catastrophizing.

A few pitchers *have* told me that coming to terms with the inevitable failures that result in baseball is like coming to terms with death. Dennis Eckersley, most emphatically. "It's like dying out there," he said to me, referring to giving up a game-winning hit—a blown save opportunity. But Eck always resurrected himself, which is a tribute to his greatness. He approached the next opportunity with vitality ("vita" = life), not with a death rattle, despite his fear. I have had the good fortune to witness, as well, closer Robb Nen's growing ability to do the same. These two outstanding performers intellectualized three major considerations: first, a closer, being human, must fail sometimes; second, the "failure" may be in not accomplishing a desired outcome, not necessarily in executing pitches poorly; third, failing at task—failing to execute—is not the same as *"being a failure."*

For some, happiness is the absence of Murdoch's demons and viruses. For me, in my experience with players, happiness is the vanquishing of them. Facing up to fears is an initial step in vanquishing them, and poet Lucille Clifton puts that step above happiness. "Honor," she wrote, "is *not* not acting because you are afraid. Nor is there honor in acting when you are not afraid. But acting when you *are* afraid, *that's* where honor is."

I feel it is important to mention "fear of success" before concluding this entry. According to many fearful pitchers, the consequences of failure are embarrassment and humiliation. However, those who fear success fear responsibility beyond their perceived capability. Though pitchers in each category arrive at the same point of limited self-confidence, they have traveled different paths to get there.

When Jeff Musselman pitched for the Toronto Blue Jays, he admittedly, "feared my next game after I'd pitched well." He turned to alcohol to escape those fears. "I was fine after I pitched poorly," Musselman recalls. "But if I won, I'd think, 'They're going to expect me to do that again.' I couldn't handle that kind of responsibility."

He learned to, after having taken care of his drinking problem by attending AA sessions regularly.

Nelson Mandella has expressed the view that "our deepest fear is not that we are inadequate. Our deepest fear is that we are powerful beyond measure." Or, as in Musselman's case, management might expect the pitcher to be so. Whichever the problem, the symptoms are the same as they are with fear of failure. All fears create feelings based on unrealistic and/or distracting anticipations. The problem usually develops at a more rapid rate than the solution. But the time spent on that solution is time well spent.

What the Pitcher Should Do...

- Know first and foremost that "fear of failure" is very common in athletes, though very unpleasant.
- Understand that "fear of success" is just a variation on the theme of "fear of failure," and that, though they are situationally different, they are psychologically the same: a problem based on self-doubt and eventual failure.
- Learn to be aware of irrational thoughts based on consequences of failure.
- Define "failure" the term as a failure to reach a goal or accomplish a task, rather than attaching to himself the personal label of being a failure.
- Recognize what does and does not constitute failure in his performance, meaning that results do not indicate performance failure. Poor behavior and execution do.
- Understand that fear impedes judgment.
- Thoughtfully script out a list of rational thoughts to replace the irrational.
- With self-discipline, practice repeating the rational, fear-confronting thoughts, preferably aloud, if alone.
- Remember that habit is powerful, and it is therefore important to create the good habit of acting fearless, despite feelings of fear.
- Learn to focus on the next performance, irrespective of physical symptoms of fear, thereby detaching himself from emotions and attaching himself to planned behavior.

- Adjust arousal created by feelings to a level desired for effective performance through deep breathing and by visualizing past successes on the mound.
- During competition, develop a "will to bear discomfort," by focusing on the delivery of the next pitch, rather than on his feeling.
- During difficulty, coach himself with positive, functional directives and appropriate arousal adjustment—up or down, based on a whether the "system" is signaling "fight" or "flight."
- Reward himself for good behavior, despite the existence of bad feelings.

■ FIFTH INNING

Three particular innings have held special psychological significance for pitchers over the years: the first, the fifth, and the ninth. [See FIRST INNING] The ninth inning has been turned over to a "stopper" in modern times. [See CLOSER] That leaves the first and fifth as noteworthy for starting pitchers.

The fifth inning gets its special significance from the fact that five innings of baseball make a game official in the record books. In addition— and no small addition, for those affected by the rule—a pitcher who goes five innings and has a lead in the game is the "pitcher of record," meaning that he is then eligible for the win. Should he leave the game after five innings and the lead be held by his team, a victory will be entered in the record book in his name; he gets his "W."

Much has already been said about behavior being the proverbial "bottom line" for a pitcher, insofar as his mental approach is concerned. But any number of major league pitchers have "owned up," with the whispered words of their id. "A win is a win," they say sheepishly. Who would not want a win? That is not the problem. Trouble arises when the pitcher's desire gets in the way of his approach to that fateful fifth inning. To that "moment of truth." The "W" is more likely to come to pitchers who are true to their philosophy of effectively executing one pitch at a time. Always. Without making distinctions based on what inning he is pitching in.

Other considerations should be discussed also.

A pitcher who "needs" a win too much can feel the need in a way that can keep him from it. I have witnessed, at every professional level, pitchers taking a lead into the fifth and not finishing the inning. The pitchers sensed the win; they wished the win; they focused on the win. They did not get the necessary outs because of those feelings and thoughts. Because they distracted themselves from task. I have heard players in the dugout, well aware of the pitcher's exaggerated need, predict his demise as he went out to the mound in the fifth. Their forecasts have been too accurate. (I, too, have made such predictions, but have kept them to myself.)

The same pitcher, having gotten himself through the fifth, tends to become very satisfied. "Relieved," in the internal sense, he hopes for relief in the external. He is happy to be taken out of the game. Assured of a win if his team keeps the lead, assured of not taking a loss in any event, he turns the responsibility for the game over to the relief pitchers. This type of attitude provokes teammates—opponents who become aware of this tendency—to label him a "five-and-diver." The term does not engender respect.

Tim Belcher is an acknowledged "bulldog." As a young pitcher, he was traded by Oakland to Los Angeles, where he immediately pitched well—during short appearances as a starter. In this case, the manager and/or pitching coach was trying to "protect" a young pitcher by getting him out of the game after the fifth inning. He would have his 'W' and carry the confidence that is supposed to go with it into his next appearance. The situation did not suit Belcher. He thought more of himself and resented going five and "diving." He did not like the treatment, and he did not like the label that would inevitably be put on him.

Belcher went into the manager's office and expressed his views. The year was 1988 (when he later beat Oakland twice in the World Series). He pitched 230 innings for the Dodgers in 1989. In 1998, Belcher was pitching for Kansas City. This I know: his manager and pitching coach dreaded breaking the news to him that he was being taken out of the game. Even in the seventh or eighth inning. Tim Belcher wants to "close the deal." He rebelled against being protected as a Dodger, and he rebels against being lifted from a game now.

Other pitchers display other reactions as they pitch in the fifth inning. The reaction is one of urgency. [See URGENCY] Once again, a pitcher's need is screaming. A sense of urgency leads him to rush his thoughts and his delivery. In his desire to reach the "finish line," he gets his "feet all in a tangle." His mechanics are thrown out of kilter; self-control and ball control are lost. He looks too far ahead and loses sight of the immediate task before him. He may battle well *after* the fifth inning, but he must learn how to get through it, before he can proceed. He is not faint of heart; he is not a five-and-diver. He is just too excited about the prospect of victory in the middle of the competition. Too much, too soon.

Again, many ways to get it wrong; one way to get it right.

What the Pitcher Should Do...

■ Be aware of any special meaning he gives to the fifth inning, meaning which prevents him from maintaining a consistent focus on the task at hand.

- Understand that, though a particular inning or situation or game may have a special significance in the broad sense, he must be consistent in his ability to concentrate exclusively on the pitch he is about to deliver. And that the aforementioned significance he gives to anything but the next pitch while competing is distracting and undisciplined.

- Develop as a goal his ability, as a starting pitcher, to pitch as aggressively and as controlled as he can for as long as he can, by working to "run *through* the finish line," not *to* it.

- Recognize that result goals are attained only through behavior—and that all behavior should lead to the effective execution of a pitch.

- Recognize also that concern for result goals during competition is inappropriate and counter-productive.

- Establish, as a competitor, the reputation for wanting to take the ball—and keep it.

■ FINISHING HITTERS

All pitching "philosophers" share the view that pitching ahead in the count is a key to success. Many pitchers struggle to integrate the belief into behavior. But of those who are very able to do so, a good number meet another obstacle en route to "getting an out." These pitchers get to two strikes and lose—abandon, is probably more appropriate a term—their intelligence and aggressiveness. From this loss comes the loss of a likely out. Pitchers who "lose outs" this way are said to be unable to "finish the hitter."

One of the reasons for this departure from his otherwise effective approach is that pitchers, having two strikes on the hitter, decide to do more—"do too much," as they say after the fact. Having lost control of their mental approach, they then lose control of their mechanics, overthrowing and missing the strike zone—until the count is no longer in their favor. Then, aware the count is slipping away, and having already lost a significant advantage, they throw "mediocre stuff" into the strike zone. The results are not usually to their liking. Neither are they to their liking when, feeling their edge slipping away, they become determined to not allow good contact and "ruin what they had going." The result is usually a base on balls.

An inability to finish a hitter can also result from a pitcher's belief that, in 0-2 or 1-2 counts, he must make a "perfect pitch." He "toys" with the hitter, trying to execute a pitch in such a way as to "force" it. Many a forced pitch becomes very hittable, since command suffers greatly. Many more are out of the hitting zone and are called balls. Very few ever qualify as "perfect pitches." Pitches not put into play allow the hitter to see additional pitches, get the count back even or in the hitter's favor, and become a distraction for the pitcher, because of his inability to execute when ahead in the count.

Some pitchers believe that if they throw a pitch out of the strike zone it will not be hit. This is not the case, and those pitchers who tend to believe it is also tend to throw "mediocre stuff" on such pitches. After all, it won't be hit, they think. They, too, frequently suffer the consequences of their approach.

When the count is 0-2 or 1-2, an inexperienced pitcher will tell himself that the best way to finish the hitter is to keep the ball away from him, whereas more success has come to pitchers who have kept the ball down. At his best, closer Robb Nen, with his 96+ mile-an-hour fastball, will get ahead in the count and snap a slider down—perhaps in the dirt. The pitch down is much harder for a hitter to fight off than the pitch away. Down and away works well for him and others.

Different personalities display different tendencies. Some pitchers "go hard" at the strike zone, establish the count at 0-2 or 1-2 and become self-satisfied. They think the hitter's at-bat is over. They relax their intensity and focus and become careless with their pitches. Good things do not happen in this scenario. "Cookies" are thrown in the hitter's zone or a base on balls result. (These pitchers frequently tend to apply the same sloppy approach to two-out situations. [See OUTS]

This final example is dramatic, but relatively unusual. In the late '80s, during a championship game in the Northwest (rookie) League, a young, effective relief pitcher was brought into the game for the Medford (Oregon) A's. A graduate of a Big Ten school, this young man entered the game in the ninth inning of a tie game. A runner was on second base; two were out. He went right after the hitter and got the count to 0-2. He then threw a wild pitch, the ball in the dirt, and to the backstop, far to the outside beyond the catcher's reach. The runner went to third. The next pitch was identical. The runner scored what proved to be the winning run, the championship going to the team from Everett, Washington, if memory serves me.

After the game I was thinking about those two pitches. It came to mind that I had seen a number of similar circumstances earlier in the season when I had visited. Same pitcher. It is not my "way" to confront players after games and immediately talk about mistakes or situations that went awry. But this was the final game of the season, and the players were leaving for their homes the next day.

I waited until after our showers and then casually approached the pitcher. He saw me coming and shook his head from side to side. "It's over," I said. "But tell me something. What did you want to do on the 0-2 and 1-2 pitches?"

He said he didn't want to sound as if he were making excuses. I encouraged him to tell me and allow me to decide for myself. In college, he said, the coach had a "rule." Pitchers were to "waste" the pitch in those counts. Any pitcher who allowed contact on an 0-2 pitch, or who gave up a hit on a 1-2 pitch, would run "until he dropped." I heard him out and asked him if this hadn't happened to him in like circumstances earlier in the season. "It happens all the time," he said. "All I think of in those counts is that there's no way the pitch is coming anywhere near the plate."

Psychology 101: stimulus-response; conditioned reflex. Baseball 101: a reason is not the same as an excuse.

A number of ways of "wasting" an advantage have been presented. Opportunities based on a hitter's vulnerability are lost because a pitcher does not know how to finish the hitter. The best "finishers" are those who simply keep going after the hitter. Certainly, pitch selection and location are factors. But "best stuff" and an attack mode are as great, if not greater, factors for these pitchers. After all, that was how they established the count in their own favor. The confident competitor will not forfeit that edge. And so it comes down to trust and behavior once more. It always seems to.

In one of his columns in the *New York Times*, George Vecsey wrote about certain athletes' "inner bully." Vecsey wrote of their "instinct that says, 'Kick 'em while they're down.' Jordan had it," noted Vecsey. "[Mark] Messier had it. Lawrence Taylor had it." Pitchers who consistently finish hitters have it also.

What the Pitcher Should Do...

- Understand that an advantage early in the count is of no value when it is lost late in the count.
- Continue to keep himself under control when working to finish a hitter, rather than trying to "do too much."
- Understand that a "perfect pitch" is not required (and most often not executed) when the hitter is as vulnerable as he is on 0-2 and 1-2 counts.
- Remember to finish the hitter by continuing to throw his "best stuff."
- Understand that a hitter will more likely be "finished" by a pitch that is down than by a pitch away.
- Keep aggressive focus, attacking with the purpose of finishing the hitter immediately, rather than prolonging his at bat by "wasting" pitches.
- Work ahead, stay ahead.

■ FIRST INNING

The first inning has been the nemesis of many starting pitchers. Successful pitchers have struggled in the first, often giving up runs in the opening inning and shutting down the opposition thereafter. Tom Glavine, has twice won the Cy Young Award, but he had a period of difficulty with first innings. Of course, if a pitcher comes to believe it to be a recurring issue, it *will* be one. [See SELF-FULFILLING PROPHECY]

Pitchers are not prizefighters. Boxers come out in the first round and "feel each other out." Typically, they do not commit to aggressive action, waiting to see the style and disposition of the opponent. The fighters are cautious as they watch and wait. That is their plan.

Many pitchers act in a similar fashion in the first inning. It is dangerous behavior—and it is *not* part of a plan. It is a form of involuntary reflex, a cautious reaction, rather than an aggressive action. Most frequently, the pitcher's behavior results in his pitching behind in the count. The next result is usually a hard-hit ball or a base on balls. Countless times I have witnessed a leadoff hitter trotting to first base without seeing a strike. A pitcher must "come out swinging" in the opening "round"—his first inning.

Why would he not? Some pitchers are tentative at the beginning of competition. "I was waiting to see what would happen out there," I've been told more than once. The pitcher's focus was on what would happen *to him*. He made himself the object instead of the subject. "What I want to make happen" never entered his mind—in the first inning. That should have been his point of view; that *is* always his responsibility. The wait to see what happens is often a short wait—with a quick exit.

Television and radio baseball commentators speak of this type of pitcher in a particular way. "They better get to this guy early, before he gets his rhythm. He's tough once he gets his rhythm," they announce to their audience. Read "rhythm" as the aggressive decision to attack the strike zone. Lack of "rhythm" is a physical discomfort that usually has as its origin a mental discomfort. A lack of situational self-trust.

Other pitchers manifest a similar non-aggressive behavior in the first inning, though their viewpoint is slightly different. These pitchers I call "hopers." These pitchers go out in the first inning hoping the day will show itself to be a good one; hoping they will have a good outing. Often, a "hoper" is a spectator at his own funeral. He always starts off as a spectator, irrespective of outcome. He, too, thinks about what might happen, rather than what he wants to make happen. If he gets outs early in the inning—in spite of, rather than because of, his behavior—"it will be a good day" (confessed to me), and he will be encouraged to participate with heart, soul and mind. If "things go against [him]," it is just "one of those days," a phrase so commonly used it is enshrined in the "Baseball Hall of Shame."

The first inning presents an issue for starting pitchers only if they approach it with caution and uncertainty. Any inning can become an issue when the pitcher is non-aggressive or aloof.

A recollection comes to me. I was coaching a basketball team with very talented players. A team that, for no apparent reason, was always behind in the score in the first quarter. The feeling grew in me that, sooner or later, we would not be able to make up the deficit, and we would lose to an inferior team. The problem frustrated and confounded me. After many failed appeals and other attempted remedies, I decided the team was "not ready to compete" when the game started. I ditched the pre-game "warm-up" from the traditional drills; the team played three-on-three "games."

We did not impress the spectators with drill-skill wizardry, but the players "worked up a lather"—and, more importantly, a competitive focus. The issue was solved.

In nine years of coaching basketball, that team was the only one to require such a preparation. Every year during my 15 years in professional baseball I have seen the need for pitchers to improve their "mental readiness" to compete in the first inning. A Russian proverb says, "Necessity taught the bear to dance." Pitchers who seek to be consistent in the maximizing of their talent, must feel it necessary to be ready to compete aggressively in the first inning. To take that aggressiveness and focus right to the "first dance."

What the Pitcher Should Do...

- Be aware of the type of attitude brought to previous first innings that may indicate "an issue" exists.
- Be determined to confront such an issue through immediate and aggressive behavior in competition.

- Create a plan and preparation (increased arousal level?) to encourage appropriate first-inning mind-set and behavior, using bullpen warm-ups as a possible instrument.
- At the end of bullpen warm-up, work a "count" on imaginary hitters, sharpening focus in the process.
- Warm up on game mound with game intensity and focus on target.
- Coach self after last warm-up pitch, getting down off mound and reminding himself to go after the first hitter by getting ahead in the count and forcing contact.
- Make things happen; bring energy into the first inning.
- Throw through the target.
- Get ahead; stay ahead.

■ GATHERING

"Gathering" is a term meaning just what the image conjures up: a drawing together—a getting together of something. For a pitcher, gathering means getting himself together. His thoughts, his self-talk, his attitudes, his focus. In a word, his composure. [See POISE] What gathering is *not* is the "waiting for everything to be all right." Gathering is the process of a pitcher making himself "all right." It is the taking charge of oneself and one's circumstance. It is another moment in time when a pitcher takes responsibility for himself and his performance.

The process is not all that elaborate. It has been alluded to throughout this book. "Gathering" allows the pitcher the time to remind himself to get back to his approach. During the process, he provides himself with whatever stimulus he needs to refocus on task and take charge of his thoughts, by using keys or "triggers" that quickly get him "back on his mental track." The duration of the process should be in proportion to how far off the track he has gone. Though it should not be a prolonged process, it must be long enough to allow the pitcher to calm and control himself.

After a young and talented minor league pitcher had a rare good outing recently, he told me he "finally had himself together out there." He did not have to be expansive. I knew "where he had come from." Prior to that performance, he had struggled with "keeping himself together" because of thoughts that separated him from his task. He had been worried about his recovery from an arm injury. He had been burdened by the expectations that come with having been a high draft choice.

During his previous performances, the young man seemed to act out

119

every symptomatic behavior of a distracted athlete. The behavior wors-
ened each inning—with each hitter, actually. Every difficulty imposed itself on the pitcher's next approach. The outings were relatively brief.

The story has been "told" before. The major point in this telling is to
emphasize how the pitcher allowed his performance problems to continue
and to grow. He stood on the rubber and watched as the snowball rolled
down the hill. The pitcher's remarks after the snowball had impacted and
stopped: "I didn't know what was going on out there. I mean, I didn't have
a *clue*. Before I knew it, I was gone [from the game]."

It has been said before, many times.

Pitchers *must* have a clue. One must know something is breaking if he
is to keep it from shattering. He must know it is broken, if he is to fix it.
The "step" off the mound is the first step a pitcher should take in searching for a clue. The stepping off the mound gives him an opportunity to
gather his thoughts, to stop the rushing [See TEMPO] that comes in times
of adversity, to stop himself—and to coach himself—until he is ready to
execute a pitch with proper focus and purpose.

The development of this habit is essential. For a time, a pitcher may
need someone to provide a reminder, by giving the pitcher whatever "key"
he wishes to use. [See CATCHERS]

When working with pitchers on gathering, I encourage them all to step
off the rubber. "Separate your environments," I say. By getting off the mound
the pitcher moves to a place where he can coach himself. Where he can
gather himself. This is difficult, near impossible, to do on the rubber, since
the pitcher, in that environment, is physically readying himself for the next
pitch. I also tell pitchers that they are two different people on the ballfield.
One is the performer; the other is the coach. On the rubber, he is the performer; off the rubber he is the coach. [See RUBBER] The more coaching
necessary, the further from the rubber he should be. Off the back of the
mound, facing toward center field is my place and posture of choice.

Getting there is that first step in getting himself together. By separating
himself from the place where trouble has formed, the rubber, he has put
himself in a place where the solution can be formed.

What he does when he is there is the other part of the gathering process.

Different pitchers have different techniques. Pragmatism tells us what
works is true. Some pitchers, unhappy with the execution of a particular
pitch, come down off the front of the mound and take a circuitous route

back, gathering themselves as they go. (e.g., Kevin Brown) Some have even squatted behind the mound, when "getting it together" requires more time and thought (e.g., Al Leiter).

Gathering, then, is the physical and mental action that, first, allows the pitcher to "get away" from what is going on by getting away from the rubber and/or the mound. Second, gathering is the internal action of calming and slowing down thoughts and body, so as to be able to use all the self-coaching techniques available to the pitcher. For example, deep breathing, positive task-directed self-talk, mental reminders addressing focus "keys" and to provoke aggressive, controlled execution. The process of gathering allows the pitcher the time and the environment for making mental adjustments. It allows the pitcher to "stop the snowball," before it gets rolling down the hill.

What the Pitcher Should Do...

- Understand the process of gathering allows him to make the mental adjustments required to stay in control of himself, i.e., his thoughts and behavior.
- Understand that gathering helps break a tempo that is working against the pitcher and for the hitter. [See TEMPO]
- Develop a routine that serves him well, first making sure to get off the pitching rubber and/or the mound.
- Understand that by "separating his environments," he allows himself to break tension, moving away from the point of distraction to a point of instruction.
- Recognize that he has two roles: he is a pitcher and he is a coach. And that pitching takes place on the mound and rubber, while coaching takes place away from them.

■ GIVING IN

"Giving in" is a term frequently heard in baseball dugouts. Words can mean all things to all people, so it seems necessary to make a distinction between "giving in" and "giving up." I do *not* consider the terms to have the same meaning.

There is good reason to take the time to make the distinction. Each of the behaviors associated with the terms stem from a loss of hope. And people—ordinary people—who lose hope tend to lose motivation. But hope should never be part of the competitor's point of view. Determination should. Persistence should. [See RELENTLESS] Nevertheless, in their humanness, pitchers have faltered, yielding to whatever sense of hopelessness they may have felt. "Giving in" is a less dramatic, if more frequent, behavior than "giving up." Neither is acceptable on a baseball field.

Though the topic of "giving up" will be treated in later pages, [See QUITTING] the definition must be established here, as a contrast to "giving in." The metaphor of traffic signs might serve. "Giving in" would be a yield sign, "giving up" a stop sign. As a driver would yield to another motorist, a pitcher would, for example, yield to a hitter, or to his own emotion of the moment. Deference in traffic and deference in competition are both defensive behaviors. In one setting, the behavior assures favorable outcome, in the other setting the behavior generally assures the opposite.

In battle, "giving in" is fighting the opponent ineffectively, because of uncertainty, distraction and/or fear. "Giving up" is surrender.

The most frequent use of the term "giving in," as it relates to pitchers, can be heard when talking about the pitcher's confrontation with the batter. "Don't give in to this guy," seems to be the phrase of choice. [See NEGATIVITY] The speaker, usually a pitching coach, can mean any of a number of things, but in the broad sense, he does not want the pitcher to yield to the batter, philosophically and behaviorally. What he *does* want is for the pitcher to be aggressive, but smart. The pitcher, it is presumed, knows what that means in that context.

In May 1998, Orioles pitching coach, Mike Flanagan, spoke about the kind of "giving in" that most frequently has come to my attention. Flanagan was explaining the travails of pitcher Doug Drabek. "In the spring," Flanagan said, "hitters reacted to Dougie. Now it's the exact opposite. He gives up a bloop single, and then he starts thinking, 'Uh oh, now they're going to get a big inning off me.' [See SELF-FULFILLING PROPHECY]

"You start fearing being hit," Flanagan continued. "Then you pitch defensively. You try to pinpoint pitches. You miss pitches. You fall behind in the count. Then you get hit." Flanagan was describing perfectly the cycle of behavior and outcome that has as first cause an attitude of "giving in" to hitters and circumstance. Loss of trust, loss of hope, loss of aggressiveness. Flanagan went on to say he saw no flaws in Drabek's mechanics. "It's all mental." It usually is.

The mental state of "giving in" is like the fungus of athlete's foot. It may be dormant, but it can reappear at any time. The first sign of its reappearance should provoke immediate attention to the issue. All pitchers are susceptible. They wear shower shoes and powder their feet. Equal attention must be paid to behavior during competition.

A batter/runner does not hustle down the line to first base. Why not? Disappointment is one response I've heard to my question. Frustration another. Fatigue. Sorry. Guilty with an explanation, but all guilty nevertheless.

A batter is extremely unhappy with an umpire's call. Strike two. The batter is blinded with rage and has no idea what he is swinging at. Strike three. "Giving in."

A pitcher doesn't back up third base after the batter has hit a double in the gap with two men on. "Brain cramp," has been an explanation. See above. An emotion of the moment was triggered by the gapper. The instinct for self-pity became stronger than the one for responsibility. "Giving in."

A close acquaintance, a major league pitcher, sheepishly admitted to me years ago that, when he became frustrated by errors behind him, he "tried to strike everybody out." Can over-aggressiveness be a form of "giving in"? When a pitcher is forced out of the approach he knows works for him because of circumstances beyond his control, he has, indeed, given in to those circumstances and to the emotions they provoked.

Bad weather, bad mounds, bad luck. These are but a few of the other forces to which a pitcher can "give in." Whatever the force, if it is stronger than his resistance to it, the pitcher has given in. He may not always have the capacity to win the battle, but he always has the capacity to fight it effectively. To do less is to expand the external forces he will always be called on to face. At the same time, he shrinks the spirit within him, and diminishes his chances of being the victor, rather than the vanquished.

What the Pitcher Should Do...

- Understand that "giving in" takes many forms, but essentially it is a yielding to external circumstance, internal distrust, and discouragement, which trigger unassertive, deferential behavior.
- Recognize that self-discipline and intelligence are the countervailing forces to fight the tendency to yield to a formidable hitter, condition or emotion.
- Reiterate the goal of going as long and as hard as he can during his performance, adding "as smart."
- During competition, be aware of any undesirable behavior (a "giving in") and of the thoughts that preceded it.
- Make immediate mental adjustments based on the awareness, using self-coaching techniques.
- Be aware that a lowered arousal level accompanies the instinct to "give in," therefore an aggressive tone of voice is required during self-coaching.
- Seek courage within himself, rather than ease in "the world" outside.

■ GOALS [See APPENDIX A and APPENDIX B]

The most successful people in the world are known to be goalsetters. The problem I have come across in baseball is that too many players set goals over which they have no control. Won-lost records, earned-run averages and the like direct a pitcher's attention to what he wants, while diverting it from what he must do. In the doing, though his behavior is exemplary, the pitcher may still not reach his goal. So many of the outcomes in the game of baseball are left to the doctrine of chance.

I am reminded of Friedrich Nietzsche's parable. "Not every end is a goal. The end of a melody is not its goal; however, if the melody has not reached its end, it would also not have reached its goal." The pitcher who focuses on the notes of the "melody" as he plays is unconcerned with its end. Unconcerned with the goal; with the result. A baseball game, like a melody, will reach its own inevitable end. The pitcher should be attentive to the means to that end.

A musician and a pitcher have as their goals the effective execution of notes and pitches. This is achieved through concentration, confidence, control—of himself, of the instrument, of the ball. Other appropriate thoughts and behaviors have already been discussed; others are yet to be discussed.

By addressing these thoughts and behaviors a pitcher recognizes that he is responsible only for what he can *do* within the context of a game. As great as that responsibility is, still greater is the pitcher's obligation to be resolute in maintaining his mental discipline throughout the competition. [See GIVING IN/QUITTING/RELENTLESSNESS] Circumstances within the game that affect "his numbers" (statistical goals)—or any result goals ("winning this game")—most often test the pitcher's mettle. If a goal appears to become unattainable, the goalsetter may "give in" to the perceived failure. The real failure is in the behavior, and in the inappropriate goal he set. [See RESULTS]

And that is why I am always so adamant with pitchers about setting very specific, individualized behavioral goals. But they must be goals that are completely within their reach. The individual pitcher can impose his will on his thoughts and acts. He cannot impose himself on bad hops, bad umpiring, bad defense, or wind direction. If those factors influence the pitcher's behavior, he has already failed to satisfy a goal. The kind of goal that lends itself to self-assessment—from pitch to pitch.

The value of goal-setting has been established by research and by elite athletes' anecdotal reports. Studies and athletes reveal that specific goals direct their attention and provoke them to physically act on this focus. In addition, goals help to sustain their efforts and enable them to evaluate themselves on a regular basis.

Players who tend to use "I'll just do my best" as a goal fail to commit themselves to a real challenge. The goal is too high in subjectivity and too low in responsibility. It is often stated in an off-handed manner.

Self-pronounced "team players" have said their only goal is to help their team win. It is a pleasing lyric perhaps, but the tune cannot be carried. A player—a pitcher—must first know how to help himself. Being a winning player requires specific individual achievement. A pitcher should set individual goals that will address his needs, as he strives to accomplish what will benefit him, thereby helping the team "to win." [See WINNING]

Goals not immediately reached should not immediately be abandoned. They should be modified—adjusted—based on the degree of progress being made. If little or no progress has been made, the goal set was probably too lofty. There is no "failure" implied by an adjustment of a goal. One of the purposes of setting goals is to help encourage the pitcher to be more confident, as a result of identifiable daily achievement. The purpose is not to frustrate effort and motivation and have the pitcher become neurotic.

A pitcher will bring on neuroses if he allows the expectations of others to become his goals. He must learn to distinguish the difference, and approach his goal-setting appropriately. It has been said that some primitive tribes believed photographs taken of them to be a "theft." The tribesmen felt their selves were taken from them through the image in the photo. The expectations of others can steal a pitcher's self. Self-image, self-assessment, self-discipline, self-control (topics specifically treated or alluded to in this book) are the ingredients of self. And a pitcher's goals must be set for himself, by that self.

At this point, it might be helpful to identify the type of goals I speak of when working with pitchers. The list that follows is not all-inclusive, by any means, and, of course, it is not one developed by *one* pitcher. A list of goals will be long or short, depending upon the needs and inclinations of the individual. In either case, the pitcher does not necessarily hold himself accountable for meeting goals immediately. This has happened, however.

Some goals are:

- Improve the ability to hold runners (better move to first, varying moves, being "quicker" to the plate—without negatively affecting control or "stuff," etc.).
- Improve throws to bases during PFP drills.
- Improve a specific fielding technique, according to individual need (e.g., fielding a bunt down the third-base line and setting feet properly).
- Be more aggressive early in the count. (The pitcher has the game charts to bear witness.)
- When ahead in the count, finish hitters before getting to a three-ball count.
- Throw inside more often, at appropriate times.
- Improve (a specific pitch) through concentrated work in the bullpen—and a willingness to throw it with conviction in appropriate game situations.

APPENDIX B is a chart effectively used by pitchers who have wanted to monitor "game behavior." The consensus from those who use(d) it has been that "when I score well on the chart, I have pitched well in the game." In other words, there seems to be a correlation. There should be.

Copies of the chart are made; the dates of each outing are noted at the top; the pitcher, according to self-assessment in the areas listed, evaluates himself by using gives number evaluations. When he "sees" he has faltered in a specific area—or areas—he mentally addresses the issue and prepares himself to improve upon the behavior during the next performance. It becomes one of his game goals. That simple. The achievement is always more challenging, he knows.

Setting goals can be a double-edged sword. I try to have pitchers avoid grandiose achievement goals that are expressed in statistical terms. They are meaningless. Some pitchers have had great years, and their numbers did not reveal the quality of their performance. The reverse has also been true. I have seen pitchers with very commendable won-lost records achieve the numbers with less commendable execution of pitches. They may have had wonderful run support whenever they pitched, or wonderful defensive support, or they may have had the "good fortune" of consistently throwing "at 'em balls"—balls hit right at fielders, many hit very hard.

But execution comes from all the thoughts and behaviors that precede it. All within a pitcher's control, and therefore appropriate as goals. So too are the pitcher's behaviors after a ball has been put into play, when he becomes part of the defense on the field. It is a long trip to perfection, and no one I have ever met has gotten there yet. However, through behavior goals and the determined behavior itself, a pitcher can certainly move closer toward perfection than he might imagine.

What the Pitcher Should Do...

- Set goals for himself, with the input of those he works closely with, based on specific, individualized behaviors and skills he wishes to improve.
- Understand that the expectations of others are not to be considered as part of the goal-setting process, nor should they be considered.
- Express goals in positive language, rather than in language that indicates what he does not want to do. (e.g., "I want to attack the strike zone regularly," rather than "I don't want to walk guys.")
- Adjust realistic goals, rather than abandoning them.
- Prioritize goals, according to need.
- Put the goals in writing.
- Keep a record of progress, in order to hold himself accountable on a daily/regular basis.
- Be reasonable in the evaluation.
- Understand that an *unattainable* goal should be abandoned, since it was inappropriate to begin with.
- Understand that goals relate to performance, not self-worth—that the failure to reach a goal does not make *him* a failure.

■ HABITS

One of my "games" with players is to have them clasp their hands and wait for me to give them a signal to undo the clasp—pulling their hands apart. They then are to quickly clasp their hands again, this time putting the other thumb on top and intertwining the rest of their fingers. Some players do it faster than others; some fumble and fix, as they look down at their hands in awkward motion. When fingers have been in place for a time, I ask the player how the second clasp feels. Responses range from "different" to "weird." Habit is very powerful.

"Winning is a habit," Vince Lombardi said. "Unfortunately, so is losing." In other words, people have good habits and they have bad habits. Bad ones are harder to break than good ones are to develop, so it stands to reason that one should work diligently at creating good habits for himself. As Mark Twain said, "It is easier to stay out than get out."

Creating a good habit is an act of self-discipline and will. If, as a Roman poet believed, "Ill habits gather by unseen degree...," good habits must be recognized and monitored diligently. Attention must be paid.

Earlier in the book, the thought was presented that acting out courageous behavior while at the same time being fearful is a form of heroism. The consistent enactment will allow the fear to dissipate; the habit of behavior will pre-empt the emotion. As Lawrence Durrell wrote, "One day you will become what you mime. The parody of goodness can make you really good." Such is the power of habit.

This truth has implications for the way a pitcher should go about his "business"—or his profession. Eating habits, sleeping habits, running, lift-

ing, his manner of practice and game-day preparation create a pattern—for better or for worse. If a pitcher has no consistent routine, he still creates a pattern. The pattern is one of inconsistency, which will represent his habits and, most likely, his performances. [See PREPARATION] If order produces security, it follows that randomness or chaos will lead to its opposite.

The more a pitcher can develop routines, the more confidence he can have in his preparedness. He will feel a greater sense of control and focus. His routines are formed through choice and consistent expression of the behaviors he understands will serve him well. These routines are the focus of his attention and help him to "stay in" good habits, so he does not have to concern himself with "getting out" of bad ones. The habits are developed in relation to directed tasks.

Without being compulsive, the pitcher can create a form of ritualistic behaviors, so very helpful in that they provide him with systematic lead-ins to his regular performances. He will have his off-field, pre-game, in-game, and post-game habits firmly established. Physical and mental preparations that are habituated will allow him to focus on what he wants to do, rather then on any thoughts or circumstances that are distracting. Good habits represent his plan, his adjustments, his philosophy. His habits also represent his character.

Habits, as Francis Bacon believed, are the "principal magistrate of man's life."

What the Pitcher Should Do…

- Understand the power of habit.
- Recognize that old habits are difficult to break.
- Determine to create new good habits through diligence and discipline.
- Set up routines that will best serve him and re-enact them daily, on the field and off, so as to create a ritual that is natural and effective, without being compulsive or obsessive.
- Remember that appropriate physical and mental habits are part of his "package."
- Understand that habits are a form of preparation and consistency.

■ HITTERS

A couple of years ago, a pitcher with whom I have a close relationship rang me up on the phone. It was early winter when he called. An American League pitcher his entire career, he had recently signed on with a National League team as a free agent. At the time, I was working for the Marlins, a National League team.

"What can you tell me about the hitters in the league?" he asked in the first minute of our conversation. "I don't know anything about them." His tone was one of conscientious concern. Great concern—not quite worry.

"The hitters aren't your problem," I answered. "You're *their* problem. They don't know anything about *you*! Do you know yourself?" I asked rhetorically. The more you know about yourself, the less you have to know about hitters. Remember?" He had heard all this before. Then I changed the subject.

If dugout conversations—serious and frivolous—were to be monitored, the phrase (in the form of a question) that would rank first in frequency of use would be one which expresses the prevailing concern of *hitters*, regarding pitchers: "What's this guy got?" Hitters feel a great need to know the answer. Pitchers realize this; they hear the question asked on a daily basis. It should help them to reinforce their psychological advantage, to say nothing (yet) of their statistical edge. Pitchers should focus their attention within, heading the advice of Shakespeare's Polonius: "This above all: to thine own self be true."

In response to a question asked by an *Atlanta Constitution* interviewer during spring training, 1999, Greg Maddux had this to say: "When you understand yourself more as a pitcher, it's easier to pitch... Hitters have been the same since I came up. You've got some righties; you've got some lefties; you've got some fastball hitters; you've got some guys that'll steal bases, guys that hit homers. They just have a different name on their back. That's why I think understanding yourself makes it easier."

Let the pitchers be the warriors and the hitters the worriers.

To know a hitter's strengths, weaknesses, and tendencies can be helpful to a pitcher, it is true. But knowing his own is of greater value. A pitcher's trust in his ability is more powerful than all the information he can gain about a hitter. This trust allows him to maintain the inherent "edge" he has over hitters. He should further realize that if a pitcher's strengths coincide

with the hitter's strength, the pitcher "wins" most of the time. On the condition that he employs his own strengths aggressively. So much the better
for him if he can execute from his strength to a hitter's weakness.

Finally, a pitcher should also heed the words of Marc Antony and
apply them to his own audience: "I have come to bury Caesar, not to praise
him." Pitchers, however, should say it in truth. They should go to the
mound to "bury" hitters, not to praise them. A pitcher's praise of a hitter
can develop into an exaggerated respect, which can lead to awe. Awe becomes deference and deference is a "giving in" to a hitter. Pitchers who
are overly concerned with hitters—and many are alive, if not well—generally will admit, after damage has been done, that they "gave the hitters too
much credit."

This brilliance in retrospect has one value: it is a mistake the pitcher is
aware of, and so has the opportunity to learn from. Sadly, man's history
indicates such learning to be the exception, not the rule. Luckily, being
exceptional is a pitcher's goal. Or should be.

The less said about hitters, the better. This has come close to the limit.

What the Pitcher Should Do...

- Understand that pitchers initiate action and hitters must react to
  that behavior.
- Respect hitters' great significance to the game, but not to him.
- Know himself as a pitcher: his own strengths and weaknesses, his
  abilities to make adjustments and his plan of attack whenever he
  performs.
- Use whatever information he has about a hitter as supplementary to
  the information he has about what he himself can do and expects to
  do during his performance.
- First and foremost, mind his own "business"—being pro-active,
  rather than re-active to the hitter.

■ INTELLIGENCE

In earlier pages, I mentioned that if a pitcher told me he could not give me *both* the intelligence and courage I had hypothetically asked him for, I would gladly accept courage. I stick to my guns with that choice.

But the talk with the pitcher was meant to establish the value of courage, not to discount the value of intelligence. During such discussions, I tell pitchers they are smart enough to know how to deliver a pitch; they have been doing so since they were small fries. I do not expand on the topic of intelligence, since I am talking with them about courage. Now is the time to talk about the importance of a pitcher's intelligence: knowing what to think and *when* to think.

Hall-of-Fame pitcher Catfish Hunter quoted his Oakland manager during the A's championship years in the '70s. "… (W)hat Dick Williams said about a pitcher…when he starts thinking, he's always in trouble. So the best thing is not to think."

Certainly, pitchers will confirm that when they are at their best, they are not thinking. "On cruise control." "On automatic pilot." These are two of the descriptions used when talking with pitchers about the phenomenon. But, as Dick Williams and others have said, thinking starts when trouble starts. No more "automatic pilot." The pitcher must take control. Of what? Of his thoughts. Thinking is inevitable. Right thinking is invaluable. Right thinking is an expression of a pitcher's intelligence, as opposed to his anxiety or frustration or uncertainty. Intelligence will short-circuit the trouble. Thinking cannot be stopped; it can be changed. [See SELF-TALK]

Intelligent thought is blood for the brain—and, in turn, for the pitcher's kinetic system.

The pitcher must be aware of what thoughts are being processed when there is difficulty during competition. He cannot make an adjustment without applying intelligent thought. Appropriate thinking will save him; uncontrolled thinking will destroy him. Is what he is thinking relevant to the circumstance? Is it based on false perception? Fear? Time must be taken to determine these answers and get the right information to the muscles. [See GATHERING] In the contest between a pitcher's emotionality and his rationality, intelligent reasoning should always be the victor.

When a pitcher is on "cruise control," he is still thinking. But it is a kind of automatic process, during which he focuses intently on task: target, delivery, get the ball back, on the rubber, sign, target again, delivery. [See TEMPO] This process indicates a task-oriented thought process—so natural that the pitcher may have no heightened sense of it. Because he is not thinking about thinking. He is thinking about task.

A pitcher becomes aware of his thinking when trouble arises. When his thoughts are based on irrelevancies (e.g., consequences), he is not using his intelligence. When his thoughts focus on himself (e.g., "What is the manager thinking about me now?"), he is not using his intelligence. They are counterproductive thoughts. Distracting thoughts. The *wrong* thoughts.

All research indicates that a person's behavior is influenced by what he is thinking. When thinking is directed internally on the pitcher's feelings and self-interest, his tension level will increase. Anxiety or fear is often the result. He may think about his discomfort ("No rhythm" or "I just didn't feel right") or any number of negative triggers ("This isn't my day" or "I can't get a break"). Behavior will be directed by these thoughts. The problem will be exacerbated, rather than alleviated. The performance will suffer, as will the pitcher.

By employing his intelligence, the pitcher can direct his thoughts to his task, thereby giving himself a chance to enact the appropriate behavior during competition. Intelligent thoughts are the medicine—the cure. Emotional thinking is the poison.

The pitcher who thinks about what the situation requires, rather than what he requires "pitches smart," rather than "stupid." (Pitching "scared" inevitably becomes pitching "dumb.") Mark Twain said that there is very little difference between man and other animals—and usually man forfeits the difference. He was talking about man's brain. A pitcher forfeits the difference when he thinks in any way but an intelligent way. Too often, his left brain takes a nap; it must always be on duty.

Every pitcher is intelligent enough to know the difference between his best thoughts and his worst. By continually disciplining his mind, he will be able to help himself out of whatever trouble may arise. The results may not always go his way, but his thoughts must. When they do, the pitcher provides himself, during the high-wire act of competition, with what Lawrence Durrell called "the safety net of logic and reason."

There are any number of inhibitors to intelligent solutions for whatever problems may exist during competition. Fatigue is one (Lombardi's line: "Fatigue makes cowards of us all"). Intelligence should tell a pitcher that conditioning is the solution. Laziness is another inhibitor, the reciprocal being self-motivation. Frustration, disappointment, embarrassment, selfishness, and fear get in the way of excellence. Reason would tell a pitcher that the countervailing forces he should muster would be maturity, knowing how to make adjustments, self-trust, selflessness, energy, and courage. Yet behavior based on intelligence is considerably more difficult to enact than behavior driven by emotions of the moment. Those who strive to be exceptional, rather than ordinary, work at it. As noted earlier, if it were easy, it would not be extraordinary.

One last very specific requirement for a pitcher's use of intelligence: he must be smart enough not to damage himself by pitching when his body is not up to the task. His body, not his mind. Two days ago, on the telephone, I told a young pitcher that he "must learn to play through pain and take the ball." I also told him to ask the trainer first if he would damage himself by going out there. "Trust your trainer. (I know him and am certain of his professional abilities). Be honest about your pain with him and the team doctor. Pain alone shouldn't keep you from competing. Physical disability should. Know the difference."

In contrast to this young man, most pitchers I have come across are too willing (for a multitude of reasons) to "pitch hurt." David Cone said it best, having gone through the ordeal himself, by "failing to make the distinction between pain and injury." He allowed his strong competitive instinct to get in the way of his intelligence, thinking he could "pitch through anything," and had to endure the consequences. Harvey Araton of *The New York Times* called the problem "a juggling act, trying to strike a proper balance between cockiness and caution, emotion and ambition." [See BALANCE] Let the pitcher beware.

If thoughts are "rays of power," as Iris Murdoch suggested, intelligent thought will provide power for the *pitcher*; unreasoned thought will provide power for the *circumstance* he is facing.

What the Pitcher Should Do...

- Understand that thinking is an on-going process.
- Understand that during an effective, well-paced performance, his thought process is hardly discernable, since the focus is both narrow and concentrated on task exclusively.
- Be very aware of his thoughts during adversity.
- Recognize that when difficulty arises in competition, an intelligent response will arrest it, whereas an emotional response will exacerbate and prolong it. [See ADJUSTMENTS, GATHERING, COACHING SELF, SELF-TALK]
- Use simple keys (phrases) to prod right thinking into his brain. ("Good low strikes," "Attack the strike zone," "One pitch at a time") [See MANTRA]
- Be determined to "stop the bleeding" by gathering and employing thoughts directed to task, rather than to consequences.
- Establish as a goal for each performance his ability to "pitch smart," and "grade" himself after each outing.

■ INTENSITY

One demonstration I have used to help players understand the meaning of "intensity" has been to hold a magnifying glass above a sheet of paper under the Arizona or Florida sun. The paper rests on the grass of a practice field. My hand holds the magnifying glass at knee level. A large, faint circle of light is spread across the paper and spills over its edge onto the grass. I move the glass closer to the paper. The circle of light becomes smaller and more defined. I then move the glass to within an inch of the paper. Smoke begins to rise; a hole is formed; the paper is now on fire.

The three circles represent degrees of a player's intensity. 1) no intensity, 2) controlled, well-concentrated intensity (heat and light) [See AROUSAL], 3) destructive intensity. Players understand what they are seeing; they themselves have experienced each level.

Too much of a good thing is a good thing no longer. Discussing an effective intensity level is much like discussing arousal. Both deal with the regulation of the mental and physical energy an athlete brings to performance. Pitchers often confuse the expenditure of energy as being solely physical and mental expression. But the discipline needed to control intensity also requires the expenditure of mental energy. The sharply defined circle on the paper strikes the proper balance. Intensity, like aggressiveness, must be controlled if the pitcher is not to "go up in flames." As mentioned in previous pages, "Nothing in excess."

Yet, my experiences have instructed me that more pitchers are in need of greater intensity than they are of greater control. Too many are trying to drive their metaphorical racecar with one foot on the brake.

In accordance with this belief, I tell young pitchers (and a few older ones) of my preference for "too much," rather than "too little" intensity. "It is easier to adjust down than adjust up," I say to them. The many distractions they bring to their game often make the circle on their paper wide and diffused.

Intensity is the calling card of every pitcher who considers himself to be a competitor. Yes, there are some bulls who must learn to move with determination, while not destroying the shop's chinaware. That ability can be developed with relative ease. For the timid or distracted pitcher, the process of heightening positive intensity can be a daunting task. But it is a core requirement in the curriculum of pitching excellence.

Intensity is both an attitude and a skill. Effective intensity is rooted in caring deeply and knowing how to be successful in the caring. Aquinas said that only intense actions develop and strengthen good habits. Repetition alone can be a mindless and therefore meaningless activity. Recall the reference on earlier pages to PFP as a repetitive drill. Without the right attitude, the skill fails to be developed. The meaning given to it on the practice field must replicate the meaning given on the playing field. Intensity can be learned.

Appropriate intensity requires undivided, controlled, and sustained attention, and both physical and mental energy. Enthusiasm is another ingredient. An intense pitcher considers competition to be fun and practice to be purposeful. [See JOY] His focus is always narrowed, concentrated, and consistent.

Kevin Brown's intensity is apparent to any observer. Journalists have noted the way he takes batting practice. "Watch Brown in a routine batting practice and he is not joking around the way pitchers often do..." This from a saved newspaper clip. I have seen Kevin Brown return to the dugout after a poor at-bat. He takes all competition very seriously—at the same time relishing it.

Said Tony Gwynn, a San Diego Padres teammate in 1998, "You see [Brown] sitting there on the bench between innings when he's pitching, and he is like in a daze [zone?] he's concentrating so hard. He's probably going over in his mind who he's facing next inning and what he has to do. Whatever, you know you aren't going to go over and start a conversation with him."

Oral Hershiser provided *San Francisco Examiner* writer Henry Schulman with textbook material during an interview a day before his second start with the Giants in September 1998. Hershiser incorporated many facets of the mental requirements for successful pitching in his talk, which initially addressed "intensity." His remarks are quoted liberally.

Hershiser began his interview by noting that prior to his last start against the Phillies he had lost the intensity for which he was recognized. He was distracted by the expectations of others, these based on the view that he had come to San Francisco to be a mentor, rather than a pitcher. "That took over my mentality on the mound," he said.

Hershiser continued, "I got my nickname 'Bulldog' because of my intensity... The last time out, I threw every pitch like it was the last pitch of my career. That's going to be my mantra for the rest of my career. See

MANTRA] Everyone wants to label you as old and more cerebral, but I've still got some good stuff left to offer. Here it is. Come and get it.

"I'm not worried anymore about how people react to my facial expressions... Not all of us got here by being robots. Some of us got here by being passionate, intense, and exuberant about what we do.

"I think I started to lose that because I was listening to what everyone was saying about me instead of listening to who I am. At some point I thought I started to lose love of the game... [Now] I just decided to give everything I've got and uncover the original source of why I wanted to play."

The interrelatedness of topics discussed between the covers of this book—intensity being but one—is made abundantly clear by Hershiser's revelation of agendas—past, present, and future.

What the Pitcher Should Do...

- Review concentration exercises and work at sustaining focus during whatever activity in which he is involved.
- Understand that intensity is closely related to his level of arousal and must be monitored and adjusted (up or down) according to need.
- Recognize that intensity should not vary according to circumstance, but rather, be consistent and sustained.
- Be aware of whatever distinctions he makes between practices and games, particularly within different circumstances during games.
- Evaluate and keep a record of his intensity (i.e. focus, energy, discipline, consistency, etc.) after practice sessions and performances.
- Establish as a goal the desired ability to be indiscriminate in the application and maintenance of effective intensity throughout practices and games.
- Establish a specific preparation and consistent mode for behavior for game days.
- Allow no teammate, media person, or whomever to intrude on this *modus operendi*.

■ JOY

At least 30 years ago, I saw a five-paneled cartoon in the *New Yorker*. The smile it brought to my face came from recognition of circumstance. I had lived the experience. The first panel showed a group of young boys playing a game of baseball on a sandlot. A more-than-middle-aged man is watching the game, standing outside a chain-link fence that surrounds the field. He is standing behind the center fielder.

Second panel: "What's the score, kid?" the man asks the center fielder.

Third panel: "34 to nothing—them," replies the boy.

Fourth panel: "That's too bad, kid," says the man.

Fifth panel: The boy is turned slightly toward the man, a smile on his face. He replies, "Don't worry about it mister. We ain't even been up yet."

For me, and for my boyhood friends, playing ball on those lots or in cemented schoolyards was, to paraphrase Henry Ward Beecher, a joy, which longed to be ours. I think these days about the boyhood baseball experiences of the professional players I have worked with. They all played Little League baseball, formalized baseball, adult-supervised baseball. There were parent/fans and adult expectations—and the consequent behaviors after the disappointment or "failure" of a poor performance or a loss. No organized play existed for the very young in those times. My father never saw me compete as a member of a team until my senior year in college. He cared; he just had his own busy life to live and left my recreation to me. As did the other fathers and mothers in our neighborhood.

Recreation. That was what baseball was for my peers and me. "Recreation: Refreshment of one's mind or body…through diverting activity. *Play*."

(Emphasis mine.) Willie Stargell used to remind those around him who seemed to have lost their joy: "The umpires say, 'Play ball!' not 'Work ball!'"

Lest this sound like a veiled treatise against Little League or parents, let me emphatically remind the reader that I am speaking *for* something, not against anything. I am speaking for joy.

Joy has not come out of the game. Rather, it has come out of many who play the game. Any number of reasons might be identified. Suffice to say the players I have worked with were precocious and special athletes when they were youngsters. They excelled in highly organized competition at an early age, dominating the opposition.

The playing field leveled somewhat for them as they went higher and higher—eventually becoming professional baseball players, competing against other professional. The ultimate level playing field, for the most part. If pressures were not put on them when they were young, pressures usually developed with time. And intensified, for many. [See PRESSURE] Joy dissipated.

The desire to make the big leagues, the desire to stay there once he makes it, the ordeal of a long season, the injuries, the poor performances, the losing teams, the responses of those around him, the media all—*all*—can take their "pound of flesh" from the body of a joyful player.

If the player allows it! That is the condition. What is "out there" can be controlled by what is "in here." (I am pointing to my heart.) [See ATTITUDE] What is "out there" can be determined by what is "in here." (I am pointing to my head.) [See PERSPECTIVE]

All of the concerns that a player develops as he plays the game of baseball indicate a loss of innocence. The innocence of the boys losing 84-0, who still are optimistic and having fun, irrespective of adult concerns. The sooner one loses his innocence, the sooner he may lose his joy. In life, and in baseball. Players, amateurs as well as professionals, who do not lose their joy for the game have developed and maintained a healthy attitude toward themselves and the game. Others have not been as fortunate. Bertolt Brecht wrote, "What's a joy to the one is a nightmare to the other. That's how it is today, that's how it'll be forever."

Brecht is probably right, yet any individual has the capacity to regain or change his attitude and perspective. Oral Hershiser told of his rediscovery of his love for the game in the previous section. On the other side of a "nightmare," thus far, is Yankees closer, Mariano Rivera, of whom *The New*

York Times writer Butch Olney wrote, "...there was always a sense that on that mound, Rivera could barely contain his grin." Rivera's catcher, Joe Girardi concurred: "He has a lot of fun out there."

"Fun." That is the synonymous cliché for joy heard in clubhouses and dugouts, especially when things are not going well for a team or individuals. "Just have fun," has been the directive of teammates, coaches, and managers over the years. Though used frequently, the term has never been defined—within earshot of me.

Once, at the end of a players' meeting in the clubhouse of a struggling Florida Marlins team, I prolonged the meeting with a query. A veteran player had provided the concluding mandate, "Just go out there and have fun!" As the players were about to rise, I asked, "How do you do that? How *do* you have fun?"

Everyone was silent. I interrupted the uncomfortable silence with an oversimplification which would allow us all to escape the room. "Trust your talent," I said. "Get your egos out of the way and *play the game*. Then you might have a chance to have fun."

Iris Murdoch wrote, "Happiness is a matter of one's most ordinary mode of consciousness being busy and lively and unconcerned with self." PLAY THE GAME. Oral Hershiser recaptured his love for the game. Maddux expresses his joy for the competition. Jamie Moyer expresses his happiness for the challenge. Todd Stottlemyre expresses his enthusiasm for confrontation. Al Leiter expresses his ecstasy for life. They play the game.

"Take all away from me, but leave my ecstasy, and I am richer then than all my Fellow Men." (Emily Dickinson) The game is still there. The joy still longs to be there also.

What the Pitcher Should Do...

- Understand that the game stays the same; players' attitudes toward it may not.
- Ask himself if he loves the game.
- Ask if he is playing the game for himself.
- Ask if he trusts his talent.
- Ask if he enjoys competition.
- Understand that if the answer to the above questions is, "Yes," he will pitch with joy.

- Ask if he thinks about the game as he pitches, rather than about himself and what may happen to him.
- Ask if he interprets a poor performance as an indicator that he is a failure.
- Ask if he negatively anticipates his next performance.
- Understand that if the answer to the preceding three questions is, "Yes," he will pitch with no joy, and should choose to change his attitude and perspective—or stop playing the game and choose to do something he enjoys. (The vast majority of professionals I know have called that choice a "no-brainer.")

■ K's

In 1998, Mets pitcher Rick Reed told *New York Daily News* writer Thomas Hill that he held nothing against Jim Leyland, his former Pittsburgh manager, for letting him go. Said Reed, "He did what he had to do. He did say last year, 'Maybe he's finally learned how to pitch.' It was a great compliment. I used to think you had to strike out ten. Now I know I don't have to do that."

Reed's adjusted approach the previous year dramatically helped his results—his won-lost record, his earned-run average, his paycheck (13-9, 2.89, $2.58 million).

Reed learned to pitch, to value contact, because it worked in his favor. [See CONTACT] Yet, it can be said that the 1997 and 1998 seasons saw pitchers striking out 6.7 and 6.6 batters for each nine innings pitched—the greatest figure in baseball history.

Are more pitchers trying to strike people out? I think not. I see more hitters getting themselves struck out. I have heard hitters' expressions of great pride in hitting home runs, and have watched the actions that went with their words. Such approaches make them more vulnerable than they ordinarily would be. Aggressiveness with little or no control fails in the long haul.

The April '99 issue of *Sport* provided these facts: "...the top five batting average leaders 40 years ago averaged 46 strikeouts that season; last year they averaged 87... Forty years ago, the top five home run hitters averaged 88 strikeouts apiece; last year they averaged 130." An "all-or-nothing approach," the article suggests. Same long haul results.

144

As mentioned previously, pitchers are the long-term beneficiaries of these hitters' approach. More discredit to the hitter than credit to the pitcher, it would seem. Yet, those who are known to be strikeout pitchers do deserve credit for the application of the philosophy advocated for all pitchers. Clemens, Randy Johnson, Kerry Wood, Pedro Martinez, Curt Shilling, *et. al.*

David Cone, himself on the top 10 list of strikeouts per nine innings in 1998, told *Sport*, "I think all strikeout pitchers have that atttack-mode mentality, trying to get ahead and then having some finishing pitches, really quality pitches, that can make hitters swing and miss. All strikeout pitchers across the board have that trait."

A pitcher must know himself and his capabilities. Though a minority of big league pitchers are considered to be strikeout pitchers, even those who *are* get more outs through contact. The leading strikeout pitcher in 1998 was Kerry Wood with 12.6 K's per nine innings pitched. Considering that 27 outs are projected over those nine innings, he would have 14.4 "contact outs." And very few pitchers come close to Wood's or Johnson's or Clemens' strikeout capabilities.

My idea of an "absolute perfect game" is one in which the pitcher gets twenty-seven consecutive first-pitch outs. Can't get better than that, for me.

Irrespective of what eventually happens in any given at-bat, the point made in earlier pages is that, as Kerry Wood has said, "...it's all about getting ahead early in the count." That should be every pitcher's agenda, whether contact results or a strikeout results. The agenda of every "*pitcher.*" Roger Clemens clarifies and finalizes the point. "I take more pride in being a pitcher than I do in being a strikeout pitcher."

What the Pitcher Should Do...

- Know himself and his capabilities as a pitcher.
- Establish the count in his favor by attacking the strike zone.
- Learn to finish hitters when far ahead in the count.
- Establish as a "rule-of-thumb" that he will let strikeouts happen, rather than try to make them happen.
- Know that when a strikeout is highly desirable because of a game situation, aggressiveness can be heightened only as far as command (control) is maintained.
- Value contact outs.

■ LEARNING [See APPENDIX A]

Simply stated, the best pitchers are the best learners. Whereas just about everyone in baseball gives and receives advice, the best learners are eager listeners. They know how to evaluate what they hear, and then how to integrate the appropriate advice into behavior. The best learners know that failure, as Henry Ford put it, "is the opportunity to begin again more intelligently." The best learners instinctively recognize that experience by itself is valueless. What one does with it gives it value.

When someone chooses to be an enthusiastic learner, he will find enthusiastic teachers. Coaches love learners. But as a person gets older, he finds that he is responsible to put information through his filtering system. A confident learner is wise enough to be discriminating. Others listen indiscriminately to everyone, trying to apply everything they hear and burying themselves under the weight of information and misinformation. The good learner is able to detect the false, the ineffective, the counterproductive and the affected (what my friend, Rene Lachemann, calls "eye wash"). Unedited advice can be dangerous.

Not to be confused with a discriminating learner is the stubborn one. A stubborn pitcher does not want to hear anything that forces him to consider changing an idea or a habit. "Consider." That's the operative word in that sentence. Good learners are open; poor or non-learners are closed. They consider nothing but the comfort of their own wrong-headedness. All error, no trial for them. I met pitcher Jim Deshaises late in his career. When he was a rookie with the Houston Astros he admitted to his stubbornness, made necessary adjustments and was a learner thereafter. Some take longer than others; some never seem to learn.

The know-it-all is another example of a poor learner. He thinks, or acts as if, he already knows whatever he needs to know. It was Josh Billings speaking in the mid-1800s who best described this type:"It ain't what a man don't know as makes him a fool, but what he does know as ain't so." Socratic wisdom with a Western flair.

But then, anyone taking the time to read these words is probably open to ideas and learning. So I will here leave the stubborn and self-impressed to their own devices, recalling the words of Francis Bacon, who said, "The unlearned man knows not what it is to descend into himself or call himself into account…" [See RESPONSIBILITY]

The pitcher who is a learner is the person who is responsible. I remember the words of WBC. welterweight champion Oscar De La Hoya, after winning a split-decision in February 1999. "I'm finding out I've been giving too much respect to my opponents. I have to be more aggressive. That's a learning process." Every mention of "process" in this book, and there are many, is grounded in the responsibility of the pitcher for integrating learning into behavior. Without process, there is no change for the better. De La Hoya included in the process: "Learn about your sport; learn about yourself." Familiar words to the reader by now.

I have been around avid learners, reluctant learners, and non-learners. The ratio in baseball is no different from the one I found in schools where I had taught. Yet, a significant difference exists as to why baseball players take their resistant stance to learning. A pitcher, for example, has already been very successful before becoming a professional. It is therefore more difficult to teach him something that calls for a change from what he considers to be partly responsible for the past success. A degree of frustration or failure, as in the case of Jim Deshaies, will deliver a more willing student to the teacher/coach. It takes time for some to recognize that ignorance is what Lawrence Durrell called "a calamity." First, they must meet on-field calamity. Then they seek a cure for the ignorance or ineptitude.

Some pitchers who wish to learn are initially frustrated in their attempts. Often, an individual has not been able to be objective about himself or his performances. Pitchers who have expressed a desire to learn have still found it difficult to examine their own faults and needs. Again, it is a trying process. I tell this type of pitcher, "It's hard to see the picture when you're inside the frame. Step out of it, and look at yourself as if you're me." And so on. They eventually realize that the very advice they may have given to others is the advice they have failed to provide themselves.

Kevin Brown has spoken about the "mirror" I hold up and make players look into. Some try to see what they want to see; the learners try to see what they need to see. "You won't fool him," Brown said. "And he won't let you fool yourself."

Yet, as avid a learner as Brown is, he can be reluctant to be a teacher. With the Padres in '98, he was showered with praise for the way he went about his business. "I don't tell anyone how to pitch," he said. "I just keep working. I hope everyone keeps their eyes and ears open and we will all learn."

Atlanta manager, pitching coach, and television commentator all admire Greg Maddux, the student. Says Bobby Cox, "The talent is not God's gift to him alone. He studies the game like mad...." Leo Mazzone said that Maddux is "much smarter than any coach I've been around. When we talk it's an exchange of ideas. I've learned a number of things from him." And Hall-of-Famer Don Sutton said of Maddux, "He is a person who goes to class four days and gives the class the fifth day."

Pitchers who do not watch other pitchers—or hitters—are losing what might be valuable information. The attentiveness to the game itself provides a great opportunity for learning. Research has shown that adults will not learn unless they see a specific benefit for themselves. Pitchers should be capable of understanding the benefit that comes from learning the game.

Learning is a prerequisite for making adjustments. Learning is a prerequisite to growth and improvement. Learning is part of self-discipline. Learning leads to confidence. "They know enough who know how to learn," said Henry Adams. Because we never know enough.

What the Pitcher Should Do...

- Be open to learning.
- Listen to everyone; be discriminating, thoughtful, and honest in using what is heard.
- Always seek better ways of accomplishing tasks.
- Give new approaches honest effort before evaluating them.

- Realize that what might have worked at one level might not at a higher level.
- Give a newly acquired approach a fair amount of time to "kick in."
- Understand that learning implies change, and that change is not immediately "comfortable."
- Learn about solutions, rather than dwelling on the problem.
- Be discriminating, using what seems to work and discarding what does not.
- Understand that in order to find out how to do something well, a good learner takes risks, rather than being fearful of doing something poorly.
- Understand that the wisest man still has plenty to learn.
- Know that ideas do not work, unless he also does, because theory may be fine, but application is finer.

■ MANTRA

By now the reader has surely recognized that positive, rational, task-oriented thoughts are prerequisites for effective behavior on the mound. Over and over this point has been made, particularly in WHAT THE PITCHER SHOULD DO sections. "Understand" this; "Recognize" that: "Be aware" of such and such… Over and over.

The purpose of these repetitions is to help the pitcher to create an understanding of a mantra—a sort of incantation, casting a spell, so to speak, over him as he "chants" the same, sound point of view. The repetition is a strongly defined and constant reference point—the star to guide the pitcher's ship by, through safe waters, away from troubled waters.

If using a mantra is a form of "brainwashing," the pitcher can be assured his brain is being "washed" by the pitcher himself. In doing so, he must be careful to choose impeccably correct messages to deliver to his brain—messages that ultimately affect his muscles. From the trust in, and the repeated expression of it, the mantra will become a countervailing force to all the wrong messages delivered by pressures, anxieties, distractions and fears. A strong, positive mantra can mute the voices of negative would-be intruders. That is why "one-pitch-at-a time" has become such a popular—and appropriate—mantra. It puts a pitcher's mind where it belongs: on the next pitch to be delivered. Simple, direct, clear. Repeat after me…

"Every time we…chant our mantra, the brain rewards us with the release of soothing endorphins…" wrote novelist John Dufresne. Endorphins help relieve pain and stress. The additional "reward" a pitcher gets from his mantra is the reminder of what focus he needs at the moment. That has very practical value. Hershiser's mantra, previously referred to, brought the veteran pitcher back to his lost focus.

Also noted previously was Greg Maddux' insistence that his sole concern is "executing a pitch." This has become his mantra. He chose it; he ritualistically verbalized it; he learned to believe in it; he is now unfailingly "spellbound" by it. "It's scary," he told me a couple of years ago. "That's all that matters out there [on the mound]."

If someone thinks about a particular thing in a singular way, he learns to own the thought—to represent it. The body hears the same directive repeated and repeated. The chant becomes he who chants it. "Scary," as Maddux said, the power our minds have, if we choose to use it.

What the Pitcher Should Do...

- Identify the major reminders he needs to keep his mind directed and focused. (e.g., "One-pitch-at-a-time"; Execute the next pitch"; "Attack the strike zone"; "Be easy.")
- Remember that his needs will change as he changes.
- Develop new/additional mantras according to new needs.
- Create mantras that are based on behavior, rather than results. (e.g., "Good low strikes," rather than "Get groundballs.")
- Be persistent in owning the mantra, rather than allowing someone (e.g., newspaper reporter) take it from you with irrelevant or distracting questions and concerns.
- Know that familiarity comes with use and time, and that time is not his responsibility—use is.

■ NEGATIVISM

I know NHL coach Ron Wilson to be a positive, upbeat person. He took a Washington Capitals team that had not been in the playoffs the previous year to the Stanley Cup finals in 1998. In 1999 the team was out of the playoffs again. Such a three-year sequence had not happened in approximately 50 years. The 1999 circumstance was not a happy one for Wilson and his team, and the coach knew that unhappiness often leads to a negative point of view. Negative behavior follows.

"I come to practice as positive as possible," he said in March of '99. "What you're trying to do is keep people from becoming cynical, thinking that they don't have a chance, that it's still a fun place to come to work. If it becomes dreary, it's ten times worse."

Cynicism, dreary attitudes, giving up, dread of what each day brings all take the meaning out of a person's life and livelihood. Negativism rules the individual and infects the environment in which he moves. Tough circumstances can challenge a person's inner strength and conviction. [See RELENTLESSNESS]

Because children are initially taught the "no's" and "don't's" of touching hot stoves or crossing streets alone or fighting with a sibling, they hear negative teaching during much of their childhood. It was written many years ago that by the time a youngster gets to high school, he has heard those two aforementioned negatives 40,000 times. I remember reading to my youngster a book entitled *No Fighting, No Biting*.

Youngsters are greatly affected by the words and deeds of the people who raise them, teach them, and coach them. Much of what they learn will come from what they hear and see in their extended environment. Precociously athletic children grow up in a very public and competitive milieu. They are coached early by people who may not be expert at teaching—and who may have their own vested interest in a youngster's performance. Indoctrination to negativity creates excessive pressure and a distorted outlook. For a young athlete, negativity becomes poisonous food for thought. And the most pronounced thoughts in a young athlete's environment will accompany him into adulthood.

One young man, who I am fairly certain will become a major league pitcher, told me of his childhood experiences playing baseball. "If I got four hits, my mom would get all over me for making an error. If I did great in the field, she would hammer me about hitting. It wore me out." Joy? Positive reinforcement? Those terms have been foreign to this young man. He is working hard at change. Small wonder he became a pitcher.

During a tenure with one of the major league organizations I have worked for, a big league utility player was called upon to play every day, when the regular he had occasionally spelled injured himself fairly seriously. The utilityman was told he would be in the lineup every day for the rest of the season, approximately two months. He responded by telling the manager he could not play. Period.

After a week or so, he did play, and he did a very respectable job, both in the field and at bat. Let it simply be said that, through great effort on the player's part, he was able to identify a junior high school coach who he now remembered clearly to have told him, "You'll never be an everyday player in the big leagues."

I will not regard here the motive behind this negative, mean-spirited and audacious remark. The adolescent boy did not regard the remark, at the time. But he carried it with him into the major leagues. The coach's words had become the player's belief. Adult opinions can have power, whether they have merit or do not.

Once the "adult" identified and discredited the coach's remark, he was able to function as an everyday player. (It was not necessary to discredit the coach, though the temptation was mine.) The "feeling" that resulted from the remark still requires regular attention, years after the individual ended his playing career.

Those are only a couple of the many examples that could be provided. The illustration is clear enough to make the point that influences beyond the individual greatly affect him and "teach" him to think in a particular way. Negative thinking and perceptions do not allow a baseball player to have the "fun" a positive thinker has in the game. Negativism does not allow him to have a life that is uplifting.

How some players manage to function at all impresses me greatly. It is a testimony to talent. But negativism gets in the way of their enjoyment and appreciation of what they possess. And some do not have what it takes to change their view of the world and of themselves. It takes honesty, and trust—and an immense effort.

The preceding anecdote provides the reader with an extreme example. Nevertheless, it illustrates something that does exist in the baseball culture and in the world at large. (A more extreme example is provided in PERSPECTIVE.) Now, let us examine the more "subtle" forms of negativity—less dramatic, perhaps, but more prevalent. Often harmful; always counterproductive.

When the gang in *Winnie The Pooh* is planning to have a picnic, the doomsayer, Eeyore, wants no part of the group's positive anticipation. "Don't blame me if it rains," he says. Eeyores can be found on every baseball roster. A negative verbalization such as the one made by Pooh's donkey friend is one of four basic types: statements that are self-critical; judgments that are negative; expectations of failure; attributions that lead down a "blind alley."

Players who degrade themselves can have a number of motives, each of them traced back to low self-esteem. [See SELF-ESTEEM]

Players who verbalize in negative terms tend to find things wrong with teammates, managers, coaches, and others. They focus on whatever they say is wrong with others. The effect on them is not a helpful one.

The Eeyores of the world expect the worst and usually produce it. [See SELF-FULFILLING PROPHECY]

The "blind-alley" players tend to disclaim responsibility. (Eeyore also did that, though in his case, he had no responsibility. Players often deny responsibility that is truly theirs.) "Blind-alley" thinking leads players' thoughts to unchangeable past events, unmanageable future events, jealousy or resentment of others. It encourages remarks that put players in the role of victim. (I have told such players, when they complained to me, that I refuse to jump into their pool of self-pity. "Take a hand, or you'll drown.")

Strategies can easily be formulated for such people. They can become positive problem-solvers, but only if they change their thinking and speaking, in a positive and resourceful way, and reject the negative and wasteful ways of their past. [See POSITIVISM]

Here are a number of destructive statements commonly mouthed by pitchers who think in negative terms:

"No way I can do well today."

"With my luck _____ ." Fill in the blank with a self-pitying phrase.

"This'll never work."

"My changeup will never be a good pitch for me."

"We don't have a chance against these guys."

"Don't mess this up."

"He never comes through when I need him."

"This guy [his catcher] doesn't have a clue."

"I can't believe they're leaving me in the game."

"I can't believe they're taking me out of the game."

"They made me throw that pitch."

"This guy thinks he can always psych me out."

"I can't do a thing right."

"I stink."

"This stinks."

"I can never get this guy out."

"I'm an idiot."

"Don't walk this guy."

"Don't give him anything to hit."

"If only _____ ." Fill in the blank with wishful thought.

"I've got no choice."

"It's not my fault."

"Why does he always do this to me?"

"Don't rush."

"Don't hang this slider."

"I'm lost out here."

"I'm a loser."

"He's a loser."

"How can such a loser be telling me how to get it done?"

"I hope they don't expect me to get it done all the time."

"I knew I wasn't going to make it through the fifth."

"I can't pitch on this mound; it's brutal."

Even when things are somehow going well, the Eeyores of the world will not be convinced: "This can't keep going so good."

Enough. The reader can add to the list, I'm sure. People who spend their time expressing such thoughts are people who, as Cormac McCarthy has written, "hold funerals before there's anything to bury." [See SELF-TALK]

The pitcher must start to listen to himself, understanding that as he expresses these negatives each day, he is increasing the chances of negative outcome—and walking around with an unhealthy point of view—diseased, if truth be told.

What the Pitcher Should Do...

- Listen to himself.
- Examine how his attitude is reflected by his thoughts and speech.
- Understand that negative influences in his youth do not have to continue through adulthood, if they are understood and rejected.
- Be who he wants to be, rather than who others have shaped him to be.
- Take responsibility for what he says and how he behaves.
- Know that what he thinks and says will greatly influence what he does.
- Learn to change negative talk into positive statements (e.g., "I'm going to work on this," rather than, "I can't do this." "Right through the target; good, low strike here," rather than, "Don't walk this guy.") [See COACHING SELF and SELF-TALK]
- Tell himself to what to do, rather than warning himself what not to do.
- Be aware of the common vocabulary of negativism so that, in identifying "the enemy," he can combat him.
- Learn to understand himself, to be honest with himself, to like and trust himself.
- Know that changing the quality of his thoughts will change the quality of his performance—and his life.
- Know that the change is a choice and requires commitment and positive mental energy.

■ NICE GUYS

When a player flies in to spend a couple of days with me during the off-season, I pick him up at the airport. Once we're en route to my home, I present a hypothetical situation.

"You go to an upscale restaurant for a good dinner. You have looked forward to it. You knew just what you wanted to order. The meal is served; you begin eating. The food is cold. What do you do?"

A considerable number (probably 13 out of 20) have answered, "I shut up and eat it." Or words to that effect. They "don't want to bother the waitress." They do not want to confront the issue.

"That's why you're here," I say to them.

I am reminded of a story that made a strong impression on me when I read it as a child. It is about a young boy and his father, who are bringing a donkey they wish to sell at a market three towns away from their home. They begin the trip with the father walking, as he holds the rope around the animal's neck. The son rides the donkey. As they go through their town, the father hears people say, "Look at that; the old man is forced to walk by a selfish son with young legs." The father and son switch positions.

They walk on and soon hear the townspeople of the adjacent hamlet say, "Look at that; a small young thing forced to walk, while a strong man rides." Father and son mount the donkey and both ride into the next town.

There they hear, "Isn't that inhumane! Two people burdening that poor, dumb animal. What insensitive cruelty." The father thinks for a moment. He then purchases a long bamboo pole and a length of heavy rope. The father and son tie the donkey's legs to the pole, then lift it onto their shoulders.

They walk into the next town carrying the upside down animal. "Look at those fools, carrying a donkey."

The most certain way to assure failure in this world of ours is to try to please everyone.

Nice guys tend to be pleasers. They may have different motives, but their agenda is not to ruffle anyone's feathers. I have found three distinct differences among players who want to please. Some just seem to want to be liked too much. They tend to have low self-esteem; their acceptance by others is their validation of self.

Others have been criticized excessively as youngsters. They too suffer from poor-self esteem and wish to prevent criticism by catering to those who have any chance of giving it. Like a waitress in restaurant. Or a plumber who botched the job in the player's home, but who the player will not call to hold accountable. Or their inept, perhaps dishonest, auto mechanic.

Still others simply have been raised to be very nice sons by very nice parents. Nothing wrong with that. Until the "son" walks out to the mound to compete. (I often ask such pitchers, "What was the last thing your mother said to you when you left the house by yourself when you were a child?" The answer is usually: "Be careful." Or, "Be a good boy." Or both.

Most of the aforementioned pitchers tend to have difficulty converting off-field niceness to on-field competitiveness. They pitch "carefully" and are "too nice."

Many with whom I have worked have what is called in semantics, "an either-or orientation." They are concerned that if they are not acting like a Mr. Rogers, they will appear to be Attila, the Hun. [See PERSPECTIVE] Not true, but if it were, Attila would be the more likely of the two to get the job done on the mound.

I am struck by the Denver Broncos' Bill Romanowski, reputed to be *the* wildest, most aggressive, nastiest linebacker in the NFL. He is also known, off the football field, as the consummate and caring gentleman. He is well-spoken, active and giving in his community. He seems to adjust his persona to what the environment calls for. He has compromised his persona. Rather, he has established it. Whoever he is, he is effective—wherever he is.

In BEHAVIOR, I spoke about Rick Honeycutt. Another ultimate off-field gentle man. He learned to be a steadfast attacker as a pitcher. It can be done, but a decision must be made.

Early in his career, pitcher Tom Seaver decided to shed his "nice guy" image, which he equated with "a losing-guy image." He knew he had to back hitters off the plate and did what he had to in order to send his message. "There is a fine line between good hard baseball and dirty baseball," Seaver said.

The line between good, hard baseball and not-so-good, soft baseball is much more clearly defined. Pitchers must be on the appropriate side of the line. If they are not, they must inspire themselves to cross over.

Greg Maddux can be the humble, self-effacing good person—when he is not pitching. But those who watched Maddux respond to what he perceived to be Jim Leyritz's attempts to distract him during the '98 NLCS, saw a fierce, competitive nature express itself. Not the nature of a "nice guy."

The Cardinals' Bob Gibson has been my favorite non-"nice guy" on the mound, but I think I would have enjoyed watching New York Yankees pitcher Burleigh Grimes perform. I was a bit too young. In the mid-1930s, someone asked Grimes why there are so many "nice guys" in baseball. (Yes, back then, during those glorified days of "hardball.") Grimes said he didn't know the answer about "nice guys," but he knew about himself: "I'm a bastard when I play."

Pitching is confrontation. Pitchers realize that and must reconcile any differences they have between their understanding and their approach. If efficacy comes from aggressiveness, and caution or timidity assures ineffectiveness, their choice should be clear to them. Their goal should be established and vigorously pursued. That is the need of every "nice guy." Otherwise, he will not be much better off than the "nice guy" in a Bryce Courtenay novel, who became "powerless as those around me plundered my spirit with the gift of themselves." Hitters especially.

What the Pitcher Should Do...

■ Understand that some of the finest, "nicest" men, off the baseball field, have been the fiercest, most confrontational competitors on the playing field.

■ Understand why so many people have as an agenda, the need to please others.

■ Identify himself and his tendencies, in this regard, as a person and as an athlete.

■ Understand that the ability to adapt to the appropriate conduct required in any given environment, without compromising his own values, is one characteristic of a self-actualized person.

■ Remember that aggressive behavior is a major attribute of every successful pitcher.

■ Set specific goals related to behavior during competition that address being aggressive and confrontational, rather than being timid and a "nice guy."

■ Live and perform from the "inside out," rather than from the "outside in," meaning, act upon what you know is right and appropriate, rather than what and you feel would satisfy and please others.

■ On the mound, develop "an infantryman's heart." [See COMPETITOR]

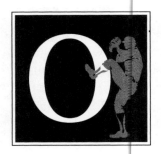

■ OUTS

Baseball is a game of outs. Twenty-seven of them, unless more are required in an extra-inning game. The 27 outs of a regulation game *all* must be made by the winning team. This elemental fact I try to impress on pitchers constantly. Irrespective of score, outs must be made. The game will not be over until those 27 outs are "in the book."

Because of this fact, a pitcher should always maintain his intensity of focus until the game is over. Truly over. That is when competition ends. That is when the winner of the game is determined. Not so in football games, which are "over" when the quarterback takes the snap and goes to a knee as the clock ticks. (The clock is still ticking as opposing players and coaches shake hands with each other on the field.)

Basketball teams maintain a lead by "spreading the court," holding the ball as the clock ticks, and their lead becomes that much more insurmountable. As the victory is more assured by each tick.

Hockey players, victory in their grasp, ice the puck—"killing the clock"—by shooting the puck down to the other end of the rink, making it impossible for the other team to score a goal in so short a period of time.

These are all strategies for using time as a weapon. The ball is a pitcher's only weapon. No clock exists in baseball. A defined terminus is built into the game, no matter how long it takes to reach it. No lead is insurmountable. No strategy should be changed. Execute every pitch. GET OUTS.

Two recollections are vivid. A few years ago, after the Marlins had completed a home game, coaches and players were watching a Los Angeles-Philadelphia game on the clubhouse television sets. After I had show-

160

ered and watched a bit longer, I started back to my hotel room. When I left, the Dodgers were ahead by eight or nine runs in the eighth. Getting out of the parking lot, driving back to my hotel, parking, and getting up to my room took approximately 40 minutes.

I turned the set on, presuming the game was over, and presuming the L.A. victory. Both presumptions were inaccurate. The game was still being played, and I saw the Phillies get their game-winning hit.

No such presumption should be brought to a baseball game. Spectators may presume, they may run up the aisles and leave the ballpark; they may shut off their TV sets; they may say what they wish about the impending result. The players, the participants—the pitchers, most notably—must continue to play the game. And play it with the same energy and singular focus they had at the beginning of the game.

The other memory is of a minor league game played in Huntsville, Alabama, where Oakland had its Double-A team. Huntsville was behind 12-6 when the ninth inning started. In order to "save the pitching staff," the manager put a position player in to pitch the top of the ninth. Based on the staff's need, the move was necessary. The "pitcher" gave up six runs. The purpose, however, based on the organization's player development philosophy, was served.

In the bottom of the ninth inning, the score 18-6, I stood in the dugout and watched our team score 11 runs all with two out. We had runners on first and third, as our third baseman, a young man named Larry Arndt, smoked a ball up the middle. The pitcher somehow made the play. Hunstville lost the game, 18-17. But what a torturous inning the opposing team had—all for want of one out.

A pitcher gets two outs in an inning. I see his approach change. Particularly if he has gotten two *quick* outs. He "relaxes" his approach, meaning his attention gets broader ("And next inning I've got the bottom of the order"), his focus gets fuzzier ('This is cake"). The parenthetical remarks are actual expressions of two young pitchers who suffered the consequences of their altered approach. The lesson is not always learned as quickly as it was by the two who I use as examples. The price for not learning can be very costly.

Though they are the subject here, outs are still the second rung on the ladder of abstraction. Down there, but not low enough to reach through a pitcher's proper approach. The execution of one pitch—"one pitch at a time"—is the bottom rung on his performance "ladder." That's the step that leads to all others. First, make a pitch. That is the mean to most the immediate end: an out. [See TASK AT HAND]

What the Pitcher Should Do...

- Remind himself constantly of the fact that every baseball game requires a specific number of outs, and that the results of the game are not determined until those outs are made.
- Know that, as a pitcher, he should maintain his level of energy and his sharpness of focus, irrespective of the score, the number of outs in an inning or the count.
- Be certain to maintain his best approach as he reaches a point in the game when he presumes outcome in his favor.
- If he has a tendency to "let up" when he senses the end is in sight, get off the mound and coach himself to "run through the finish line," rather than anticipating when that "end" will come (i.e., the end of his outing).
- Set as a goal the ability to "go as hard as he can, for as long as he can."

■ PERSPECTIVE

"[I]t is true in culture as in optics that if you hold a large object close to your nose, it will block out the sun, moon, and stars. But that is the very reason why large objects should be viewed from a proper distance. We must work for perspective, under pain of never seeing more than one thing at a time..."

I use Jacques Barzun's words to direct the pitcher's thoughts toward whatever limited perspective he may have of the world. Yet, a limited vista is exactly what a pitcher *should have*—on the mound. The fuller view indicates to a pitcher that there is more to life than baseball. The reduced view allows him to pay full attention to his task at hand.

Those two perspectives are essential for him.

A perspective is a point-of-view. A pitcher can see the world one way; his friend can see it another way. The pitcher can see himself to be something other than what the friend sees. The difference is based on all that has happened to each of them over his lifetime—for better or for worse. The positive reinforcement and the negative reinforcement. The failures and the successes. But ultimately, the perspective the pitcher has of his world, of baseball, and of himself is entirely his responsibility.

Much of my professional concern has, of course, been for athletes whose rational and emotional systems have adversely affected their mental health and performance. Their perspectives have been distorted by their experiences and by their interpretation of them. Even "healthy" people at times develop perspectives based on invented scenarios (not nearly as dire as the inventor "paints" them) and highly unlikely consequences, (Shakespeare's "horrible imaginings"). The person with a distorted perspective is an un-happy person. His unhappiness is inevitable, because his point-of-view is at odds with "reality."

The following words of Karl Albrecht beg inclusion:

"The chronically unhappy person seems to labor under the cruel de-lusion that he is unhappy because of unfortunate circumstances, events, and processes happening in this world. He doesn't realize that he is un-happy because of his evaluation of these circumstances, events, and pro-cesses. The unhappy person fails to grasp the all-important fact that positives and negatives do not exist in 'nature'; that 'success' and 'failure' do not exist as elements of the flow of reality processes outside his head. This person doesn't realize that these are mental constructs, which he su-perimposes on his perceptions of the world. The chronically unhappy person fails to grasp the fact that *one decides to be happy or unhappy*." (My emphasis.)

People "evaluate" according to their point of view. People have choices. Adult people. In the section NEGATIVISM, I gave an example of a player being "taught" by a coach. The player carried a negative perspective of him-self into adulthood—into the big leagues—as a result of that "lesson." Also alluded to was a more dramatic example of such "teaching." It follows.

A five-year-old boy is atop a brick wall, which is eight or nine feet in height. The boy is walking slowly and carefully along it, as his father walks below, on the cement sidewalk. The father speaks to the boy, opening his arms as he turns toward the wall underneath the boy. "Come on, jump. I'll catch you," the father assures. The boy is hesitant. Reluctant. "Come on; I'm right here."

The boy jumps; the father steps aside. The boy hits the pavement, fracturing an arm. The father stands over him and says, "That'll teach you not to trust *anyone* in this world."

"Bless the Beasts and the Children," the song says. They have "…no voice, no choice…" The boy referred to in the above anecdote is now a man in his 40s. He learned his father's lesson all too well. His perspective of the world and of himself was bleak because of it. The ordeal of change is painful, but, in this case, less painful than living with such a troubling and persistent perspective for 30-plus years. Perhaps each day now his eyes open with more of the grace of the adult in him, and less of the grief of the child in him.

Counterpoint to the preceding is the anecdote about a Frenchman who told his gardener he wanted a tree planted. The gardener did not like the idea, since, as he pointed out to his employer, the type of tree to be planted grew very slowly. The Frenchman listened and then told the gardener that if that were true, he'd better not lose any time. "Plant it immediately."

Two polar opposite perspectives. The father and the Frenchman.

Pitchers with healthy perspectives have been "taught" by parents, coaches, and by their own experiences to trust themselves, to trust others, to trust this about the world: it was not created to undo him. [See POSITIVISM] Some are more self-actualized than others, but every healthy person can be "stung by a flu bug." Each person's resistance will influence the seriousness of the sting.

The view I express to players is that they should work on their health, rather than worrying about the "bug." In terms of mental strength, I suggest that the people best off are those who have the best coping mechanisms. "I would rather have a number of issues (the term 'problems' is resisted) and many coping mechanisms, than have only one issue but no coping mechanisms," I say. "Difficult issues can fog up our perspective; coping mechanisms help clear away the fog."

Distorted perspective results when players think they cannot cope with situations they are facing or will be facing. The ability to cope with these difficulties is influenced by the context in which we view them. The more contexts a player can choose from, the less likely his perspective will reveal to him an inevitable and insurmountable difficulty.

In the section on FEAR, I spoke of the technique of "catastrophizing"—determining what the worst possible happenstance could be for a player. The process allows him to determine that he is capable of coping with that "awful" possibility. The difficulty usually dissipates, not because it entirely lacks validity, but because the player realizes he can cope with it. And what he was originally "worrying about" is not even close to the construct of worst scenario. "I can deal with this," is his music to his ears.

When All-Star shortstop Walt Weiss was interviewed some time ago, he spoke about a time he and I applied the process, in the early '90s. Weiss was injured at the time, and he thought Oakland's management was losing its patience as they waited for him to recover. "I was really getting depressed," Weiss told the interviewer. "I mean, I hadn't played for close to a year. Harvey simply said to me, 'Okay, what's the worst case scenario here?

What's the worst that can happen?'...He got me thinking not just about baseball, but about my life in general. He gave me the bigger picture, the larger view... And once I did start to put things into proper perspective, I found that I could cope a lot better with the ups-and-downs of my career."

What if a young pitcher is "taught" at an early age that he is an inspiration to others? Isn't that a positive, a jump-start for a wonderful self-image? Well, it may not be all that wonderful, from the youngster's perspective, if the burden of being an inspiration is "a large object too close to his nose."

Such was the case with Jim Abbott, who became a major league pitcher despite having only one hand. Abbott made a comeback in 1998, after having taken a year off from the game. His earlier performances had suffered, as had his perspective. He used the time off to "move the large object."

Abbott talked to *Arizona Republic* reporter, Paola Boivin, in March, 1999. "I took the perception of me too seriously," Abbott said at the Milwaukee Brewers' spring training site. "I felt that because I had a bad year and was playing for a team [Anaheim] in the community where I lived, I was embarrassed to go places.

"I thought that my record was my name. [See SELF-ESTEEM] I thought when I walked into places, people would think... [negative thoughts]. What you learn is that people don't care that much. I had created this unrealistic world, and I think as baseball players we tend to do that.

"It's fun being here, and I know it's a choice for me. When you look at it that way, then all the other stuff you used to complain about doesn't matter. I tell myself, I don't have to be here. I want to be here.' I enjoy the competitiveness, and I look forward to pitching instead of dreading it."

A textbook unto itself. As Emerson wrote, "It is the eye that makes the horizon."

"... Baseball players tend to do that," Jim Abbott has allowed. Pitchers tend to do it most. If Mariano Rivera sees the baseball world as one happy place, it is, in part, because he saw the unhappy prospect of being a fisherman in the little village in which he grew up. Will the game eventually change his perspective? If his perspective changes, it will be because *he* changes it.

With that in mind, every pitcher should understand that his career prospects for the future, a "big" game, an injury, a crucial situation, an imposing hitter to face, all can block his vision of what is beyond—which is—his life. He must know that the limits of his field of vision are not the limits of his world.

Ironically, on the mound, the pitcher must limit his field of vision. As noted, he has strategies available for doing just that. They help him to execute his task without the distraction of such other concerns as those mentioned above. On the mound, he narrows his world to the next pitch he will deliver. "Nothing matters at that time but that pitch," I tell pitchers. That is his perspective of function. And he must know he will be responsible for creating "threat" or "challenge," as he competes.

At his home, he must know there is a world beyond baseball. A struggling player is interviewed on television. He has just become a father. "It [the birth of his child] helps me have a better perspective." The same thought is expressed when a family member or teammate develops a serious health problem—or dies. It would enhance his perspective if he were able to recognize the boundary between reality and perception without having to wait for dramatic events to clarify it for him.

That is the purpose of this rather lengthy presentation. To help provide that clarity. To assist the pitcher in his coming to an understanding that he is affected not by "things," but of the view he takes of them.

What the Pitcher Should Do...

- Understand what perspective is and how he has developed his.
- Understand that he can choose to alter his perspective to be one grounded in reality, rather than in imagination.
- Employ the "catastrophizing" technique, when burdened by a troubling perspective as a "person," thereby understanding that he has the ability to cope with "worst scenario" possibilities.
- Recognize the unlikelihood of these possibilities becoming realities.
- Employ the mental strategies of a pitcher, when competing. [See CONCENTRATION, GATHERING, POSITIVISM, SELF-TALK, etc.]

■ POISE

Hemingway called it "grace under pressure." Writer Paul Theroux used a term that is a favorite of mine: "Un-get-at-able." As in the dugout expression, "You can't get to this guy." Poise is their subject.

A pitcher who has poise is able to maintain his composure during "times that will try his soul." That is not to say he will not entertain some distracting internal responses. But he will not externalize them. He will "keep his powder dry." Two-time Cy Young Award winner Tom Glavine comes immediately to mind. His demeanor is impeccable. No observer knows what he is thinking or feeling, and that is the way it should be. He is methodical and consistent in his behavior on the mound. He will not let anyone "see him sweat." Peter Gammons described Glavine's mound behavior to me, with pride in his eye and tone, as "good old New England stoicism."

But poise is more than outward appearance, though that is important enough. [See BODY LANGUAGE] The Vikings believed that no good purpose could be found for showing fear. Such display, they felt would signify to observers that they had lost their independence—freedom. A pitcher's display reveals himself, and the loss of self-control. A pitcher who has "total" poise has the ability to control his emotions, his thinking, and his *behavior*. His is a serenity of mind over chaos.

Many pitchers have "partial" poise. When speaking of Tom Glavine, I refer to what observers may see. He is not a "stalker" on the mound. His serenity is total, insofar as the observer can tell. Yet other pitchers may stomp around the mound when matters seem to become "unglued." As long as the *pitcher* does not come unglued, the situation can be dealt with effectively. By that I mean, the proverbial "bottom line" is how the pitcher behaves as he executes the next pitch. Glavine exemplifies "total" poise. His performance seems to be effortless.

His teammate, John Smoltz, is an example of "partial" poise. Smoltz can be seen making facial expressions or body suggestions, but he seems to regain his composure—his poise—quickly, before delivering the next pitch. That is what truly matters.

The danger for young pitchers is to believe that regaining poise during competition is easy to do. For a pitcher who habitually expresses his emotions on the mound, the likelihood of getting it back is less. For some, it is easier to maintain poise than regain it. Often, a pitcher who "loses it" does not get it back until he is in the shower. Having lost his poise, he lost his self-control—to the extent that he could not have "his wits about him" and gather himself. "I just flat-out forgot everything I had to do to fix myself," I have been told, by a pitcher who showered early.

Such a statement as the one above, indicates one of the mental skills that can be lost in the heat of the moment. Panic, anger, or frustration can result in loss of "memory." Those emotions can also produce vague or distorted messages in the brain. The pitcher's judgment suffers as well ("I'm going to unload this pitch as hard as I can"). Doubt and indecisiveness result. [See SELECTION] Irrelevant and distracting thoughts gain control.

Physical effects also result from loss of control. Breathing is adversely affected (I have seen pitchers hyperventilate on the mound). Muscular tightness inhibits proper blood flow. Range of motion is reduced and the arm becomes less "free." The ability to focus on the target is reduced or eliminated.

The loss of poise has a ripple effect. A pitcher should always strive to have an internal peace, in spite of adverse or chaotic conditions outside him. [See ADVERSITY] The poem, "If," by Rudyard Kipling lists the conditions for manhood, as delivered by a father to his son. The first condition reads: "If you can keep your head when all about you are losing theirs..." The last line, after all the other conditions have been stated, is: "And...(then) you'll be a Man, my son!"

Poise helps make the man.

What the Pitcher Should Do...

- Understand that poise is an indicator of self-control.
- Understand that body language indicates attitude, and attitude, at such times, will dictate behavior.
- Be aware of the mental and physical effects of loss of poise.
- Remember to gather himself and his thoughts when conditions begin to affect him adversely.
- Work diligently at harnessing emotional responses to external events. [See DISCIPLINE]

■ POSITIVISM

The term "positivism" is not meant to be applied as a doctrine referred to in philosophy books. Rather, it is a reference, in these pages, to a thinking "skill" that is a countervailing force to "negativism."

Nor is "positivism" a synonym for "optimism," which is a tendency to expect that "everything will work out for the best." For a pitcher, positivism is the utilization of appropriate thinking patterns—task-oriented directives, stated in positive language. "What to do and how to do it." The "best" may not result, but the pitcher will be "at his best." He will deliver his pitch effectively (plan, focus, execution, response) by employing positive self-coaching techniques. [See SELF-TALK]

If a pitcher is not predisposed to speak in positive terms, he must learn to do so, acquiring the behavior as a skill is acquired. It is bad enough that negative language reflects an unwholesome attitude. Worse is the fact that the negative thoughts a pitcher may have, expressed silently or aloud, are translated into negative approaches. A pitcher, in telling himself what *not* to do, focuses his attention on just that—and increases the likelihood of the very behavior he wishes to avoid. Positive directives provide a pitcher with a focus on what he should do.

If I did not know how to properly drive a nail into a piece of wood, and I wanted to learn how to be a carpenter, I'd seek out a carpenter, someone who knew how to *do* what I wished to do.

"Let me see what you've got. Here's a hammer and nail; there's the wood. Drive the nail into the wood," he might have said to me. Despite my not really knowing how to go about the task, I gave it my best attempt. The nail went in sideways and bent, because of my inept attempt at driving it. "Good grief!" the carpenter exclaimed. "You can't do it that way. Don't bend the darn thing; don't swing the hammer sideways; don't come down with it from so far away. Can't you do it right?"

He did not tell me how to accomplish that. He knew how to *do* the task, but he couldn't *teach me* how to do it. He certainly told me what I shouldn't do.

I sought out another carpenter. The nail looked the same after I demonstrated my lack of skill to this fellow. "OK," he responded. "Let me show you what to do. To begin with, you held the nail at an angle; hold it straight up and down. Good. Now, keep your hammer stroke short and come right down over the nailhead. You hit too rapidly and lost control of your stroke the first time. You want to use short, deliberate swings over the top. There you go."

It would take a while for me to become a master carpenter, but I would know what kind of teacher I needed. A "positivist." One who would teach me what to do and how to do it.

If it is true, as I will say to a pitcher, that he is the most important coach he will ever have, the need for him to be positive in his coaching should be obvious. If a pitching coach tells him all the right things in all the right ways, but the pitcher translates it into negative terms, the coach has been of no use. Conversely, if a pitching coach is not skillful at presenting his messages appropriately, but the pitcher converts what he needs into positive language, all will be well that ends well. Every external message must run through the pitcher's mental filter. If he does not have a filter, problems are very likely to result. If he himself provides the contaminated internal message, problems are assured. He must be an exemplary self-coach for his pitching self.

The battle to express all thoughts in a positive way must be fought—if it needs fighting. The first campaign is to employ general language such as: "I will"; "I'll find a way"; "I'll adjust." Rather than, "I can't"; "I'd better not…"; "I hope." A pitcher who tries to "find a way" looks for a positive strategy, rather than saying, "It can't be done." The pitcher who employs positive language is a seeking excellence. A pitcher who speaks in negative terms is seeking an escape from failure. One pitcher is likely to find what he is seeking; the other is likely to be found by what he is fleeing from.

A pitcher grows by what he feeds on. Positive language allows him healthy growth. He affirms himself, rather than degrading himself. He examines possibilities, rather than pronouncing impossibilities. He seeks ways to improve himself, rather than seeking ways to judge others poorly. He is grounded in reality, rather than floating in imaginative thinking ("If only …"). He expects the best, rather than being certain of the worst. He looks for solutions, rather than wallowing in problems.

The development of appropriate behavior is a process. It takes longer to habituate desired behavior than it does to determine the behaviors. To say, "OK, I'm going to speak in positive terms as much as I possibly can," is a simple enough plan. The execution is the challenge. Someone once said that his greatest inspiration was the challenge to attempt the impossible.

My inspiration is to declare this challenge difficult, but very possible.

What the Pitcher Should Do...

- Understand that to be a positive thinker is to think of what to do and how to do it, rather than thinking everything will work out to his satisfaction.
- Understand that the best coach/teacher instructs by revealing and reinforcing strategies that help the pitcher/learner to accomplish his task.
- Recognize the importance of self-coaching. [See COACHING SELF]
- Accept the responsibility of coaching himself in a positive, constructive manner.
- Listen to himself thinking and speaking, in order to monitor his language, then converting negative thoughts and verbalizations and reinforcing positive ones.
- Be persistent in the pursuit of positivism in thought and expression.

■ PREPARATION [See APPENDIX A]

The instinct of highly successful pitchers runs parallel to all research—and with the view held by Boy Scouts: be prepared. Research shows that confidence and self-belief are greatly enhanced "when systematic plans are developed and employed."

While researching the topic of preparation for *The Mental Game of Baseball*, I spoke with Tom Seaver about the game's persistent "chicken-and-egg question." Which comes first, confidence or success? The best resolution, it would seem, is indicated by the research referred to above. A pitcher has his own preparation within his complete control. The most he can do for himself is to prepare himself optimally. His preparation can be definable and clear-cut. "Confidence" and "success" are abstract terms, always open to discussion and debate. He should not have to debate with himself—or anyone else—about whether or not he is "ready" to pitch.

I have already mentioned that the two words I hear most from players are, "I know." Players are, for the most part, aware of what is required in order for them to be effective. They also know that a gap often exists between their knowledge and their behavior. There are pitchers who usually do what is necessary; others often do what is necessary; some rarely do... Those who never do what is necessary are not around long enough to be otherwise convinced.

Excellent athletes always do what is necessary, meaning they behave in ways that will enhance their performance, rather than detract from it. Their consistency is the lock on their performance. Preparation is the key to that lock.

Pitchers who wish to be consistent must make a commitment. First, they should formulate goals, which will help them determine what it is they need to work at. Then they should develop a program of routine, which will allow them to habituate behaviors, so that these behaviors will become "second nature" to them. Learned instincts. They then must have the mental discipline and stamina to follow these routines, irrespective of how they may be "feeling" at a given moment or on a given day.

The story that will always stick out in my mind was presented in *The Mental Game of Baseball*. It deserves repeating—summarizing, at least. Because of poor weather conditions on a particular day in Montreal, Tom Seaver was forced to miss his regular opportunity to pitch. Circumstances dictated that he would miss his start. His regular routine would be affected.

The New York Mets' flight back from Montreal that night arrived in New York after midnight. Seaver drove to Shea stadium, changed his clothes, got a security guard to turn on a light in the bullpen, set up a screen for himself behind the plate, got a bucket of balls—and, at one o'clock in the morning, prepared for his next outing. He got his throwing in.

A goal, commitment, mental discipline, routine. Seaver would not be denied his preparation.

A pitcher's preparation should become all the good and appropriate habits he has on and off the field. [See HABITS] His eating, sleeping, and conditioning habits should come as a result of a plan put into action. If they are habits of default, they will be habits of failure. Sloppy thinking is not the characteristic of successful pitchers. Preparedness developed through positive and determined thinking succeeds and endures.

Preparation related to performance is required during the performance itself—with each pitch—before the performance and between performances. (The "after" and "until.")

A pitcher should develop a reliable sleeping schedule. For example, a starting pitcher knows he will be pitching on certain days, and he can determine a plan for the nights between his performances. He may or may not make a distinction between the night before his start and the other nights. But whatever he decides, it will be his plan. It can be adjusted according to its effectiveness—and according to unforeseen and uncontrollable circumstance. (He should not be obsessive about any plan he cannot completely control.)

A relief pitcher must develop a pattern appropriate to his role. He should presume he will be called on to pitch each day and form an appropriate sleeping plan, based on this presumption.

Part of a pitcher's preparation may be affected by the social demands of others—including teammates. Another presumption is that the pitcher knows what is best for him—better than others do. He should act upon what he knows. Commitment and self-discipline are required. So, too, is courage. Not everyone can easily say, "No." The pitcher must decide what is most beneficial to him and make a choice based on that understanding.

Conditioning is part of preparation. A pitcher should, in accord with the weight trainer and medical trainer, establish a regimen that works for him as a pitcher, not as a professional wrestler.

In the clubhouse, a pitcher should have a routine. Snacking, reading, doing crossword puzzles, chatting with teammates, putting on headphones, and the like. This is especially important for starting pitchers on game days. He should have his "readying place" and his "readying procedure." He can choose to be somewhat sociable or entirely reclusive. Whatever works well for him. [See AROUSAL]

As the time nears for a starting pitcher to go out to stretch and warm up, he should be in his "quiet place" (if he is not there already) and internalize all the mental keys he uses. He may go over the opposition's lineup in his mind. He may give himself reminders, based on possible mental deficiencies in his last performance and/or whatever else merits review. [See VISUALIZATION]

The bullpen is a preparation, not an indicator. The pitcher gets loose, works on execution of his pitches, reviews mechanical keys—and uses his last few pitches to establish "game focus." He leaves the bullpen with the thought of being aggressive, under control, and determined. He does not deliver messages such as, "My stuff stinks today," or "I'm unhittable." Both are irrelevant and/or absurd. "Attack the strike zone," or "Establish the count," or "Force contact," are more constructive thoughts, to put it mildly.

Enough has already been written about on-the-mound thinking and behavior. Positive, task-oriented thinking; narrow and sustained focus; aggressive, controlled actions; poise; the ability to "regroup" through self-coaching—all prepare a pitcher for his next pitch.

Closers at the major league level have their own unique way of preparing. Though their individual procedures are not likely to be applicable to the situation of the reader, one note should be struck. When Trevor Hoffman of the San Diego Padres was asked how a closer should prepare for a game, he answered simply, "By having the same routine every night." Some come out from the clubhouse into the dugout after four innings, then go to the bullpen in the seventh. Others have different times for their appearance in different places. Some have a certain kind of rubdown. Others do not want a rub. But they are all consistent in their routines.

"It's not superstition," explained Hoffman. "The discipline helps me to focus. My father got across to me early the importance of approaching a task with an idea and discipline…"

Curt Schilling is an acknowledged "battler." But he also takes great pride in his preparation. He credits a conversation he had with Nolan Ryan for clarifying that need. Schilling recalled, "(Ryan) said there are things I can and can t do on days I pitch. He said I can't control the weather, the umpires or the emotional state of the other team. But I can control one thing. I can be better prepared than the hitters I face that day."

Preparation is his getting ready for battle. The military purpose is to have an advantage over a warring opposition. The baseball purpose is to have the pitcher perform at his best. Still, to compete is to battle [See WARRIOR], so I succumb to the temptation of employing a military metaphor. "The more you sweat in peace, the less you bleed in war."

Be ready.

What the Pitcher Should Do...

- Understand that appropriate preparation will help him be a more confident and effective performer.
- Understand that a major ingredient of his preparation is consistency.
- Establish away-from-field, off-field, and on-field routines, making behavior compatible with circumstance.
- Prepare mentally by reiterating all the keys he previously developed, according to need and time.

■ PRESSURE

Important, critical, extremely significant, essential, imperative, must game, must pitch...Shakespeare's "the be all and the end all." These are words used to describe a situation.

Must, have to, got to, need to, expected to, had better...These are words used to describe an attitude. An attitude held by a person who interprets a situation to be as described above.

Words of pressure; words of weight.

In a psychology class I was teaching, the subject of "pressure" (and stress)—because of problems real and imagined—was to be discussed. I brought a big, tin, empty linseed oil can into class the day the topic was to be treated. And an air pump. At the beginning of the class, I gave a demonstration. First, I took the cap off the opening of the can and put a rubber stopper into it. Then, the thin hose from the air pump was inserted into a hole in the stopper. The pump was to be used to extract air from the can.

Slowly I pumped the air out of the can. A crackling noise began to sound as the can's shape gradually changed. The sides were collapsing. I pumped faster; the noise became more pronounced and the can collapsed and shriveled. When I stopped, the can's shape was completely distorted.

"What happened?" I asked.

"It collapsed because of the air pressure outside," came an answer.

"It folded because there was nothing left inside," I responded.

Prior to the demonstration, we had noted that air applies 15 pounds of pressure per square inch on every surface. The pressure put on the can's external surface was 15 pounds per square inch. The pressure inside the can had been the same—until I sucked the air out of the can. Because there was no longer any air inside, to "combat" the pressure from the the air outside, the can "folded."

"The same physical principal applies to us," I said to the students. "We have air inside us that keeps our bodies intact. Our psyches follow the same principle. The 'pressing' problems or issues we have all can create 'pressure.' But these issues won't 'dent' us or 'buckle' us if we have what it takes to stay whole. It takes coping mechanisms. The can's internal force is air; our internal psychological force is whatever coping mechanisms we have," I said. Though oversimplified, the point seemed clear to them.

Part of the oversimplification is that "pressure" is a perception. What pitcher A perceives as a threatening situation, pitcher B sees as an exciting challenge. This point has been made often. So, when Orel Hershiser signed with the New York Mets in March '99, he said of playing in New York, "I love the pressure..." Well, *is* it "pressure" then? That point is moot. What matters more is that different pitchers interpret the same environment and circumstance differently. I know pitchers who "buckled" in New York. (I refuse to say New York "buckled" them.) And I know pitchers who have thrived there. A person's reality is what he believes it to be. (Karl Wallenda once said, "Being on a tightrope is living; everything else is waiting.")

Still, if the environment truly presents difficult situations that must be dealt with, a pitcher who has "the right stuff" will survive at least, and thrive, at best, in spite of the whatever external problems exist. He will cope. He will manage himself and, to that extent, "manage" his environment. He will not control the externals, but he will control the internals—thereby applying equal pressure from within. He will not cave in.

I am certainly not cavalier about the various issues pitchers must face—many presented by particular factors of environment or circumstance. But I have heard too many people pay too much attention to too many problems, rather than paying attention to possible solutions. The "problem" of pressure is just one more misdirected focus. "How can we deal with it?" That is the question I ask pitchers on a regular basis (after we determine that the issue is real, rather than imagined).

What a pitcher is forced to deal with is an internalization that inhibits his ability to relax, to enjoy what he does and to do it well. Crucial games, important performances, "must" pitches—all the descriptive terms noted in the very first paragraph above—lead to the responses in the second paragraph. [See URGENCY] By defining his world thusly, he creates his "monster." By dwelling on his creation, he feeds it. By confronting it, he will have a chance to starve it.

"Baseball is not pressure," Sammy Sosa has said. "Pressure is when you're seven years old and, and you don't have food to eat. So when you've come from nowhere and have all that I have now, I sleep like a baby every night." [See PERSPECTIVE] Nevertheless, if someone else has decided baseball *is* pressure ...

Veteran outfielder Paul O'Neill has been known for being very hard on himself throughout his career. In 1984, O'Neill played for the Vermont

Reds, Cincinnati's Double-A team. At the time, I was doing a newspaper feature—about "pressure." O'Neill told me, "I feel pressure on me when I go 0-for-5. Sure it affects me... The eight-hour bus rides you take in the minor leagues keep you thinking about it. It adds to the pressure. I need time with other things, other interests, to relieve the tension. It isn't easy."

"The rides...keep you," "It adds to..." Pressure given life by a bus ride. Or by O'Neill himself? It is the human tendency to give pressure life without understanding the life-giving process. Pitchers, again, must develop more enlightened tendencies if they wish to be exceptional. O'Neill apparently did.

Entire teams can be affected. I have seen it firsthand. [See JOY] So has Detroit pitcher Jason Thompson who, in September '98, with his team at the bottom of the American League standings, saw young players "feeling the pressure of all the losses." Said Thompson, "It's just really weighing on everybody. You can see it in the way everybody's playing. It's just been real tough. You've seen things you normally wouldn't see. I think we're all starting to think about it too much. We just need to go out there and play."

Easier said than coped with.

I am adamant about this point: players put pressure on *themselves*. The reader has heard many athletes express this exact viewpoint. Yet, privately, the very athlete who will make such a public pronouncement can express his resentment of the circumstances that, as one pitcher described to me, "...always seem to rock my house." A building without solid footings will tend to rock. [See RESPONSIBILITY]

The pitchers with the greatest sense of responsibility consistently come at difficult situations with the understanding that what they think is the countervailing force to "what's out there" to be faced. The pitchers with the best mental discipline face it best—and best cope with matters they cannot control.

Everyone will feel "the pressure." My first concern is that the pitcher properly identifies its source. Himself. Then, feeling it during competition, my concern is to help him cope with the feeling effectively, by transferring his thoughts to function—to executing a pitch. That is always the bottom line. And it is most often the solution—if the pitcher can help himself to reach it. The focus is on the pitcher and what he does for himself, rather than the circumstance and what it is doing to him.

The linseed oil can has the air taken out of it; a pitcher allows it to be removed. He gives it up. The can has no say in the matter; the pitcher has all there is to say. He has the responsibility of giving himself the right messages. [See POSITIVISM] He must develop the capacity for being mentally strong. [See COURAGE]

What the Pitcher Should Do…

- Understand the perceptions and language that encourage the creation of pressure and help to prolong the feeling.
- Take the responsibility for having created whatever pressure exists, and the further responsibility of coping with it effectively.
- Develop coping mechanisms away from the field, such as alternative thinking processes and alternative activities.
- During competition, separate himself from the rubber/mound, when feeling the pressure of a situation—breathe deeply, relax his muscles by moving shoulders and arms, concentrate his focus on the rosin bag (for example)—and then articulate his task-oriented key, before stepping back on the rubber.
- [See PERSPECTIVE]—again.

■ QUITTING

My belief that "giving in" and "giving up" are distinctly different behaviors has already been expressed. [See GIVING IN] "Giving in" is defer-
ring, I said. "Giving up" is surrender. Quitting.

While neither behavior is acceptable for a competitive athlete, quitting, in my view, marks and scars a pitcher, who most visibly enacts behavior on the "stage" in the middle of the baseball field.

A pitcher accurately identified as a "quitter" might just as well wear a
scarlet "Q" on his uniform. His will be a lonely baseball existence. It is to
be avoided. It *can* be avoided—with forewarning and the pitcher's determination to be a competitor, rather than a "caver."

Earlier in the book, I made reference to a pitcher who gave in to a
circumstance in a game by "trying to strike everyone out." He was trying,
albeit ineffectually; "giving up" is not trying at all. It is the "letting go"
poet Emily Dickinson referred to. The release from a fight for life.

In the pitcher's case, it is a letting go of responsibility, competitiveness, dignity, and self-respect. On the mound, it is a release and a relief. A
linseed-oil-can-like collapse. Nothing within.

Thomas Tutko, an early and important influence in the field of sport
psychology, felt that "it is in the very nature of a player not to participate
when all is lost, not to put out totally." If this view is accepted, the question remains, "When does a pitcher concede that 'all is lost'?" Answer: For
the pitcher, not until he's en route to the shower. For the rest of the team,
not until the game is over.

Baseball, *by its nature*, teaches players and spectators alike that all is not lost until the last out is recorded. As previously noted—strongly noted, I hope—baseball has no clock. Still, a pitcher's nature may lead him to the conclusion that all is lost for him. Giving up early runs may weaken his resolve. It should not. But it sometimes does, because at a lower level of consciousness, he may dramatically reduce his competitiveness to protect his ego against the great disappointment that comes with what he perceives to be a failed outing.

Having given up those early runs, let us say, the pitcher sees less significance in his performance—in the game itself. Many of us have seen it happen. I have spent much time altering a perception based on two runs given up in the first inning. "Hold them there, and we'll win the game," is a frequently used provocation. Perhaps we won the game; perhaps we did not. The issue is how the pitcher competed. Or stopped competing.

The pitcher's ego, if he quits, is readying itself for the pain of perceived failure. Science tells us that this is done to reduce that pain of that failure. In other words, the ego protects itself by saying, "This isn't really important to me." The message allows the pitcher's body to shut off intensity, to stop "caring"—to shut down output. Hence, the disgusted comment may be heard in the dugout: "He's not putting out any effort at all."

To battle, to fight the fight, would be to fight the relief the ego now seeks. It would be to say that the game still matters. Such a self-statement would result in the ego feeling the pain and anguish that comes with what is, after all, a failure. Basic psychology. A pitcher's ego encourages him to quit in order to protect itself in the short term.

This is a very "normal"—ordinary—pitcher. But what his ego gains in the short term, becomes a loss in the long-term. Excellent pitchers understand both the focus of the moment (short-term) and the perspective of time (long-term). Extraordinary competitors [See WARRIORS] behave accordingly. They prepare their egos to "take the hurt."

I am pleased to have the acquaintance of many pitchers who would sooner "eat their egos for lunch" than allow them to be gratified by quitting.

Many players have told me what is now commonly expressed in the world of sport. "The agony of losing is greater than the ecstasy of winning." This is exactly because of what psychology confirms. Players who do not quit hurt more, because they invest more. They are proud of their investment—and it pays off in a significant way. It reinforces behavior, irrespective of outcome. It is the mental toughness every competitor is proud to call his own. He trains his ego, whether he knows psychology or not, to be pained by *poor effort*. That is the competitor's pride. Never giving in—never giving up.

Every pitcher must know what can happen to a person when expectation meets disappointment. At that line, he will fight many battles. He should fortify himself. First, with perspective. [See PERSPECTIVE] It is not a quality, as courage is, but it allows a young pitcher, especially, to prepare himself in a philosophical way, at least, for occasional failure in the game—and more frequent frustration.

Whether he prefers to listen to James Brown, or Aretha Franklin, or Frank Sinatra, he might wish to listen to a rendition of "That's Life." Food for thought. When at his or her best in the lyric, the singer declares:

> "… Each time I find myself flat on my face,
> I pick myself up and get back in the race…

> "…I thought of quittin',' but my heart wouldn't buy it."

On November 10, 1998, one of my favorite pitchers died. As a boy, I was fortunate enough to see lefthander Hal Newhouser when he pitched in Yankee Stadium. He won consecutive MVP's in the American League in 1944 and 1945, when I was nine and ten years old. I was old enough to admire his tenacity. I was attentive enough to know his record: 29-9 in '44; 25-9 in '45. (He was 26-9 in '46.)

In the obituary that appeared in *The New York Times*, one of Newhouser's former catchers, Joe Ginsberg, was quoted. "You couldn't get the ball away from him—he hated to be pulled from a game."

Newhouser himself once said, "I remember one game when I pitched in Yankee Stadium and gave up five runs in the first inning. It would have been easy to quit, but I shut 'em out the rest of the way and we came back and won the game."

Newhouser, who was elected to the Hall of Fame, is the only pitcher to win two consecutive MVP's. (Not many pitchers win one these days.) When asked his philosophy, Newhouser replied, "Never give up and never give in." Admirable. Exemplary.

What the Pitcher Should Do...

- Understand that, during competition, athletes can sometimes believe—incorrectly—that "all is lost."
- Be aware of his own tendencies in this regard.
- Understand that quitting reinforces a sense of incompetence or inadequacy in the long term, whereas relentless competing produces the opposite.
- Adopt a philosophy that "all is never lost" while competing in a baseball game.
- Train his ego to be rewarded by effort and persistence, rather than results.
- Compete until the ball is taken from him.
- Be prepared for the times when performance expectation meets disappointment.
- Value impeccable behavior through mental discipline at such times.
- Evaluate his responses to adversity and disappointment on a regular basis, making appropriate adjustments as required.
- Battle always. [See RELENTLESSNESS]

■ RELAXATION [See APPENDIX A]

The setting was Medford, Oregon, an hour or so before the opening game of the season in the Northwest Rookie League. I was leaning on the dugout railing, watching the opposing team taking infield. A young pitcher came over to me, joining me at the rail.

"I can't relax," he said to me. "Do you have any relaxation techniques you can give me?"

"Sure," I answered. "But tell me, why aren't you able to relax?"

He gestured toward the opposing team's players. "Those guys are pros," he said.

I turned toward him and pulled at his uniform jersey. "So are *you*," I said. "And those are the guys whose butts you kicked in the Little [College] World Series."

He looked at me in dropped-jawed amazement, the possessor of a newly discovered perspective.

Perspective. A must, if a pitcher is to be able to perform in a consistently relaxed state.

Every pitcher performs more effectively when he is relaxed. His perspective suffers when he has anxieties or fears about consequences. His muscles also suffer as a result. One of my standard "lines" to a tense and anxious pitcher is, "You know, your muscles convene every night, have a beer, and share this thought with each other: 'If this guy would only trust us and leave us alone, we'd be fine.'" I get no argument from the pitcher.

A pitcher cannot function effectively in an overstimulated or excited state. [See AROUSAL] He needs to get back to what is called homeostasis—

a state of physiological equilibrium. [See BALANCE] The pitcher with perspective and poise is able to maintain his equilibrium. He controls his tension level, thus avoiding a pervading feeling of apprehension.

When tension does exist, the pitcher must learn to release himself from it through deep breathing and self-coaching during competition. It is important for the pitcher to relax the antagonistic muscles in order for his delivery to be sound and fluid. "Free and easy."

Away from the field, he can work with a variety of techniques. But first, the pitcher should understand the internal forces that cause whatever anxious state may exist. He should build a solid foundation of reason and controlled behavior, rather than emotion and dreaded consequence. [See CONTROL and RESULTS] As was the case with the young pitcher discussed above, a distorted view of circumstance is a problem; anxiety is a symptom. Solve the problem and the symptom disappears.

More than 30 million "unrelaxed" people have high blood pressure, resulting in an inability to function at an optimum level at their job. More than 25 million work days are lost each year. And these workers do not have to stand on a mound and perform in front of thousands—millions if television audiences are included—each day. A pitcher, who does his "work" in full public view, can find it helpful to have a few relaxation techniques available to him.

The "skill" of decreasing the heart rate can be learned and practiced in the privacy of a one's room. The voluntary slowing of his heart rate can be very beneficial to a pitcher who must face stress-inducing game situations. Tension brings on muscle tightening, which the pitcher is very often unaware of. Through what is called progressive relaxation techniques, he can learn to relax these tensions.

A muscle group is first tensed, then relaxed. Doing this allows the pitcher to develop an awareness of his muscle tensions and distinguish those tensions from a relaxed muscle state. The "progressive" aspect of the exercise is achieved by following the same procedure from one muscle group to another.

An example of technique: the pitcher should sit comfortably in a chair and relax himself as much as possible. After having achieved that relaxed state, he should close his fist, clenching it tight, then tighter, until he can feel the muscle tension in his hand and arm. After maintaining tension for a few moments, he should relax the hand, opening the fist and moving the fingers to make them "free and easy" again. He should repeat the process, doing the same with his other hand and arm.

This exercise can be done with facial and neck muscles, chest and stomach muscles, back muscles, hip and leg muscles. Eventually, the whole body can be "worked" this way. The duration of each exercise should be approximately five minutes.

When the pitcher has learned how to relax his muscles, he will be better able to release his body tensions during performance. This can be done during his gathering, off the mound. He should move his head and shoulders, stretch his body slowly by bending and/or moving side to side. He should employ positive, calming self-talk—and breathe deeply.

Deep breathing patterns during competition will be enhanced by exercises incorporated during progressive relaxation exercises. In his chair, the pitcher can work on specific breathing exercises, inhaling and exhaling regularly and slowly—counting from 1,000, eyes shut, mind clear. (Especially good for inducing sleep at night.) He should create a consistent breathing pattern on the mound, as part of his pitching approach. [See BREATHING]

Legendary UCLA basketball coach John Wooden defines happiness as "being at peace with yourself." With *self*. Inner peace despite outer turmoil. Such a peaceful internal state will significantly increase a pitcher's ability to relax, which, in turn, will signal his muscles. All systems will then be in an "easy go" mode—an optimal kinetic state for performance. A reasoned perspective will encourage the muscles to "do their thing" with naturalness and ease. Happiness.

Should unhappiness set in, the pitcher should use the acquired techniques to relieve tension and relax his muscles.

What the Pitcher Should Do...

- Understand that tension is a symptom, not a problem.
- Recognize the source of tension and address it with objectivity.
- Develop a point of view based on reason, rather than emotion, and therefore conducive to relaxation.
- Monitor and adjust pre-game arousal in order to keep his kinetic system in a relaxed state.

- Learn and apply off-field progressive relaxation exercises and teach himself body awareness, in order to be able to relax and control his muscles.
- During competition, separate himself from the source of stress by getting off the mound and stretching slowly, employing self-talk and breathing deeply.
- Talk out loud while coaching himself, using a slow, deliberate, and calming tone.
- Concentrate for a few seconds on an outfield sign or the rosin bag, moving focus away from stressor.
- Get focus back to task ("Nice and easy; good, low strike here").
- Get back on rubber, concentrating only on pitch selection, location and the target. [See RUBBER]

■ RELENTLESSNESS

Relentlessness is the antithesis of quitting. It is an aggressive, persistent, attack-mode attitude. It defines a warrior. [See WARRIOR] The relentless pitcher gives himself intensely, entirely, and constantly to competition.

"Paralyze resistance with persistence," Ohio State football coach Woody Hayes used to say. The relentless pitcher works consistently to do just that, offering an internal persistence to his opponent. He has "left nothing out there," after his performance. He is fully extended. Spent. He may be beaten, but he will never surrender. His ego is rewarded by this unyielding behavior. [See QUITTING]

A relentless attitude combats distractions, such as minor pain, fatigue, weather conditions—the score. [See RESULTS] "When you can't pitch with your arm, you go with your heart," said Yankees pitcher Orlando Hernandez. (His manager, Joe Torre, once claimed he "had to pry his glove open and take the ball out myself," when removing Hernandez from a game.)

Pitchers with severe flu symptoms, for example, have pitched effectively and been in a state of virtual collapse—*after* the performance. Their sympathetic nervous system gave them as much as they demanded of it. Those who make no demands, get little in return. Bob Gibson made demands. He was able to pitch with a broken leg.

"You just pitch," Greg Maddux explained to a reporter who noted that his team had "supported" him with only two hits in the game. "You don't worry if you're up ten runs or down ten runs. You just make pitches. Regardless of the situation, you just have to get guys out. So who cares what the situation is?"

On one occasion before a game a couple of years ago, Maddux, in thinking about the relentless execution of pitch by pitch, said to me, "It's scary. Nothing else matters. I've learned that if I let down, it can all turn around in a heartbeat." He does not let down.

Steffi Graf has had a reputation of being a relentless competitor on the tennis court. Monica Seles described Graf's approach with admiration. "Steffi will never give you a free point, even when it's 5-0, 40-love."

Never giving a "free pitch." That is what Maddux was talking about. Irrespective of score, of circumstance—of feelings. Keep executing pitches. Keep competing. Keep bearing down. Stay focused. Relentlessly.

All pitchers have the capacity; not all have the determination. [See WILL]

I have seen pitchers who battled through adversity, working to "find a way to get it done." They appeared to be hanging on with suction cups. Japanese players would describe such a quality as *gambate*—working hard, never giving up.

Goethe wrote, *"Ohne Haste, ober ohne Rast."* Without haste, but also without rest. Under control; slowly but surely. Relentlessly.

What the Pitcher Should Do...

- Value the behavior of competing fully until the performance is completed.
- Develop a philosophy that recognizes relentless behavior as its own reward.
- Understand that execution should have nothing to do with score or circumstance.
- Evaluate his behavior after each performance, setting as a goal the relentless execution of pitches, irrespective of any internal or external factors.
- Recognize that the development of any attitude is a process—and continue to work diligently and consistently on the development of a relentless attitude.

■ RESPONSE

"Approach, result, response." That is the sequence of the three events that take place on the mound, I tell pitchers. It is actually a cycle, these "events" being repeated throughout performance.

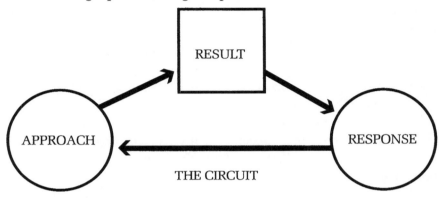

THE CIRCUIT

"Approach" has been discussed in previous pages. A pitcher's approach, remember, is entirely within his control. "Result" is yet to be discussed. It is not within the pitcher's control.

A pitcher's response is pivotal. How he acts after the previous "event"— the result of a delivered pitch, a batted ball, an umpire's call, a fielder's error—will often dictate the quality of the pitcher's next approach. Meaning that if a pitcher's response is a poor one—loss of poise, loss of purpose, loss of focus—he is likely to take that distraction into his next approach. That next pitch, therefore, will not be executed with maximum effectiveness, to say the least. The pitcher has complete control of his response. However, he may lose control of his thoughts and behavior. If he forfeits them, he forfeits whatever edge he hopes to establish as a competitor.

Every pitcher faces challenges to his makeup and attitude. When all is going well, a pitcher may respond well with continued focus—or poorly with a complacent loss of focus. [See COMPETITOR] When he faces difficulty, a pitcher may respond with frustration, anger, submission. Any response that is focused on the problem, rather than the solution, will perpetrate that problem. [See ADVERSITY and ADJUSTMENTS]

The relentlessness spoken of earlier is an attitude that must be developed. It is the response a pitcher should demand of himself if he wishes to be exceptional. The intellectual response to adversity, once again, is simple enough. Three questions, asked off the mound. "What was I trying to do?" "What went wrong?" "What do I want to do next time?"

In looking at those questions, the reader will see this: if a pitch is well executed, *nothing went wrong*. That is the proper response. Of course, the result might not have satisfied the pitcher. Stuff happens. The pitcher must recognize that there is nothing he can do about it—and deal with it by relentlessly executing the next pitch.

That is the only acceptable response. Courage, intelligence, and mental discipline are required if a pitcher is to have consistently appropriate responses during his performance.

If a pitcher should react to a result with an emotional response, though not ideal, it is not necessarily harmful. On the condition that he quickly purges himself of that emotion, and regains his composure and focus before getting back on the pitching rubber. No negative response should be brought there. Ever.

"So, if you have a good approach, and there is a bad result, then you have a related bad response, what is likely to happen to your next approach?" I will ask a pitcher rhetorically.

"Bad," I answer. "So the sequence will be: good approach, bad result, bad response. Leading to a bad approach and, most likely, another bad result. And down the drain the performance swirls.

"On the other hand, consider this sequence," I say. "Good approach, bad result, good response. What is the next approach likely to be?

"Good. So we have an ongoing sequence in which the two things a pitcher can control will always be good. That is all he can do to give himself a chance to succeed. And those who are disciplined enough to do that are very likely to be successful. That is the understanding and trust every pitcher should have. [See CONTROL] Good results will come, if approaches and responses are good."

Every sensible person knows he will face situations he will either take for granted or be troubled by. He understands that intellectually. But in order to handle these situations well, he must have his emotional responses under control. He must get his answers from his rational system. "What do I want to do here?" That is his operative question—his appropriate response.

Many, many years ago, Diogenes was asked why he begged money from a statue. He replied, "I am practicing disappointment." He was working on his response.

What the Pitcher Should Do...

■ Understand that his response to any "event," situation, or circumstance is entirely within his control.

■ Understand that a negative response during competition—whether it be frustration, anger or any other distracting reaction—will adversely affect his approach to the next pitch, if that response is brought to the pitching rubber.

■ Understand that disappointment is inevitable, and that the manner in which he handles it will determine his level of maturity, mental "toughness," and efficacy as a pitcher.

■ Respond to adversity by making adjustments that are within his control through self-coaching, rather than self-pity.

■ Disregard what he cannot control, i.e., results.

■ Trust that a good approach and a good response will most often bring about a good result.

■ RESPONSIBILITY [See APPENDIX A]

In *The Mental Game of Baseball*, the subject of responsibility is treated at length. The salient point made is that people are responsible for their thoughts, their words, their deeds. They are responsible for the choices they make. Pitchers have the choice to learn or not learn, to be dedicated or disinterested—or lazy. To be cooperative or not cooperative. To be rational or emotional; disciplined or undisciplined; selfish or unselfish. Any attitude is a choice. [See ATTITUDES]

In his book, *Wind, Sand and Stars*, Saint-Exupery wrote, "To be a man is, precisely, to be responsible." "Precisely." So a pitcher who would be "a man" would welcome responsibility, knowing that it means being accountable for the good and the bad in him. But knowing also that the accountability itself defines him first and foremost.

The topic EXCUSES provides a common defense mechanism athletes employ in order to avoid responsibility for negative consequences. The behavior, according to those who share Saint-Exupery's view, is "unmanly." Others see through it easily.

At this point, I would like to focus on still another aspect of attribution that avoids personal responsibility. It is very common, in baseball particularly. I have always expressed my views to players about the subject—and have tried, often without success, I'm sure, to keep from being a constant irritant about it.

I recall Ambrose Bierce's ironic entry in his book, *The Devil's Dictionary*: "Responsibility, n. A detachable burden easily shifted to the shoulders of God, Fate, Fortune, Luck or one's neighbor. In the days of astrology it was customary to unload it upon a star."

Many baseball players "unload" much of their responsibility on superstition. They "unload" a trust in their talent through their reliance on superstition. They lose a sense of control and self-determination. They yield to forces—imagined, at that—outside of them. They forfeit their freedom.

Superstitions, essentially, are fears in camouflage. A person who lacks confidence will rely on ritual behavior, without which, he believes, "luck" or forces will work against him, and with which, these same forces will be appeased and work in his behalf.

Luck, chance, hazard—whatever one calls it—is at work out there in the world, to be sure. But it is indifferent by nature and definition. The player who personalizes these forces will fear them—and focus on ways to avoid his victimization. So, he will act like a potential victim, rather than a warrior. If he believes superstition to be weapon, he is right. But, alas, it is a boomerang.

My major goal with players is to have them understand what they are doing with their superstitions. A player who constantly curses or blesses his "stars" has little chance of learning and making necessary adjustments—or developing a great confidence in himself and his talent. And there are many who do just that. It is clear to me that superstitions can make a player "more comfortable," a phrase they often use. But I rail against players who put the responsibility of outcome on a talisman, whether it be a jockstrap or tee shirt, or on any ritualistic behavior. "Go ahead and do what you wish, if it makes you feel better," I'll say (grudgingly) to a pitcher. "But after all is said and done, take responsibility for your performance. Attribute what happens to the way *you* execute pitches. Prepare yourself as a competitor, rather than as someone trying to avoid disaster by pleasing the false idols of baseball."

It is easier to value freedom than to achieve it. It is easier to understand responsibility than to enact it. A late 18th century poem entitled "Nathan the Wise" (G.E. Lessing) said, "The superstition in which we grew up, / Though we may recognize it, does not lose / Its power over us.—Not all are free / Who mock their chains."

More than awareness is required to get out of the chains. Attaining excellence is an ordeal. The choice always remains: "to be or not to be...?" Everyone has the responsibility to make that choice and the freedom to make the attempt.

Someone once said, "Success is just a matter of luck. Ask any failure." It is not evident to "failures," I presume, that the most diligent and successful pitchers seem to be the "luckiest." Mature pitchers take responsibility for their behavior; the immature point to an indifferent universe that they believe is orchestrating their performance. Nothing paralyzes intelligence more than the deception of excuses and superstition. And man's desire to deceive himself can be a powerful one indeed.

Yet, some deceptions can be well intentioned. Many pitchers take more responsibility than they should—or are able to. Taking too much responsibility, whether with bravado or exaggerated martyrdom, is unrealistic and ineffective. It is enough of a "burden" to be responsible for oneself, without taking on the entire pitching staff or team. Common phrases heard from such pitchers are: "I let everybody down." "I feel like it's all on my shoulders." "I'm the go-to guy, and they expect…" "I've gotta save the staff." And so on.

These are the pitchers who, as Henry Adams said of J.P. Morgan, try to "swallow the sun" when they perform. Their effort is beyond efficacy. Their expression of responsibility beyond reason. [See BALANCE and PERSPECTIVE]

Then there are the fellows who blame fate when things go against them, but take credit for good results. It is a loftier form of fingerpointing, aimed toward the sky, instead of at the shortstop who booted a groundball in a key situation.

Greg Maddux was interviewed a few years ago, after a game in which he lost a shutout over the Dodgers because of errors by outfielders Ryan Klesko and Marquis Grissom. The interviewer was sympathetic. Replied Maddux, "I just pitch, man. Seriously, I don't care if they make a diving play or have a groundball go through their legs. I still have to pitch to the next guy. I mean, I hung a fastball to Piazza. I hung a slider to Mondesi. I've got to look in the mirror first."

When Kevin Brown came in to a 1998 NLCS game to pitch in relief against the Atlanta Braves, he was excited about the "new"—and controversial—responsibility. Brown retired the side in the seventh inning, but in the eighth, Michael Tucker hit a three-run homer off him, and the Braves won the game, 7-6.

Brown's first expression after the game was, "I feel bad because people are going to second-guess [San Diego manager] Bruce Bochy. I feel bad because it's nobody's fault but my own."

The word "fault" should read "responsibility." Brown was responsible enough to take the ball, and he was responsible for the pitch he threw. But the term "fault" is too often used to replace "responsibility," and that tendency helps perpetuate an idea that works in opposition to a willingness to "own up." People do not like being at fault—being blamed. Too much finger pointing by media, teammates, coaches, and managers, will not encourage young players to take responsibility. [See NEGATIVISM] Rather, it will encourage self-defense—and all the creative and unhealthy mechanisms that the pitcher thinks will protect him. Such as excuses and bad luck.

To be sure, luck and chance are out there. But they do not stalk individuals. Good things happen; bad things happen. Things beyond our control. People either learn to accept that or live in fear and distraction, trying to control the uncontrollable and neglecting to take responsibility for what they can control. A "Catch-44," one might say.

Giuseppe Verdi wrote an opera entitled, "La Forza del Destino." The power of fate. Fate is powerful, but it is beyond the individual's ability to manipulate it. Whether with a particular pair of sanitary socks or a rub of a clubhouse boy's head before a performance.

The "real" ritual for a pitcher should be to take good care of himself physically, to take the ball when asked, to give an honest and relentless effort—and to take responsibility for the consequences. To learn from those consequences, and to make the necessary adjustments. Which does not mean—to change "sani's" or rub someone else's head before the game, in order to encourage a favorable outcome.

Responsibility is power; it is part of the glory of self-fulfillment. Players have asked how a person gets that power. "You don't get it, you take it," I answer. "But it's easier to give it away than to take. That's why the first power is to make the right choice."

The conscious acceptance of responsibility is one of the greatest indicators of a pitcher's maturity and personal "make-up." The immature will try to attribute difficulty to circumstance, others, managers, family history, persecution, or plain bad luck. He externalizes responsibility and so shuns making choices and living with the consequences of his own behavior. He waits for a lucky accident to get him what he wants—or he tries to force the luck through superstitious ritual.

The mature and well-adjusted pitcher will, as Maddux said, "look in the mirror first." He will also understand what he cannot control, and take such fate like Saint-Exupery's "man."

Philosopher Viktor Frankl saw the strong connection between freedom and responsibility. He recommended that we all be reminded of it by having the "Statue of Liberty on the East Coast... supplemented by a Statue of Responsibility on the West Coast."

What the Pitcher Should Do...

■ Understand that taking responsibility expands him, while pointing to external factors diminishes him.

- Understand that taking responsibility—or avoiding it—is a choice, at whatever level of consciousness it is made.
- Recognize that excuse making and superstition are grounded in feelings of fear and inadequacy, whereas personal responsibility is grounded in freedom and self-trust.
- Realize that taking legitimate credit for good work done is as important as taking legitimate criticism, since one enhances confidence, while the other provides an opportunity to learn and improve.
- Understand that responsibility is forfeited when he "thanks his lucky stars," or bemoans "all the bad breaks" that went against him.
- Remember intelligence can be paralyzed by excuses, superstition, and the invoking of "bad luck," so no adjustments are possible, since no personal responsibility is taken.
- Be responsible for his physical condition and habits, for taking the ball, for giving a sincere and relentless effort—and for taking the consequences with proper perspective and attitude.
- Listen to himself and be determined to express the language of responsibility, thereby fostering responsible behavior.
- Look first in the mirror, with honest intent.

■ RESULTS

"Everything we do has a result. But that which is right and prudent does not always lead to good, nor the contrary to bad." The words spoken by Goethe are as applicable to baseball as they are to life in general. Perhaps more so to baseball.

A pitcher executes a great pitch. Slider low and away. The batter goes down and gets it. He hits the ball on the end of his bat, and the ball loops over the infield, down the line. A hit. Good pitch; bad result.

A pitcher executes a poor pitch. A cookie—a BP fastball right down the heart of the plate. The hitter pops it up to the third baseman. Bad pitch; good result. Thank you, Mr. Goethe.

The history of baseball is rich and fully recorded. Books of statistics abound. Averages of all sorts are broken down, analyzed, discussed and debated. The baseball boxscore was invented in the 1870s. Young boys read and memorized players' statistics, reading *The Sporting News*, which printed boxscores of major and minor league games in the 1940s, my time to be an avid young fan. Everything a player did was documented statistically, for better or for worse.

Well, not everything. The boxscore does not tell all. A won-lost record does not tell all. Nor does an ERA. They do not tell whether the pitcher executed his pitch well, only to have the batter fight it off even better. They do not tell whether a pitcher got away with a number of poor pitches, because batters had worse approaches. They do not tell about wind-blown flyballs, or line drives hit right at fielders, or "seeing-eye" groundballs.

Statistics do not tell a true story about behaviors. They only tell about the results of the behaviors. And even that depends on how one interprets the term "result." For example, if a pitcher executes a pitch well, he might consider the good execution a result. He might, but it's not likely.

The game is historically based on "numbers." Way back when, before television and radio coverage, the boxscore was all fans had, unless they bought a ticket to the game. Jim Gates, the director of the Hall of Fame Library has said, "The boxscore is deeply ingrained in the American sports culture." Today, the statistical nuances and volumes added by Bill James, *et. al.*, are even more "ingrained." "Numbers" still rule. Ask any participant in a fantasy baseball league. Ask almost any player in the minor leagues. Ask any agent or arbitrator. Ask a pitcher.

Mark Davis won the Cy Young Award when pitching in relief for San Diego. "Numbers" became his nemesis. "I hate numbers," Davis said in May 1990, after having signed a big contract with Kansas City during the previous winter. "I don't look at them this year. I didn't look at them last year or the year before that. Numbers are in the past, and they don't help me get anyone out. I just know what they can do when they get into your mind and make you think things you don't need to think," he said.

"When your numbers are good, then a pitcher puts pressure on himself, and says, 'I've got to keep it up.' When a pitcher's numbers are not good, he puts pressure on himself, by saying, 'I've got to get it down.'"

Davis delivered a sermon I have given many, many times—to pitchers who told me, "I have to put up numbers." And to those who were desperately trying "to keep their numbers from slipping away" from them. Davis knew too well the danger of numbers and pressure. After having signed a big contract with the Royals, he struggled mightily and never came close to the level of performance he had reached with the Padres in 1989.

Statistics are the results that fans, lawyers, and management scrutinize. A pitcher is none of the aforementioned. But if he accepts what happens to a batted ball as a result, rather than how he executes a pitch, he must then have an understanding or two beyond his interpretation.

First, he should reconcile himself to the fact that he has no control over results that take place after the ball leaves his hand. Second, he should reread the words of Goethe above. If he executes a good pitch and gets a bad result, he must *respond* by understanding that he did what he wanted to do (and could control) and that he should do it again. And again. Irrespective of the result, which he knows he cannot control.

Pitchers who talk to me with a sense of urgency about their won-lost record get no support. I tell them that Cy Young lost 316 games and had an award named for him. "He was a 5-3 pitcher," I say. "But if you have the staying power to come close to 800 decisions, you'll be the richest man in baseball."

Years ago, a young left-handed pitcher, originally with the Toronto Blue Jays, came to the Oakland organization. A Harvard graduate, Jeff Musselman had talent and intelligence. But he lacked an essential understanding, in regard to the cycle of approach—result—response. While discussing the topic, he revealed this lack. "When I execute a great pitch but get a bad result," Musselman said, "I think, 'Now what do I do? I just threw this guy a great pitch and he hit it hard.'"

"Throw another good pitch," I said. Instead, Musselman tried to throw a "better pitch," which invariably was overthrown and ineffective. Common and unacceptable. My answer, he said with a laugh, was "too simple." He had been seeking something more profound. [See SIMPLICITY]

Robb Nen takes his responsibility as a closer very seriously. When he first assumed that role, with the expansion Florida Marlins, he had no experience to back up his conscientious attitude. His sensitivity to results was even more acute than the typical closer, which is dramatic enough. "You either get the save or you blow the save," Eckersley would say matter-of-factly, while dying inside when he blew one.

In a particular game early in his career, Nen was called on to protect a 2-1 Marlins' lead. The bases were loaded with one out. A double play would save the day. Words of encouragement came from the dugout. "C'mon, Robb, get a groundball." "Throw a two-ball, Robbie." Nen executed a fine pitch. The hitter rolled his bat over it and hit a groundball between third and— short. The fielders crossed each other as they attempted to get to the ball— which rolled into left field. Two runs scored. The Marlins were behind, 3-2.

"Do it again," came a shout from the dugout. The remark was as shocking to Nen as the result of two runs scored. The "it" in his mind was the two-run single, not the well-executed pitch.

If one would ask Robb Nen about that situation today, with years of experience behind him, the questioner would get a different answer from the one Nen gave himself that night. Yes, after all those years, it was still a blown save. (It's in the record book as such.) But Nen's response is more cerebral than emotional now. He is much more likely (absolutes strain belief) to respond to the pitch thrown, rather than to the result. He did as much as he was asked to do on that day years ago. He could not guide the grounder into a fielder's glove. Nor can any pitcher. (Please see Goethe's words above—once more.)

Disappointing consequences may seem limitless to a pitcher. Too frequent, imposing, ill-fated. But in the short term—clock time, that is—they are reduced, weakened, and made irrelevant by the immediate focus on behavior. On the execution and the next pitch.

Centuries ago, Euripedes wrote, "A bad beginning makes a bad ending." Though he cannot control a result, a pitcher can certainly influence it, as Euripedes suggested. A bad approach will lead to a bad result. A good approach, one that does not regard result, will greatly enhance a pitcher's performance—and most likely provide him with a satisfying result.

What the Pitcher Should Do...

- Understand that he has no control over results, if by results he means outcome after the ball has left his hand.
- Recognize that good results are most likely to come from good approaches and responses.
- Recognize that statistics become part of an historical baseball record, but they are results, which are not part of his focus during competition.
- Be aware that it is inappropriate to set result goals, since he has no ability to control them, as he does behavioral goals. [See APPENDIX B]
- Know that when he effectively executes a pitch, he is doing his job, irrespective of the result after the ball leaves his hand.
- Understand that mental discipline is required to consistently execute good pitches, despite possible poor results.
- Take responsibility for his approach and response, and disregard results during competition.

■ RUBBER

Though little need be said about the pitching rubber, what little there is has significance.

When the pitcher stands on the rubber, his mind and body should be ready to deliver the next pitch. His thoughts should be exclusively on pitch selection, location and then directed—with his eyes—to the target. Any intrusive thoughts should trigger the pitcher to back off the rubber and redirect his focus.

Typical of pitchers' tendencies is the one expressed by veteran Doug Drabek, when he was struggling during the 1998 season. "You can't stand on the mound [read 'rubber'] and try to figure it all out," he said.

The pitcher must recognize that he has two roles on the baseball field. He is a performer (a defensive player once he delivers the pitch), and he is a coach. On the pitching rubber, he is a performer. Whatever self-coaching is required—whatever "figuring it out" must be done—takes place off the rubber. The more dramatic the adjustment, the further from the rubber he goes, getting down off the mound and gathering his thoughts and his composure, if necessary. Off the rubber, the pitcher becomes a coach.

Many pitchers have not come to this understanding. They "think too much" about mechanics or the previous pitch or possible consequences, while standing on the rubber. All those matters are irrelevant and distracting. Even effective self-coaching techniques become ineffective when the pitcher is on the rubber. It is a pitching rubber, after all, not a coaching rubber.

The pitcher should use the rubber as a "key"—a trigger to remind him of what his focus should be. When he feels his foot on the rubber, he should be reminded that his head should be clear of all thoughts but three: selection, location, target. That is the mantra of the rubber. Selection, location, target. Anything else should provoke him to step back off the rubber and replace the extraneous thought(s) with appropriate ones.

Too many pages would be required to catalog all the examples of "thinking too much" that I have heard from pitchers over the years. Negative or positive. All are counterproductive if expressed on the rubber. [See TASK AT HAND] They force the pitcher to "think big," instead of encouraging him to "think small." These distracting thoughts focus on a topic, rather than on a target.

Selection, location, target. The awareness of inappropriate thinking will develop from the habit of invoking that mantra. And when a pitcher is able to develop a consistent thinking pattern on the rubber, he will be better able to center his attention on where and how he delivers the pitch. He will be rewarded for thinking less by the ability to control the ball more.

What the Pitcher Should Do...

- Understand that when his foot is in contact with the rubber, he is a pitcher exclusively.
- Understand that all self-coaching takes place off the rubber.
- Be aware of what thinking and focus he has on the rubber.
- Understand that distracting thoughts will divide his attention and reduce his focus on the target.
- Develop a "feel" for the rubber, using it as a key to limit his thoughts to selection, location, and target.
- Develop the habit of allowing himself to think only of the pitch about to be executed.
- Utilize the mantra to habituate that narrow focus: "selection, location, target."
- When intrusive thoughts enter his thinking, step off the rubber (the mound, if necessary) and coach himself, redirecting his thoughts and focus before getting back on the rubber.
- On the rubber, strive to breathe deeply and consistently before each delivery. [See BREATHING]

■ SELECTION

Little will be said about pitch selection; little should be thought about it while the pitcher is on the rubber. Determine it; trust it; execute it. The end.

Unfortunately, the topic is a bit more complex than that—only because pitcher's thoughts are more complex. [See SIMPLICITY] Hall-of-Fame pitcher Sandy Koufax captured the essence of the issue. "It is better to throw a theoretically poorer pitch wholeheartedly, than to throw a so-called right pitch with feeling of doubt—doubt that it's right, or doubt that you can make it behave well at that moment. You've got to feel sure you're doing the right thing—sure you want to throw the pitch you're going to throw," Koufax said.

In the section, ANALYSIS, an anecdote was provided about Bruce Hurst as a young Red Sox pitcher. His "thinking too much" led him to say to himself, in the midst of delivering a pitch, "I shouldn't be throwing a slider here." The thinking was related to pitch selection, to doubt in and lack of commitment to the pitch he had "chosen" to throw. It was a reluctant choice, if it was a choice at all. His attention was divided, his muscles and eyes did not work with a free and aggressive certainty of purpose. The pitch was poorly approached—and poorly executed. It happens often—to many pitchers.

When a pitcher senses the doubt he has about a pitch, he must step off the rubber and commit himself to whatever the selection ends up being. Either he shakes off the pitch he is uncertain about, or he quickly accepts the selection, gets back on the rubber, and executes with that commitment. The quicker the process, the better. All this should be part of his established pitching approach. When it breaks down, he knows what adjustment to make. [See ADJUSTMENTS]

The first thought when stepping on the rubber should be about pitch selection. The catcher gives the sign, the pitcher accepts or rejects the offering. It is the pitcher's responsibility to make the decision—and commit to it. The tiresome excuse that "the catcher has stupid fingers" does not work. I tell pitchers, "Your head shakes from side to side as well as up and down. Throw the pitch you want to throw. Know the pitch you want to throw."

It is certainly helpful to be on the "same page" as the catcher during an outing. But it does not always happen. The pitcher is ultimately responsible for turning to the "right" page. As Koufax said, the right pitch is the one the pitcher believes in at the moment. How many times have pitchers, in retrospect, realized that they got easy outs on pitches which could have been second-guessed? Many times. But they executed those pitches well. And how many times did they throw the "textbook" pitch of the moment and get hit hard? Many times. Poor execution, for any number of reasons.

If a young pitcher has pitches being called from the dugout, that becomes his reality. He still must make a choice. Does he take responsibility for executing the pitch he, in this case, *must* throw, or does he deliver the pitch with resentment and doubt, allowing himself to internalize the excuse that, should the pitch be hit hard, it wasn't *his* selection? In fact, it *became* his selection. In that process, he had no choice. His real choice was to commit to the pitch (maturity) or not to commit (immaturity).

Remember the mantra: selection, location, target? The selection process should become a rapid one—often anticipated before the pitcher even gets back on the rubber. No extended "thinking." When pitchers are having an effective performance, that tends to be the case. The game flows; all is well. [See TEMPO] But when doubt creeps in because of the circumstance of a game, the pitcher must be able to understand its possible effect on the selection process—the possible slowing of tempo, which allows "too much thinking," much of it an internal debate about what pitch to throw—usually, what pitch *not* to throw. At such times, he should gather himself and coach himself, providing reminders based on the way he functions when things are going his way. [See ADVERSITY and CONSISTENCY]

To doubt one's pitch selection is to assure a cautious, reluctant, distracted approach. As Kevin Brown has noted on earlier pages, "...if you make a bad pitch timidly or cautiously, that's when you get nailed." [See

AGGRESSIVENESS] Aggressive behavior begins with aggressive thinking. Make the selection—and attack with that pitch.

What the Pitcher Should Do...

- Commit to the pitch he selects and execute it aggressively.
- Make the selection with a consistently good tempo, rather than a deliberate one, stemming from an analytical thought process.
- Learn to anticipate the pitch he wants to throw before getting back on the rubber.
- Make the selection according to his own conviction, being responsible to shake off the catcher's sign when he feels it necessary to do so.
- If the pitch is called from the bench, take responsibility for its effective execution, rather than predetermining an excuse for its ineffectiveness.
- Understand that the "right pitch" is the one thrown with trust, commitment, focus, and aggressiveness.
- Step off the rubber and coach himself when doubt exists regarding the pitch selection.
- Remember that an aggressive thought pattern is a prerequisite for the aggressive execution of a pitch.

■ SELF-ESTEEM

Initially, my instinct was to consider "self-esteem" to be a redundancy on these pages. After all, BELIEF and CONFIDENCE have been already been presented. But there is an extensional meaning I wished to clarify, based on experiences with precocious athletes over the years, and this attempt seemed important.

"It is difficult to make a man miserable while he feels worthy of himself ..."Abe Lincoln said in one of the many speeches he delivered as President of the United States. "Worthy of himself." That's the operative phrase. When talking with athletes, my subject is usually "performance" or the athlete as a performer. Players wear uniforms, but I must often remind them that there is a "self" under each uniform.

A youngster who is precocious, whether it be as a musician, a mathematician or an athlete, has his precocity in front of others—and himself—always. He is identified for his great and exceptional talent, rather than for whatever "self" is behind it. Behind it—hidden from public view, and, very often from the person "himself." What seems to matter is what he does, rather than who he is. And this is how his early years train him.

He may have great "confidence" in his talent and skill, especially at early stages when others around him cannot come close to being as skillful. He may have great "belief" in his ability to achieve, especially when there is, in an athlete's case particularly, little to no competition to truly challenge him. But, alas, his "self-esteem" is most often based on his singular achievement and the exaggerated approval of others.

On this, his identity is based. He feels "worthy of himself" when he performs to the level of expectations. For a baseball player, the level is indicated by statistics—averages, numbers, victories. That is part of the youngster's learning curve. He is an avid and eager learner, in this regard. But does he learn much about self-worth as a "whole" person? The more precocious he is, the less likely he will be considered a "whole self."

As a young baseball player, he may never fail. He is too good. But as he rises, through Little League, high school, college, professional ball, the playing field "levels." The competition becomes as elite as the individual. Initial failure to dominate on a regular basis can be devastating. The interpretation of and response to this "failure" will influence the performer's perception of "himself."

When a person considers his entire "self" to be a performer, failure becomes very personal and very dramatic. Self-esteem plummets. Players say, "I'm a failure." I try to correct them. "You've failed at a task, but *you* aren't a failure." It's a hard sell, and often requires the building of a foundation of self that had not previously existed.

Many examples come to mind. One particular player, a glaring example of a person who had low self-esteem, had a very fine major league career, and was recognized as being an outstanding ballplayer. As a man, he is intelligent, kind, considerate, trusting, handsome, and articulate. At the end of his playing career, he was very troubled. He had always had social insecurities, based on the fact that he did not recognize all his personal attributes; he only recognized his efforts on the baseball field—his statistics. Those around him during his youth focused on his baseball prowess. So when his "numbers" began to identify him as significantly less than the player he had been in the past, his self-worth became significantly less as well. He had little (nothing?) to fall back on. It was an emotionally exhausting ordeal he went through, in order to gain a new—and healthier—perspective.

This is not an isolated or exaggerated example. It is "out there." Let the young player beware. If he does not develop and identify an early "self," he will become a symbol of his performance, rather than the substance of who he really is. And he will fail to recognize his substantial self, giving himself approval only when his "numbers" allow and confirm that approval.

Earlier in the book, attention was given to players who had been mentally abused as children, and who suffered through the consequences of a poor self-image. But mental "abuse" can be much more subtle than the case of the boy who jumped off a wall, broke his arm, and "learned" thereby "to trust no one."

Unrealistic expectations, subtle but constant criticism, one-dimensional treatment (as a baseball player, rather than a person), the burden of others' needs being satisfied through the precocious young player—all will inhibit the development of a healthy and self-actualized self. It can distort the boy's view of himself and influence the view of the man he becomes.

"Public influence is a weak tyrant compared with our own private opinion," Thoreau wrote. "What a man thinks of himself, that is which determines or rather indicates his fate." But when a person is a public figure at an early age, the public opinion all too easily becomes the private opinion. If baseball statistics help shape public opinion, they will invariably influence the player who has come to believe he is defined by them.

A few words about public opinion. First, in general, people "out there" are more considerate and less interested in us than we think. In addition, judgments of celebrities, athletes included, are fickle and fleeting. People have more to do than spend their time judging and condemning. Their immediate expression of opinion is neither objective nor sustained. Nor should it be an influence on the individual player.

The self-consciousness that an athlete might have is a false pride, a form of egotism which persuades him that what others think and say about him has more meaning than what he says about himself. Naturally, the player with high self-esteem, then, is fortified. The player with little self-esteem is under siege and vulnerable. He must recognize that he, not the "public," is the problem and the solution.

A pitcher who continually refers to his inadequate statistics is, to use Lawrence Durrell's metaphor, "tied to the wheel in the sinking vessel of [his] self-esteem." His "belief" and "confidence" are already submerged. The pitcher comes to discount his successes and magnify his failures, thus always confirming a negative self-image. He will be cautious, rather than aggressive. He will be distracted, rather than focused. He will expect to do poorly, rather than expect to do well. And he will "tip-toe" through life, intimidated by car salesmen and plumbers, never realizing his own self worth, despite being a good son, a good friend, a good teammate, a good husband, and father. A good man.

Maxwell Maltz, in his marvelous book, *Psychocybernetics*, wrote, " Of all the traps and pitfalls in life, self-esteem is the deadliest, and the hardest to overcome, for it is a pit designed and dug by our own hands..." Under the influence of others, we may accept a "design" created by them—but we, most certainly, "dig our own pit."

Pitchers who so frequently seek to be "comfortable"—on the mound and off—should also heed the words of Mark Twain. "A man cannot be comfortable without his own approval."

Abraham Maslow studied the lives and behavior of people he believed to be "self-actualizers." People such as Lincoln, Einstein, Jefferson, Jane Addams. He extended his study to college students, and selecting those students who fit his description of self-actualizers, he found the group to be in the top percentile, in terms of good mental health. These people made full use of their talents and capabilities. Some of the behaviors of self-actualizers are included below.

What the Pitcher Should Do...

- Understand that he has many dimensions as a person, beyond being just an athlete.
- Recognize that self-esteem should be based on all the traits and behaviors of an individual, rather than on a singular, albeit highly developed, ability and skill.
- Understand that his identity is related to his substance (who he is), rather than the symbolic representation of him (what and how he does).
- Work at being more "well-rounded," valuing more in life than just baseball performance.
- Learn to play the game for himself, rather than for others.
- Learn to diffuse the effect of public opinion by understanding its nature: exaggerated, self-gratifying, subjective, and temporary—and less interested in him than he thinks.
- Perform regular "reality checks" on himself, assessing daily behaviors—on and off the field—in order to evaluate himself fully.
- Set his own standards and goals, based on his values, and hold himself accountable through the daily evaluation noted above.
- Use affirmative language when talking about himself, rather than the language of self-disparagement.
- Be an advocate, rather than an apologist, for what he values and believes.
- Look people in the eye during conversation (regardless of his "stats").
- Take responsibility, rather than blame.
- Look at life and himself objectively.
- Express his sense of humor.
- Learn to tolerate uncertainty.
- Take risks.
- Be honest, rather than being deceptive or a "game player."
- Identify his defense mechanisms and have the strength to work at breaking them down, recognizing that he does not need to continually justify himself to others.
- Like himself—and deserve it.

■ SELF-FULFILLING PROPHECY
[See SELF-TALK]

If people are, indeed, what they think, the importance of an athlete monitoring his thoughts should be clear. [See BELIEF] And if belief is an engine, prediction is a fuel. A pitcher who predicts outcome—for better for or for worse—is preparing himself and his muscles to play into that prediction.

Physicians and psychologists—and research—all confirm that a patient's belief in the likelihood of his healing will significantly affect his health. There is psychological and physiological power in prophecy. The self-fulfilling prophecy is so named because of the correlation between the belief and the behavior. If a pitcher says something is going to happen, he will behave in such a way as to confirm his prophecy. In baseball, it often seems, more often for worse than for better.

The pitcher with a healthier attitude is more apt to see positive outcome than negative. He will therefore use more self-affirming language and focus positively on what he wants to do, rather than on forces that will inevitably bring about adverse consequences.

The tendency is linked to control, responsibility, mental discipline — positivism and/or negativism, to name a few related topics. A pitcher's perspective will determine the nature and direction of his prophecy. [See NEGATIVISM and POSITIVISM]

Sitting in a dugout on a May afternoon at Phoenix Municipal Stadium, in 1985, I was chatting casually with the Tacoma Tigers (Oakland organization) Triple-A pitcher, Steve Mura. Mura was a 29-year-old veteran who had spent six seasons in the big leagues, winning 12 games for the 1982 Cardinals. A bright, dependable person and pitcher, Mura was the scheduled starter for this night's game.

He shook his head silently, and I asked him what that meant. "I can never win on this mound," he said.

The reader will be spared the entire lecture, but my first response was to the language Mura had employed. "There is a difference," I said, "between, 'I have not won and I cannot win...'" And I expanded the point.

When questioned further, Mura complained about the height and slope of the mound. I asked what kind of adjustments he could make because of it. Being intelligent, he thought for a while and produced a strategy. He never had—and he couldn't understand why that had been the case.

"You don't think about strategies when you think that outcome is inevitable," I said. "That's what self-fulfilling prophecies are all about. You've pitched right into your certainty that you can't pitch here." And so on.

Mura pitched seven innings that night, giving up no runs on two hits. He threw the ball well. After the game, he was more embarrassed than elated. Understandably so.

Many pitchers have held similar points of view. Early in his career, Greg Maddux felt he couldn't pitch well against a particular team in the Eastern Division, and felt he just had to "throw my glove out there," and he would beat another particular team in the same division.

Day games, bad weather, opposing pitchers, opposing hitters—all present possibilities for formulating prophecies. More often than not, it is a negative prophecy. "I can't," "It's going to be one of those days," "I've got no chance," "This isn't going to be pretty..." These are the phrases of predicted doom, almost certain defeat.

On the other hand, having a positive anticipation of outcome will enhance a pitcher's belief system and likelihood for success. That is fine. But an indiscriminate and determined approach to every external factor will, to my mind, best serve a pitcher in his desire to be consistent and responsible for his own performance. Rather than regarding the forces of fate and outcome, he will focus on task and behavior.

In other words, it is better for a pitcher to believe in positive outcome than negative outcome. But it is best for him to believe in his talent and his ability to make adjustments and execute pitches.

What the Pitcher Should Do...

- Understand the power of his belief system. [See BELIEF]
- Anticipate positive behavior, irrespective of external factors.
- Make necessary adjustments based on external factors, rather than predicting failure because of them.
- Listen to the language he employs.
- Be certain to use self-affirming, functional language, rather than the self-defeating language of negative prophecy.
- Focus on behavior and task, rather than on circumstance and possible outcome.

Self-Fulfilling Prophecy   213

■ SELF-TALK

At the point where the reader is in his life, he responds to situations based on his past experience and the habit of reaction from those experiences. His memory of similar circumstance and their effects on him provokes a patterned verbal response. That self-talk is most often a help or a hindrance as he faces a current situation. (It can be, but rarely is, neutral.)

Self-talk is what a person says to himself, either silently or aloud. The habit, as noted above, is established according to situation. For example, if a person spills his coffee at a restaurant, what does he say to himself and/or about himself? Does he scold himself? Disparage himself? Condemn himself? The harsh self-criticism is a language of self-diminution. It does not build self-confidence or self-esteem. Yet, it is regularly invoked out of habit. [See HABITS]

On athletic fields, as a youngster, my singular emotional response to a mistake I made was to say to myself, "You jerk." It was not helpful. The measure of maturity and efficacy is the length of time it takes for an athlete to recover from his emotional unhappiness. On earlier pages, it was suggested that it is acceptable to be angry ("You jerk") and purge oneself, so long as the expression is brief and the recovery swift. A recovery through adjustment and refocusing on task, rather than the non-recovery of sustained frustration over what just transpired.

If a pitcher is to function effectively, his self-talk must be grounded in reality and rationality, rather than in imagination and irrationality. The latter leads inevitably to emotional disorientation and poor performance.

Again, the pitcher is called upon to examine his tendencies and work at developing good (new?) habits. With positive self-talk, he can train himself to focus on what will enhance him and his performance, rather than on what will diminish both. He must, of course, first be aware of what thoughts and self-talk he employs during his preparation and during the actual performance. It is an arduous process, as noted often.

One major league pitcher expressed the following thought to me, having worked diligently on changing the nature of his self-talk: "I try to get through the tough times [situations] by talking myself into acting like I've got things going for me. Deep down, I know it's not necessarily true, but if I keep talking right things seem to work out." Brainwashing at its best.

But talk alone is not enough. What a pitcher says is important. So is *how* one says it. An instructive tone is more desirable than a critical one. *Listening* to what he is saying is an imperative. Pat Rapp said all the right things to himself during a difficult circumstance, while pitching for the Florida Marlins. But he did not *hear* himself. (The anecdote is elaborated upon in TARGET.)

I used the following illustration with him the next day. A man is sitting at a breakfast table reading the sports page in his morning newspaper. His wife is talking to him. He responds to her with appropriate remarks and answers, still focusing on the sports page. Twenty minutes after breakfast, she says to him, "It's time we got going, dear." He has no idea where they are going, though that was her topic at the breakfast table. The husband assimilated only what he had been truly attentive to—the information on the sports page.

While self-talk may be positive, neutral or negative, it can also be classified as follows: that which is irrelevant to the task at hand, that which is focused on the task at hand, and that which is related to the pitcher himself. Two of those three do not serve him well at all. [See TASK AT HAND]

When thoughts are focused on himself, they diminish the pitcher's ability to adequately see what is going on around him. He cannot interpret what must be done, nor make adjustments. Nor can he properly focus on the target. He is mired in self-consciousness and, most likely, anxiety. Two days before I write this, a major league pitcher told me of such an experience he had had the previous day. "I felt numb out there. I didn't know where I was or what I was doing." I asked him what he had been thinking about to start with. "Myself," he answered.

Irrelevant self-talk proliferates. On the mound, anything that *is not* related to the task at hand is irrelevant. Listed below are some—but not all—of the most common irrelevancies I have heard coming from pitchers' mouths. They include self-talk related to self and self-talk related to externals. These, the most frequent expressions, are negatives.

"Idiot," "loser," "dummy," "gutless"—and profane variations on the theme.

"I stink," "This always happens to me," "I can't believe this crap," "What's new?" "He's [manager/coach] jacking me around again," "It's not fair," "The hell with it all," "I can't," "I don't have it," and "I'm clueless."

A sampling which, in what is known as semantitherapy, would be considered as "language of maladjustment."

These are a far cry from the pitcher "trying to get through tough times..." noted above. The ease of "giving in" has been established on earlier pages. So has the difficulty of being relentless in the pursuit of efficacy. Positive self-talk is the tool. But the tool is only as good as the worker who uses it.

The "worker's" task is simple enough to understand. He must be aware of the language he uses and work effectively at thought changing. "Blocking out a thought" does not work. The command becomes a negative one. For example, if someone is thinking about a pink elephant and he wants not to think about it, he will attempt to "block it out" by saying, "Don't think of a pink elephant." The image of a pink elephant is still in his head. He must *change* his thought. He can say to himself, "Think of a black swan." He has a new image in his head.

Pitchers hold great disdain for pitching coaches who come out to the mound and say, "Don't walk this guy." Or give other directives based on what *not* to do. Yet, they do it to themselves, saying things such as, "I better not hang this slider," or "I can't hit this guy by going too far inside." Their talk of what they do not want to do becomes the focus of what they are about to do. Rather, they must train themselves to use self-talk that encourages focus and positivism. "Good low strike here," is much superior to "I'd better not get behind this guy." "Slider away," much better than the expressed fear of hanging it.

What the Pitcher Should Do...

- Examine and monitor his internal "conversations" related to circumstance, competition and himself.
- Understand that self-talk indicates what he thinks and feels about his "world" and himself—and should be grounded in objective reality.
- Recognize that positive self-talk and expectations will enhance his ability to perform, whereas negative self-talk will focus on and encourage failure.
- Understand that positive self-talk should be accompanied by involved attentiveness to what is being said.
- Know that self-talk should be expressed in a positive and encouraging tone, rather than in an impatient and urgent tone. [See URGENCY]
- Talk about himself in self-affirming, non-judgmental language.
- Anticipate performance with enthusiasm.

- During competition, talk about the task and how to approach it.
- Understand that he is human and therefore fallible—less than perfect—and must learn to coach himself accordingly, with appropriate self-talk, rather than with inappropriate self-condemnation.

■ SHUT-DOWN INNINGS

Managers and coaches put great emphasis on shut-down innings. They value the shut-down inning because, they say, it maintains the "momentum" their team has established after having "put runs on the scoreboard"—and then, in turn, held the opposition scoreless in their next at-bats.

Certainly, it is desirable to do just that. In baseball, the pitcher's object—and the manager's joy—is always to keep the opposition from scoring. [See ZEROS] But the psychological "boost" an opposing team gets by coming back and scoring runs immediately after the other team has scored "changes the momentum." Though this is not empirically validated, in the baseball world it is a widely held generalization, worthy of attention.

The attention given to the shut-down inning is similar to that given to stopping the big inning. [See BIG INNING] In pointing out an inning's uniqueness, coaches and pitchers often seek to achieve the goal of shutting down the opponent by searching for methods that are complex, rather than simple. [See SIMPLICITY] Such an attitude will take the pitcher out of the consistent approach he has established or wishes to establish. It leads him to believe he must behave differently, "try harder." The change will prove to be counterproductive.

Randy Johnson, when pitching for the Houston Astros, responded to a reporter's question about post-season play. His response is perfectly applicable to any situation or circumstance for a pitcher, shut-down innings included. Said Johnson, "You do the same thing you've done all the time to make yourself successful. You don't change things."

No sense of urgency should be attached to shut-down innings. [See URGENCY] I will allow myself to repeat the words I use at pitchers' meetings, already presented in BIG INNINGS. "*Anytime* the focus is put on the definition of an inning, the perception of it, the concern for runners and runs, the idea of making special a particular situation, something very important—most important—will be pre-empted: the pitcher's focus on executing the next pitch."

The actual purpose of calling pitchers' attention to shut-down innings is based on the tendency of some pitchers to get "comfortable" after their team has scored runs. Those pitchers tend to go out to the mound with less intensity, because of that illusionary feeling of comfort. Complacency sets in. Concentration suffers, aggressiveness is diminished. It happens; pitchers recognize the truth of it—after damage has been done.

So, a pitcher *should be* forewarned of the possibility/tendency. But the warning should be this: be consistent, keep competing. Stay under control. Maintain your concentration. Think small; stay aggressive.

The pitcher should do no less than he had been doing just because his team "got him some runs." Nor should he attempt to do more.

This is simply preparation for the next inning. Appropriate behavior is reaffirmed in the dugout before the pitcher ever goes out to the mound. Like showing a racehorse the whip, in order to keep his mind on the right business.

During the presentation of TASK AT HAND (on later pages), an anecdote about pitcher Bruce Hurst is presented. The theme of that story can also be related to shut-down innings, as it can to pitching in general: execute one pitch at a time, with exclusive focus on that task.

What the Pitcher Should Do...

- Recognize the value of a shut-down inning.
- Understand that a shut-down inning is an end, not a means.
- Understand that a shut-down inning is too large a concept to manage during competition.
- Understand that outs are achieved through consistent, focused, controlled, aggressive execution of pitches.
- Be aware of tendencies to "let up"—allowing concentration and intensity to diminish—because his team "scored some runs for him."
- Prepare himself before leaving the dugout to maintain a consistent approach and a similar focus on the task at hand.
- Compete without regard to the scoreboard.

■ SIMPLICITY

Keep it simple, stupid. That is a widely held philosophy. But Albert Einstein said, "Everything should be made as simple as possible, but not simpler." Meaning, not stupid. Intelligence is valued in a pitcher, though too often that intelligence is converted into imagination. Matters become complicated, not because of information, but, rather, because of interpretation. Matters are further complicated when significance is given to irrelevancies.

Simplicity means knowing what matters and what does not matter. That is what Einstein meant. Quite often, however, pitchers tend to complicate their world with their needs, their fears, their desire to succeed. My expressed view to them is that the game of baseball is simple; people are complicated. Many of them tend to think that there must be more to the game than executing a pitch. In terms of behavior, there is not. Each singular pitch has a "perfect simplicity [that] is audacious." (George Meredith)

The greatest truths are the simplest, and so are the greatest pitchers. Not simple-minded, but simple in their approach. They think small; they are focused on task. [See TASK AT HAND] They do not allow extraneous issues and circumstance to take them out of their game plan—which is *simply* to attack and execute.

Pitcher Jim Abbott, in his comeback attempt before retirement, understood the difference between what he had done in the past and what he wanted to do in the future. "… I'm not going to make it as complicated as I used to," he said. Stated in positive terms: "keep it simple."

Inexperienced closers I have been associated with have often complicated their thoughts with the responsibility of saving another pitcher's runs and saving the win for the team. Such thoughts, on the mound, qualify as irrelevant and, therefore, are distracting. Too big, too complicated.

Much of the success of San Diego closer, Trevor Hoffman, comes from intelligence and a narrow focus. "When I come in," says Hoffman, "I know how I feel, what I've got going, how many good pitches I have. I go from there, depending on the situation and the hitter… I try to keep it all as simple as possible."

Ron Darling was an Ivy Leaguer before he was a major leaguer. A very smart man, Darling tended to use his intelligence to complicate the process of pitching. His Oakland manager acknowledged Darling's intelligence, but said the pitcher lacked "common sense" when he was on the mound. Common simplicity.

Pitcher Mike Flanagan was given credit for pitching intelligently until his "stubbornness" got in the way of his brain and complicated his approach.

But smart and simple can be synonymous. Less can be more.

Hans Hoffman, no relation to Trevor, wrote, "The ability to simplify means to eliminate the unnecessary so that the necessary may speak." The "necessary," allowed to speak, will say, simply, "Execute the next pitch." That's smart. That's simple.

What the Pitcher Should Do...

- Recognize that a simple approach allows him to more easily manage his thoughts and control his approach.
- Understand that complications arise only when he "thinks too much," entertaining distracting irrelevancies on the mound.
- Realize that simplicity means reducing focus to what is necessary for effective execution of the next pitch—selection, location, target.
- When "things get complicated," coach himself during competition by getting off the mound and making an adjustment to a narrow focus.

■ STRIKES

The standard question and answer: Question—What is the best pitch in baseball? Answer—Strike one. [See COUNT]

The value of throwing strikes—establishing the count in the pitcher's favor, forcing contact [See CONTACT], being aggressive in the strike zone—is statistically evident and philosophically agreed upon. The behavior is the hallmark of successful pitchers. The fact that being ahead early in the count will dictate an entirely different at bat than being behind in the count has been well established.

Bobby Cox has waxed poetic about Greg Maddux' ability—read "determination"—to throw strikes early in the count. "He can go strike one with the best of them," Cox has said. "That's a huge advantage if you can do that. You can talk about pitching and mechanics all you want, but strike one is the first step to success."

While pitchers will not dispute this viewpoint, many will avoid the behavior that validates it.

"I hate to use the word 'fear,'" Yankees manager Joe Torre has said, "but sometimes it seems they're afraid to challenge the hitter. They don't want to put the ball over the plate on the first pitch, and then they're behind." [See FEAR]

Fearing failure is one thing; acting out the fear is another. Dennis Eckersley has been noted in earlier pages as an exemplar in this regard. Though he admitted to a fear of failure, he did not allow this fear to negatively influence his approach. On the contrary, he used it to provoke a behavior that he knew intellectually, would help him to succeed—to avoid the failure he dreaded. He relentlessly threw strikes.

Eck attacked the strike zone aggressively. He did not "pick" or "nibble" around the strike zone. He did not "just" throw strikes, putting less than his best stuff in the zone, for the sake of having it qualify as a strike. He "went after it."

Attacking the strike zone takes a commitment, especially by a pitcher who tends to be defensive when he pitches. The understanding he has about the importance of throwing quality strikes must be integrated into his behavior. He must have the courage of that conviction.

Glenn Abbott is a minor league pitching coach with the Oakland organization. Abbott told me of a situation he had witnessed while pitching in the big leagues. We had been discussing "throwing strikes."

A particular pitcher was having an awful outing, constantly behind in the count, reluctant to throw strikes, "walking the ballpark," as Abbott put it. The manager was furious. He sent his pitching coach out to the mound, and the coach delivered the message that the pitcher had better "throw strikes or else." The coach returned to the dugout.

The pitcher understood the ultimatum. He guided pitches into the strike zone and, in Abbott's words again, "was whacked." Continued Abbott, "I mean, doubles were banging off the walls, line drives were flying out into the gaps."

The disgusted manager sent the pitching coach back out to the mound to remove the pitcher from the game. The pitcher didn't even wait for the coach to reach him. He walked toward the dugout, flipped the ball to the coach, and said, "So much for your bleepin' strikes!"

Aggressively thrown strikes, "best stuff" strikes are quality strikes. Aimed strikes, guided, dart-throw strikes are "bleepin'" strikes.

In 1996, Al Leiter was pitching for the Marlins. The Florida team that year—the year before they won the Championship—had trouble scoring runs. Leiter, particularly, received little run support. That fact, coupled with his tendency to be "effectively wild," would create games with little margin for error on Leiter's part.

During one of his mid-season home starts, Leiter set the opposition down easily in the first inning. One, two, three. He had, in his words, "great stuff." In the bottom of the first, the Marlins, uncharacteristically, scored six runs. Leiter went out in the top of the second inning, walked two batters and hit one. He escaped from the bases-loaded jam without allowing a run.

In the dugout, he explained that, with the luxury of six runs, he went out there to "just throw strikes." It did not work. The idea of steering the ball kept his delivery from being free and loose. The actual steering of the ball kept him from being aggressive. He returned to his usual approach the next inning. With the "great stuff," he pitched a no-hitter that night.

In May 1999, 25-year-old Phillies pitcher, Carlton Loewer, pitched a five-hitter for his first career shutout, defeating San Diego, 3-0. Loewer had been inconsistent during his brief major league tenure. In the first inning of the game, he had an epiphany. After having walked Tony Gwynn and Wally Joiner with two outs, he determined that his approach was based on "not walking guys." Many of the hard hit balls over the course of previous outings, he felt, resulted from "defensive strikes" being thrown. (See Abbott anecdote above.)

Loewer determined to change his focus from avoiding walks to being aggressive with all his pitches, all the time. On that night, the philosophy was well integrated into behavior. His goal was to bring that approach out to the mound on a consistent basis. The process is enhanced by the determination. [See WILL]

A strike can be an eagle or an albatross for a pitcher. The pitcher who feels he 'has to' throw strike one will be bound up by the tension that accompanies that feeling. [See URGENCY] Young pitchers who want to please their coaches feel that burden. I can recall many, particularly young pitchers in major league spring training camps, who, having thrown ball one, became disoriented by their "failure to get ahead of the hitter." What followed was usually an unhappy result for the pitcher.

Pitchers *can* get outs despite having thrown a ball on the first pitch. Or on the first two pitches. Perspective is needed. Urgency is not. A pitcher must learn the difference between what is desirable and what is disastrous. He should attack the strike zone, not himself. Process. Balance.

What the Pitcher Should Do...

- Reaffirm the value of throwing aggressive strikes early in the count. [See AGGRESSIVENESS and CONTACT and COUNT]
- Understand that strikes thrown with less than his "best stuff" or with an aggressive purpose are usually counterproductive.
- Realize that "aimed" or "steered" strikes are not thrown with commitment and are not generally quality strikes, if they are strikes at all.
- Understand that throwing strikes in order to avoid walks is "defensive," ineffective pitching.
- Make a commitment to attack the strike zone early in the count.
- Recognize that trust, rather than urgency, is the foundation of his approach.

■ TARGET

"Tunnel vision is how I explain it," Nolan Ryan has said. "You become isolated from all outside distraction…and there's only you…and the catcher. It's the most satisfying feeling I've known."

Daisetz Suzuki explained the mastery of archery: "The archer ceases to be conscious of himself as the one who is engaged in hitting the bull's eye which confronts him." Ultimate focus on a target.

Whether it is pitching, or archery, or skeet shooting, or lasso throwing, or completing a pass in football, the eyes attend to the object—to the target. Every physical "throw" requires an aim—a visual direction. The catcher's mitt best serves the pitcher as his target.

In order to develop a consistent command of pitches, the pitcher should develop consistent habits related to his approach. His breathing should be patterned, his tempo should be regular, his delivery should be replicated with each pitch. And so, too, should his focus on the target.

Inappropriate thinking distracts a pitcher from all or some of the elements of his approach. Very often, it takes his mind—and eyes—entirely away from his target. Without a narrow focus, his pitches are delivered into an expanded area, one seen with "soft focus" or no focus. If the pitcher sees the target at all, it is with a cloudy vision. The target is fuzzy, rather than sharp.

The same result follows a lazy or casual mental approach. A lack of intensity will take a pitcher's attention away from the target, just as a particular distraction will. (Recall the magnifying glass anecdote. [See INTENSITY]

Two examples can be provided to illustrate the above tendencies.

225

Pat Rapp, when pitching for the Florida Marlins, was having a fine day against the Cincinnati Reds. He had pitched four and two-thirds innings at Joe Robbie Field, and had a 4-0 lead. The third batter in the top of the fifth inning was Dion Sanders. He bunted, and Rapp came off the mound with enough time to make the play and retire Sanders. But he slipped—then grabbed desperately for the ball without being able to come up with it. Sanders was on first. Man on first, two out. No big deal.

Except for the fact that Rapp made a big deal out of it. He was upset with himself for not having made the play and getting five shutout innings—with a lead—"in the book." He then threw 11 consecutive balls. Bases loaded, 3-0 on the hitter. Rapp laid one in the strike zone. Double into the left-field corner. Three runs scored; the manager took Rapp out of the game. He left with a 4-3 lead but was not eligible for the win.

He was furious. The next day, just before stretching, I saw him coming toward me. Before he got close he shouted, "I said everything you always told me to say out there, but it didn't work."

"Let me ask you one question," I said. "What did the target look like while you were going through all that?"

After a long pause, he said with a laugh, "I've got no bleepin' idea."

Rapp had been so unhappy with his failure to field Sanders' bunt, that, in spite of what he was trying to tell himself, he maintained an inappropriate focus—and never saw the target.

The sidework done by pitchers in the bullpen has provided me with many opportunities to point out casual or lazy approaches. Sidework is preparation. Habits are formed by whatever a pitcher does on a regular basis. That is enough ammunition for me.

Many times I have asked a young pitcher to turn around and face away from the catcher. I then asked him the color of the catcher's mitt. Many wrong answers, many correct answers—before some admitting to guesswork. Purposeful sidework should include practicing breathing patterns, mechanical consistency—and picking up the target.

This is a form of rehearsal for a pitcher, as actors have their stage rehearsal. An actor rehearses his lines, his inflection, his stage presence—his entire "delivery"—in the manner he wishes to perform. So, too, does a pitcher rehearse. Picking up the target, one aspect of his performance, requires his conscientious attention.

Joe Sambito made his big league debut for the Houston Astros a while ago—in 1976. For a young pitcher, he had unusually good control—good command. Not the night of his debut. Recalled Sambito, "I was just hoping to throw strikes. I kept telling myself, 'Just throw strikes,' but I couldn't. [See STRIKES] Later I realized what I had done to myself. I didn't have a target. I didn't even think about where I wanted to throw the ball. I was just hoping the ball would go into the strike zone."

"Soft eyes" were mentioned above. In this context, "soft eyes" mean "too soft'" not allowing for sharpness of focus—on the object being attended to. "Hard eyes," in contrast, are "locked up"—causing tension to the muscles in the face, probably a result of tension and/or too high an arousal level.

Not too soft; not too hard. The ideal focus on the target is gained with a relaxed intensity. This means relaxed muscles (including the muscles in the face) and a narrowly directed vision (on the target). Many pitchers are naturally able to bring this focus to their game. Others learn to develop it. Once again, good habits are developed through diligent practice.

Finally, pitch *through* the target, rather than *to* it, meaning aggressively attack the target, rather than steering the ball to it.

What the Pitcher Should Do...

- Understand that the eyes are the muscles' guide, and should be properly used during the delivery of each pitch.
- Develop the habit of "being on target,"—i.e., the catcher's mitt.
- Recognize that distracting, irrelevant thoughts will adversely affect his concentration and "cloud" or obscure his sharp focus on the target.
- Make the necessary adjustment during competition, when he has a sense of divided attention through gathering and self-coaching—off the mound.
- Develop a consistent, disciplined approach to picking up the target during sidework in the bullpen.
- Focus on the target with a relaxed intensity.
- Pitch through the target, rather than to it.

■ TASK AT HAND

The mother of all pitching mantras is "one pitch at a time." Rightly so. The concept brings a pitcher's focus to the most important, immediate, manageable task at hand: the next pitch he will execute.

It has been said that all we have is "the now." The "now" for a pitcher is the very task of delivering his next pitch. All else in a pitcher's head is extraneous, whether it is an historical past or an hysterical future.

Living in and for the moment makes it easier for the pitcher to adapt to situations as they change. His focus is narrow; the requirements are limited to that time and space. All attention is concentrated on delivering the next pitch. He can understand that; he can control that. It is small and elemental. That task at hand is his exclusive concern, and always should be.

In 1983, while interviewing players for *The Mental Game of Baseball*, I spent some time speaking with Wade Boggs in the Boston Red Sox dugout hours before game time. Bruce Hurst, a young pitcher who had won seven games over the past three years with Boston, was sitting nearby.

After I had completed my interview/discussion with Boggs, Hurst came over and said that he had been listening, and that he was interested in talking about "the mental game." "I can use that information," he said. We talked. He was particularly interested in the concept of focusing on one pitch at a time. His concentration had been less than he would have wanted it to be.

Hurst's next start was to be in Anaheim in a couple of days. He would be pitching against Tommy John and was "looking forward to the challenge." He was enthusiastic about following the principle of taking care of the singular task at hand—the execution of the next pitch.

At the end of seven innings in Anaheim, the score was 0-0. In the top of the eighth, the Red Sox scored three runs. The Angels scored five runs off Hurst in the bottom of the eighth. Bob Stanley relieved him. (Boston tied the game in the ninth and won it in extra innings.)

When the team returned to Fenway, I was there, doing more interviews. Hurst greeted me with a guilty smile. "Do you know what happened?" he asked.

"One of three things," I said. "You were focusing on one pitch at a time all game, until you got three runs. Then you went out in the bottom of the eighth thinking either, 'Six more outs and I beat Tommy John,' or 'Two more innings and I have a win,' or 'Two more innings and I have a shut-out.' Which one?" I asked.

"All three," Hurst replied.

He had gone from thinking small to thinking big. From focus on the target and the execution of one pitch, to focus on the unmanageable and distracting future. From process and behavior to result, albeit an imagined "happy" one. Irrelevant to task, nevertheless.

The only life a man can lose is the one he's living at the moment. To forfeit the moment, for a pitcher, is to relinquish his control and ability to effectively accomplish his task. If great wisdom is in knowing what to do next, a pitcher who is attending to anything other than the moment—the next pitch—forfeits his wisdom as well.

Previous topics have also addressed the need for this concentrated attention to task. That concentration, as has been noted, will be pre-potent. It will power the pitcher's mental energy—his mind, his muscles, his eyes—toward the execution of a pitch. Nothing else will matter. Nothing else will intrude on the pitcher's "now."

The greater his ability to establish such focus, the more often he will—naturally and without effort—"be in the zone." Some pitchers will achieve it more naturally than others. But it can be an acquired instinct. The acquisition is through the process of disciplined preparation. Of adopting mantra number one: *carpe momentum.* Seize the moment. Deal exclusively with the task at hand. Execute the next pitch.

That execution is what the pitcher should be thinking about. And talking about—to himself, to the media, to whomever attempts to expand his thinking beyond what is relevant and controllable.

What the Pitcher Should Do...

- Adopt the mantra of *one-pitch-at-a-time*, which is always the pitcher's immediate and essential concern on the mound.
- Understand that whatever other thoughts are in his head during competition diminish his ability to concentrate appropriately on that task.
- Remember that his behavior is within his control; results are not.
- Recognize that he should function in the present—the "now"—rather than fretting about the past or fantasizing about the future. [See YESTERDAY and "X"]

- Reiterate the philosophy of dealing exclusively with the task at hand, especially when media or others wish him to conjecture on matters beyond his control.

■ TEMPO

In 1990, the Oakland Athletics had a good pitcher and an even finer man on their roster. He won 17 games for the A's. But teammates were not enthusiastic about playing behind him when he pitched. His tempo was excruciatingly slow. The games he pitched in seemed interminable. As effective as he had been as a pitcher, the A's sold him to another American League team after the season. The defense was not unhappy.

A slow tempo has infielders playing back on their heels, rather than on their toes. Their concentration, they are very willing to admit, wanders because so much time is taken between pitches.

Beyond that, a slow tempo allows the pitcher time to "think too much" and/or to have his mind wander. His approach does not "flow." Neither does the movement of the game.

Pitchers who slow their tempo also give the impression they do not want to throw the next pitch. Such a reference was made to a pitcher in BODY LANGUAGE. In fact, he did not want to throw that next pitch. He had lost his aggressiveness, and this was evident to everyone watching him, including the opposing hitters. And, perceiving the pitcher to be vulnerable, a hitter bolsters his own confidence and has ample time to "get comfortable." As a result, the hitter, rather than the pitcher, is establishing the tempo. That should not be acceptable to the pitcher.

A steady, regular tempo is desirable. Deliver the pitch; get the ball back from the catcher; get up on the rubber; take the sign; deliver the pitch. That pace keeps hitters from having all the time they wish to get ready. It rivets the pitcher's attention. It dictates the movement of the game. It gives the appearance that the pitcher is control. And, when a pitcher establishes such a tempo, he *is* in control.

A time does comes when pitchers must slow the tempo. Herein lies an issue for many who, when circumstance goes against them, accelerate their tempo.The tendency for many pitchers is to work faster when they are in trouble. They are anxious to extricate themselves from the difficult situation, so they rush. "The faster I work, the sooner this will be over," they are saying to themselves. They "rush." Their thoughts swirl; their muscles tighten; they jump out of their regular delivery. In the process, the difficulty mounts.

A pitcher should realize that when he is in a difficult situation, a situation that requires him to make an adjustment, he must break the tempo that is working against him, get off the mound and gather himself, coach himself, and re-establish the desired tempo.

Pitchers who have told me they were "lost out there," or "numb," or had the sky fall on them "before (they) knew it," neglected—for a variety of reasons—to "stop the bleeding" by breaking the tempo and "taking care of the wound."

Bob Welch, already a Cy Young Award winner, still had a propensity to rush himself when he was annoyed or distracted. An aggressive competitor, Welch could not wait to get the ball back from the catcher and go at the hitter. Literally, he could not wait. A high-energy, hyper-kinetic athlete, Welch would, at times, rush himself into difficulty because of his great desire to attack it.

A particular tendency would show itself at such times. If Welch went 2-0 on a hitter, he too often threw ball three and ball four on consecutive pitches. Being 2-0, he would come down off the front of the mound, reach his arm toward the catcher impatiently waiting for the ball to be returned, get it, and deliver ball three. Repeated act, then ball four. Further annoyance; further distraction. The cycle needed breaking. [See URGENCY]

I discussed with him an idea for changing this pattern, one that included the catcher's participation. Welch, being the open person he is, thought it worth a try. A simple plan was devised. Whenever the count went to 2-0, or whenever he sensed an out-of-control tempo, Steinbach would hold the ball for a moment, rather than immediately returning the ball to the impatient pitcher.

Terry Steinbach, Oakland's relatively inexperienced catcher at the time, laughed when he understood the rationale behind the idea. "You know," he said, "I've been throwing gas on the fire. We're both so competitive, and I see him pumped up out there, so I'm shaking my fist at him, saying, 'Come on, let's go,' and firing the ball back to him, when I should be calming him down."

They both changed their behavior at such times. Welch, standing in front of the mound with his arm extended, would see Steinbach holding the ball, not returning it to the impatient pitcher. A couple of clock ticks later, he would understand the key. Steinbach might sometimes put his palms down, in a calming, slow-down gesture. Welch delivered the next pitch with a greater sense of purpose, rather than with a greater sense of urgency.

There are two ends of a continuum. At one end is the pitcher who works with painstaking and pain-inducing slowness. At the other is the pitcher who is rushing aimlessly through an inning, without regard to the singular requirements of each pitch. The place to be is at the spot where each pitcher establishes a balance. A consistent, steady pace when all is well. An effective deliberation time to correct what is not going well. Break the unfavorable cycle; re-establish a favorable one—one that keeps the game moving, makes the pitcher's aggressiveness evident, keeps his mind on his business, and keeps the defensive players on their collective toes.

What the Pitcher Should Do...

- Understand the advantages and necessity of establishing a good tempo.
- Recognize the effects a poor tempo has on him and the defense.
- Recognize any possible tendency to rush himself, when an inning is beginning to go poorly.
- Know how and when to slow the tempo, in order to gather himself and make necessary adjustments.
- After self-coaching, re-establish the regular tempo, rather than continuously stepping off the mound and delaying the execution of the next pitch.
- Use the catcher, if necessary, to provide keys—gestures or language—as reminders related to appropriate tempo.
- Remember that rushed thinking adversely affects his focus and his mechanics, whereas a consistent and focused approach brings a sense of purpose to each pitch.

■ UMPIRES

God and Satan get together to form a baseball competition, in order to "liven up" the afterlife. Satan, as is his nature, is bragging, expressing his certainty that his team would defeat God's team.

"You can't be serious," God replies. "Don't you know what kind of pitching I have? Among other outstanding pitchers on the staff, I have Cy Young, Walter Johnson, Christy Mathewson, and Don Drysdale," says God. "And now I have Hal Newhouser."

"And *I* have the umpires," answers the devil.

The devil, it has been said, is in the details. And an important understanding a pitcher should have about his game is that the homeplate umpire is an external detail. Umpires, therefore, should be irrelevant to his approach.

The problem posed by umpires is based on pitchers' *responses* to them, as it affects their next approach. I have witnessed pitchers who lost their focus, because they were so affected by umpires they thought were "squeezing" them. Not giving the pitchers strikes they thought they deserved to get.

"He [the umpire] took me out of my game," more than one pitcher has explained to me. My response used to be, "You allowed him to take you out of the game." After a time, my more accurate answer has been, "You took yourself out of your game."

Umpires have been easy excuses for irresponsible pitchers for a long time. Fine umpires do their jobs consistently and effectively. Others are inconsistent. Still others are consistently ineffective. The same is true of pitchers, teachers, and auto mechanics.

What a poor umpire brings to bear on a pitcher is just another test of the pitcher's ability to recognize what he can and cannot control. A test of the pitcher's ability to control himself—his emotions, his focus, his poise.

After a frustrating experience with the calls of a homeplate umpire, young pitchers have appealed their case to me—an eyewitness. I invoke the words my father used when, as a boy, I made such an appeal to him: "You can hope for justice, kid. But don't expect it." Indifferent Fate will not intervene on the pitcher's behalf.

To a pitcher who expresses his frustration to me *during* a similar "bad experience" with an umpire, I simply say: "Shut up, focus, and compete." End of sermon. A pitcher's need for sympathy at this moment, if satisfied, would become a long-term cruelty.

Umpires are part of the environment of the game of baseball. The great umpires from the past declared that they were best doing their jobs when they went unnoticed. The issue is not whether or not that remains the modern-day umpires' agenda. The issue is that pitchers must adhere to that agenda: the umpire should go unnoticed.

Many external distractions can be found in the environment of the baseball world. The umpire is right there behind homeplate. If the pitcher cannot adequately deal with a possible distraction that is so immediate, proximate and repeated, he need not be concerned with any others. He will be out of "his" game—and out of *the* game.

The most successful pitchers are pro-active, rather than re-active. They attack the strike zone, rather than reacting to the person who may determine it on a given call. On a given day.

What the Pitcher Should Do...

- Understand that ideals in this world, in this case an umpire's ball-strike calls being consistently "accurate," are not to be expected.
- Understand that an umpire's call is one of the many things the pitcher cannot control.
- Realize that the response of frustration over a call will impede the effective mental set that helps him execute the next pitch.
- When frustrated by circumstances involving the umpire, get off the mound, gather himself and go through all the procedures of self-coaching—required at that time, because of that circumstance.

- Remember that nothing or no one can "take his focus away" without his consent.
- Remember, as well, that his efficacy as a competitor is evidenced by his self-discipline, not by self-destructive behavior.

■ URGENCY

Conventional wisdom speaks to the point that athletes perform better when they are in a relaxed state. This view is supported by much research on the topic. [See RELAXATION] A sense of urgency, so common in pitchers, is the antithesis of relaxation. At best, a pitcher's urgency inhibits his ability to function well. At worst, it makes him dysfunctional.

A feeling of urgency can have as many causes as there are pitchers. Each individual brings his perspective and needs to the mound during every outing. If one pitcher feels the need to do well to "save his job," he can manifest this need by "trying too hard." If another is pitching a "must game" for his team, his urgent response will work at cross-purposes with his intention—"to win the big one." He will "try too hard," becoming too aggressive and less controlled.

As mentioned previously, some pitchers have a sense of urgency kick in as soon as they fall behind in the count—or put men on base—or have runs scored against them. They always seem to be pitching to "get something back," governed by a vague perception of having lost something. What has actually been lost is their good approach.

This excessive concern or worry or fear produces the same symptoms: a loss of a controlled mental and mechanical pattern. Desperation sets in, and thoughts become disjointed and scattered. Muscles tighten, the delivery quickens.

A relaxed state speaks to the pitcher by saying, "Be easy, trust it, stay on task, let it flow." Urgency speaks another language: "Hurry up, force it, I'd better ..."

The "language of maladjustment" was mentioned in SELF-TALK. It is not difficult for the reader to recognize the distinction between the language patterns above. One expression is conducive to adjustment and an effective approach to performance, the other to maladjustment and an ineffective approach. A sense of urgency rushes a pitcher's thoughts toward judgments related to consequences. His concentration and muscles follow those thoughts—all going in the wrong direction.

Urgency is "I have to" and "I must." Urgency is tension and fear. Urgency is "or else." Urgency is "do or die."

Urgency induces loss of control, loss of purpose, loss of balance, loss of focus, loss of tempo, loss of trust—to name a few losses. Illustrative behavior can be seen just about every day, in just about every game. It happens, to varying degrees, to just about every pitcher. The greater the sense of urgency, the greater the loss of all the elements of a good pitching approach.

Real crisis tests mental discipline. Perceived crisis tests the pitcher's view of the world and of himself. Whichever tests him, a controlled behavior helps him to pass. Urgent behavior induces failure.

The passing "test key" is a reaffirmation of a healthy point of view and a renewed understanding of what works and what does not work on the mound. First, a pitcher who performs with a heightened sense of urgency has made everything "matter too much." The "or-else syndrome" takes over. Dire consequences are always close to his surface thinking. A healthier perspective is required.

Second, the pitcher, having gone through the experience of performing at this high level of urgency, understands its power over him. He must further understand what measures he should take to transfer that power. In my experience with pitchers, this has been done with constant and frequent reiteration of a desired approach. The "brainwashing" referred to in earlier pages. [See MANTRA]

Daily work on mental discipline and preparation helps train the pitcher to A) establish a healthier, more effective approach, and B) to recognize when it breaks down during competition and to make an adjustment. This, rather than allowing the urgency to "cut off his head," and have him pitch like the proverbial chicken.

Finally, regular relaxation exercises are appropriate for a pitcher who regularly performs with a feeling of urgency. Philosophy deals with the issue; techniques deal with the symptoms. An urgent pitcher should deal with both.

What the Pitcher Should Do…

- Understand that a sense of urgency will take him out of the relaxed state that helps him to maximize his ability.
- Recognize the causes of urgent behavior and work at developing a more realistic perspective.
- Reiterate and/or review his philosophy of effective pitching on a daily basis.
- During competition, be aware of any tendency to accelerate his tempo and rush his delivery.

- Make the necessary adjustments at such times, gathering himself, slowing his thought process, using calming self-talk and refocusing on task.
- Use the catcher to help him with keys or triggers when urgent behavior is evident.
- According to need, develop a routine for using relaxing exercises and techniques.
- Re-read RELAXATION.

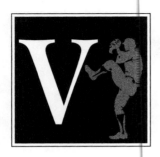

■ VISUALIZATION [See APPENDIX A]

Visualization is the technique of recalling information in images and physical forms, rather than in language. Some people learn more effectively with their eyes than with their ears. With others, the opposite is true. My approach is to present the concept and process to players, allow them to see how simple the procedure is, and encourage them to give it a try. The rest is up to them. The reader should allow himself the same opportunity, an opportunity for "mental rehearsal."

The first and most obvious value of visualization is in the fact that it can be utilized away from the field. On a living room chair or reclining in bed. Each provides an environment for using the technique.

Having recognized the ability to "rehearse" away from the field, the pitcher can be further encouraged to use the practice by knowing that research has found mental practice often to be more useful than physical practice. Stories abound to verify these studies, including the one about a POW who had never played "actual" golf in his life, but who spent years playing "visualized" golf—36 holes a day—to make his days in captivity more tolerable. When he became a free man, he also became a very respectable golfer. Immediately. His mental rehearsal had prepared him well.

Athletes who conscientiously prepare for performance wish to include some form of visualization in their program. Prerequisite for its successful use is that the player understand what makes visualization work and that he then believes in its value for him. Some pitchers are initially skeptical about their ability to visualize. I simply ask them to recall what they were wearing at their wedding or their senior prom. "What was your wife/date wearing?" I then ask. And I ask for other details. That data, stored in the subconscious, is easily recalled by the player.

His conscious mind determined that this information was significant to him, and he filed it for future reference, should it be needed. Sensory experience was thereby registered at the conscious level and stored at the unconscious level. "Memory in pictures," I tell them to simplify the idea, sparing them an explanation of Karl Albrecht's definition. Visualization, he wrote in *Brain Power*, is "all non-verbal thought forms that [the] brain organizes into a spatial pattern, *not just a mental picture*." (Emphasis mine.)

The POW who played "mental golf" had pictures of people swinging golf clubs in his memory bank. He had observed, therefore he had the images. His eyes had seen golf being played, his conscious mind stored the images for future reference, and he recalled them when he "needed" them. He was able to "re-create" dog legs to the right, dog legs to the left, water hazards, sand traps, and a good golf swing. He had these pictures, though he had not had the physical experience.

Pitchers *have* had the physical experience, and therefore have kinetic memory, as well as visual memory. Another experiential advantage. Visualization will help the pitcher to program his nervous system and his muscles. And, as noted, he has an experiential reference point to assist him in "getting it right," especially in regard to mechanics.

Joyous or traumatic memories are so vivid that the emotions from those moments are often reproduced—an example of memory controlling muscles and nervous system. This power can be utilized before the fact. The pitcher sees himself participating in the event—the game or the singular pitch. He can mentally simulate crowd noise, tension level, circumstance. Called subjective visualization, this technique allows the pitcher to include and adjust his emotions within the experience. (Being a spectator is objective visualization.) He then directs his intentions with self-talk. "Good slider here, down and away." And he sees the execution of that pitch.

The pitcher decides whether this is done at the kitchen table or behind the mound. Jack Nicklaus claimed he visualized every golf shot he took before he took it. But the movement and time between golf shots allows for that. The pace of a baseball game does not—on a regular basis.

My recommendation to pitchers is that they rehearse either the night before they pitch (starters) or in the clubhouse before each game (relievers). "When your head hits the pillow, use the next 10 minutes for putting in a tape of your best performances," I tell pitchers. "See yourself kicking butt, establishing good tempo, putting the ball just where you want it. You'll usually fall asleep with the tape still playing."

In 1991, a youngster, Gavin Osteen, was pitching for Huntsville, Oakland's Double-A team in the Southern League. The team was playing in Greenville, and Osteen and I were shagging in the outfield. Ryan Klesko was playing with Greenville that year, and the previous time Osteen had faced him, Klesko hit the ball hard in every at-bat. Two doubles and a home run, if I recall correctly. In any case, Osteen was concerned about facing Klesko the next night.

Knowing that Osteen was very effective in his use of the visualization process, I asked him why he was so concerned after one bad game against Klesko. "Aren't you preparing by visualizing good location and execution?" I asked. A long and pregnant pause followed the question. Then he responded, "My gosh, that's what's bothering me. I've been visualizing, but I keep seeing the pictures of balls going off the wall every time I deliver a pitch to him [Klesko]. I've got the wrong pictures working."

That night Osteen processed the right pictures. A left-handed pitcher, he struck out the left-handed hitting Klesko three times the following night. Klesko has been a major league player for a number of years; Osteen, at this writing is still in Triple A. So this is not meant to be a "Jack Armstrong" story. But it is simply a true one—about mental rehearsal, not relative physical talent.

Visualization requires concentration. A pitcher who begins the process and soon loses interest will not benefit from an activity he cannot sustain. Just as every concentration exercise requires mental discipline, so too does every visualization exercise. It should be clear that visualization serves more than one master.

Many exercises can be used to develop and practice the technique, through observation, imagination, invention, and recall. A keen observer sees much. When entering a hotel/motel room in which he has never been, the pitcher should notice the spatial relationship of the furniture, the window and door locations, anything unusual about the room. He should be attentive to detail, observing all, rather than just being another "piece of furniture" in the room. He should see colors (bed spread, picture on wall), feel texture (curtains), smell fragrances (wood, room freshener). He should "get the picture."

A different setting can be invented. The pitcher can sit and visualize himself water skiing, riding a horse, playing golf, or eating a favorite meal at a restaurant. The accompanying sights and sounds should be included. And smells. And tastes.

The pitcher can imagine finding a gemstone in his travel bag, for example. He senses its color, observes its size, and feels its texture.

He can recall past events and recreate the setting and images he has retained at a lower level of consciousness. A gathering of friends, a skiing experience. A wedding or prom, as mentioned above. Some special visit during childhood. Any vivid recollection will serve.

The above are examples of exercises that can be helpful in developing a pitcher's ability to create and sustain visual images. Their ultimate value is in the developing and enhancing of the pitcher's ability to "see" himself perform—to visualize the execution of effective pitches.

Don Carman, who pitched in the big leagues with the Phillies and the Texas Rangers, developed a "picture" of an alley, much like the gutter on the side of a bowling lane. The alley went from his release point to the desired location of the pitch. "I just put the ball in the alley," Carman would say. Simple and clear to him. The hitter was irrelevant to him, as was the case with Carman's Hall-of-Fame teammate with the Phillies, Steve Carlton, a master at visualizing—and pitching.

The pitcher himself will learn whether he is able to utilize visualization during competition. Visualization off the field is certainly easier to master and manage. As in every case, the pitcher will make his choice. A good understanding allows for a better ability to make that choice.

What the Pitcher Should Do...

- Understand the concept and purpose of visualization.
- Understand the technique used to visualize.
- Understand the value of visualization.
- Do practice exercises in order to enhance his ability to visualize effective performance.
- Utilize and further develop his sensory abilities through keen observation, imagination, invention, and recall.
- Visualize peak performance from his past, seeing himself in "flow" experiences of delivery and execution (possibly "feeling" the muscles and emotion during that performance).
- Incorporate mental rehearsal into regular preparation program.

■ WARRIOR

In 1992, I read a book written by Oriana Fallaci entitled, *A Man*. A passage struck me at the time. It referred to the protagonist, who was a political prisoner. The major part of the passage follows:

"...[T]he true hero never surrenders ... [H]e is distinguished from the others not by the great initial exploit or the pride with which he faces tortures and death but the constancy with which he repeats himself, the patience with which he suffers and reacts, the pride with which he hides his sufferings and flings them back in the face of the one who has ordered them. Not resigning himself is his secret, not considering himself a victim, not showing others his sadness or despair..." Exploiting whatever psychological weapons are at his disposal, the author added.

Just last week, seven years after having read Fallaci's work, I completed John Katzenbach's, *Hart's War*, which included the following: "It is easier to guard a man who thinks himself as a prisoner than it is to guard a man who thinks of himself as a warrior." Though the above references are to politics and war, the descriptions speak to my view of a baseball warrior, as well. A warrior pitcher. "A man."

The subject of competitive spirit has already appeared in earlier pages. As have the topics of aggressiveness, relentlessness, and control. So spending time writing about warriors seemed unnecessary to me, until I considered how much the term is used in the game of baseball. And in athletic competition, in general.

Most recently, Dodgers general manager Kevin Malone used the term to describe Kevin Brown and used it as a rationale for the rich contract he gave Brown. The same label was attached to Roger Clemens, when he went from Toronto to the New York Yankees. People in both organizations called Clemens a "true warrior." Baseball people use the term glowingly but sparingly. They say things such as, "This guy will find a way to beat you." "This guy will leave it all on the field." "This guy will gut it out." "This guy will always take the ball." (My own minor adjustment to that statement is that a warrior doesn't only "take the ball," he "always wants the ball.")

Scientist Louis Pasteur attributed his success not to his brain, but to his "tenacity." It is this tenacious approach which truly distinguishes a great competitor from a mediocre one. Red Sox pitcher Pedro Martinez speaks of his approach in such terms and recognizes the ball as a weapon. Martinez speaks of using his fastball to intimidate hitters, hoping to cause what Sun Tzu, in THE ART OF WAR, called "psychological dislocation" of the opponent. Warrior talk.

All this considered, one should have an idea of what behavior is characteristic in a pitcher who is considered to be a warrior. To serve that purpose, a list is provided. These traits are integrated into behavior, irrespective of circumstance, adverse or favorable. The behaviors begin with the first pitch and are manifested until the last pitch has been thrown.

- Courage
- Intensity
- Competitiveness
- Consistency of focus
- Confrontational attitude
- Aggressiveness under control
- Relentlessness
- Responsibility to do what the situation requires
- Responsibility for own behavior
- Honesty
- Self-sacrifice—a commitment to the team's agenda
- Self-trust
- Ability to make necessary adjustments
- Positive approach to task and circumstance
- Mental discipline
- Ability to cope effectively with adversity
- Indifference to hitters' presence or posturing
- Ability to "do what needs to be done"

Not all-inclusive, to be sure. But just as surely, a pitcher who "checks off" all of the above as being representative of his own 'make-up' and approach qualifies as a warrior—and a winner.

Is anyone *always* the consummate warrior. I think not. Perfection may be desirable, but it is not attainable. Its pursuit, if realistically approached, can help a pitcher to enact the desired behavior more consistently and more emphatically.

Certain warriors come to mind, other than the ones noted throughout the book. My own stated favorite was Bob Gibson. I also admired the tenacity of Don Drysdale and Dave Stewart. Current candidates include Todd Stottlemyre, who is not a quiet warrior. And Mike Mussina, who is.

In a 1999 confrontation with Kevin Brown and the Dodgers, Phillies pitcher Curt Schilling faced a bases loaded, no out situation. Twice he went 3-0 on batters, and twice he came back to strike them out. The Dodgers did not score. Schilling and the Phillies won the game.

After the game, a reporter asked the pitcher whether he would have been happy to get out of the inning with only one run scoring, what with the two 3-0 counts he had reached, and so on.

Schilling responded, "I concede nothing. I wasn't looking to give up any run, even with a 3-0 count. Nothing will happen until I throw the ball, and I won't give in on any pitch."

Spoken like a warrior.

Warriors do not always win. But they reveal their identity to their opponents as pitchers who, if they do not stand as winners of a particular game, have "gone down fighting"—while still standing as "winners" in the competitive arena of baseball. Those pitchers are mentally unconquerable.

Confucius' suggested that "he who conquers himself is the mightiest warrior." One issue comes to mind, based on my experience with warrior-like pitchers. They want the ball, and they take the ball, as established. But sometimes, they should not have the ball. Too many pitchers have damaged themselves by "sucking it up" and pitching hurt, with a hurt that caused (further?) physical injury. Some intelligence is required. Ego and excessive pride are not helpful to the pitcher. A trainer and physician are. Conquering the self includes conquest of all the emotional factors that lead a pitcher to poor decision making. A fallen warrior cannot do battle. An aspiring warrior must beware. The "weapons at his disposal" when he is hurting are honesty and courage. The courage to tell the necessary truth and deal with the consequences—his inability to take the ball at that time.

What the Pitcher Should Do...

- Recognize the advantages of warrior-like behavior in any competition.
- Be aware of the traits and behaviors that define a warrior-pitcher.
- Understand that his ability to be self-actualizing is prerequisite for effectively competing at an optimum level.
- Work at integrating positive, warrior-like behaviors into his pitching approach.
- Remember that the development of desirable traits and habits is a process, requiring consistent monitoring and conscientious effort.
- Know that warriors, who tend to "do too much," must maintain self- control.
- Understanding this, recognize that pitching with pain may cause physical damage.
- Share the decision-making responsibility related to physical injury with trained professionals.
- Be rational, keeping his ego out of all decision-making processes.

■ WILL

Will is power. Will is determination and resolve. It is the imposing of desire onto behavior. Many value it; not that many exert it.

A study of people who made New Year's resolutions was conducted quite a few years back. I remember some of the findings. Enough to support the statement above. In the large "study group" of those who pronounced their intention to enact specific changes in their behavior, 25 percent abandoned their resolutions after two weeks had past. Fifty percent "gave in" after three months. All they seemed to have was what Saul Bellow called "a warehouse of intentions."

The intentions, unfortunately, were more strongly expressed than the peoples' resolve. "Men are distinguished by the power of their wanting," wrote novelist Barry Unsworth. Their wanting, without will, achieved little or nothing.

The undistinguished behavior of broken resolutions is "normal." But it is a normalcy other than what elite athletes seek for themselves. Ordinary people have, as Durant wrote in *The Reconstruction of Character*, "a thousand wishes but no will." Ordinariness is not a goal of pitchers who wish to excel.

"Warrior" is the person—the athlete; will is his psychological weapon. The designation of an individual as a "tough pitcher" is a reference not to his physical capacity, but, rather, to an indomitable will. Most of the misfortunes a pitcher faces during competition are a result, I believe, of weakness of will. He has gone into battle with a blunt weapon—or with no weapon at all. The strong determination a pitcher has for "getting it right" connects him to his appropriate concentration. As it does to positivism, aggressiveness, and all the other traits and behaviors he values. The expression, "He wills himself to win," speaks to that point.

Even when a pitcher's internal system is invaded by self-doubt or fear, his determination enables him to disregard these intruders. He redirects thoughts and immediately regains control of his approach and performance. Self-control requires a strong expression of will.

Much has been written about people who have performed remarkable feats because of their expression of will. An anecdote is provided in *The Mental Game of Baseball* telling about a European pistol shooter who was favored to win a gold medal in the 1968 Olympics. A year before the games, he lost his right hand (his shooting hand) in an accident and disappeared from public view. People presumed his despondency and a desire for seclusion. He reappeared before the games, now shooting with his left hand. He won a gold medal.

A story of Native American origin tells of the ordeals an adolescent boy is required to face and conquer before his tribe considered him to be a man. A long, solitary walk was one of the requirements. Five miles. Before he departed, an elder would tell him, "If you can walk five, walk six." After a will becomes strong—it becomes insistent.

"When will is as taut as a bowstring, the ant can overcome the lion." An African tribe's "lesson" to their boys with "manly" aspirations.

Cancer patients have offered many examples of the assertion of will extending life, as opposed to resignation—"giving up"—assuring death. More often than a "normal" person thinks, he is able to take himself beyond that norm. With will power. Tour de France winner Lance Armstrong beat the disease and all other opposition in 1999.

FIRST INNING addressed pitchers who are "hopers." Hopers want good things to happen to them. "Doers" take responsibility for making things happen. The difference relates to the statistics of failure in people who make "resolutions." Most were probably hopers. Goal-setters are more likely to be people who establish what they want and hold themselves accountable for getting it.

The goals I most value for pitchers are behavior goals, for the very reason that the individual has complete control over these goals and can impose his will daily, working to achieve what he wants. The "power" Unsworth spoke of above. [See APPENDIX B]

The ability to think appropriate thoughts during competition and to behave in a way that is compatible with his understanding of what is required distinguishes the ordinary pitcher from the exceptional. His thoughts and focus and right decisions are part of a man's act of choice. When he makes the right choices, a pitcher senses the control he has over himself and his performance. The resultant self-confidence rests on the foundation of a confidence he has in the power of his mind. Such a pitcher is much more capable of "doing what it takes."

Certainly, as has been mentioned many times, the development of this mental discipline is an arduous, trying, and exhausting process. It is many cultures' right of passage from boyhood to manhood. For baseball pitchers, the metaphorical passage is from soldier to warrior. An implacable will can make all the difference.

What the Pitcher Should Do...

- Be aware of the power of a strong will as it imposes itself on behavior.
- Understand that ordinary people most often express intentions without expressing the resolve required for those intentions to become reality.
- Re-establish his broad goal of being extraordinary, rather than ordinary.
- Be certain his specific goals are expressed in behavioral terms, allowing for their achievement through his determination and daily attention.
- Recognize that the expression of a strong will affects all aspects of his pitching approach in a positive way.
- Remember that self-improvement as a person and as an athlete is a process, an arduous one for those who are determined and persistent.

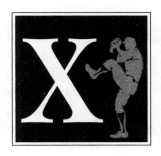

■ "X"

"X"—the 24th letter in the alphabet. In *The American Heritage Dictionary* it is defined as "any unknown ... factor (or) thing ..." As students learn in algebra class.

The future is an unknown. It is the pitcher's "x".. It will remain so for him—and everyone else—until it is revealed in the immediate present, by actually becoming the "now." The "now" is what the pitcher can know, can manage and can address. His musings on the future are surely distracting and potentially anxiety producing. That unknown, wrote H.L. Mencken, "sits...calmly licking its chops," ready to devour the pitcher who has lost his way—who has strayed from the path of the next pitch he is to deliver.

As has been said, the "now" is all a pitcher truly has. What he does with it will determine the extent of his effectiveness. Past and future must not intrude. [See YESTERDAY] The pitch about to be delivered is the most important pitch he will ever throw. That is the viewpoint he should bring to it. Having done that, he then focuses on the next pitch, the new "now." Then, and only then, on the one after that.

In such a progression, the irrelevant unknown becomes the relevant known. The "x" is no longer "x." It has been transformed by action, not by time. The action was the delivery of the previous pitch.

So the pitcher will always have an identifiable "now" to deal with. He need not and should not deal with the "x-factor." Because he cannot—except in his distracted mind.

The reader might wish to review the anecdote in TASK AT HAND, telling of Red Sox pitcher, Bruce Hurst, and his distraction with the unmanageable future. Hurst's focus went from a focus on one pitch at a time to entertaining possibilities two innings into the future.

One young pitcher minor league pitcher I had been talking with in 1984, a Double-A pitcher in the Cincinnati organization, strayed just two pitches into the future. The unknown was lurking there as well, "licking its chops."

The day after his relief appearance, he approached me and revealed what "had happened" to him during the previous night's game. He explained that, after having taken the sign for the next pitch, he brought a thought and picture into his mind and his "mind's eye." They were related to the pitch that would follow the one he was about to execute. "I was about to throw a fastball inside—move the guy off the plate. Then I saw myself throwing a slider away after that—while I'm on the rubber! I was thinking about that slider when I threw the fastball. It was away, where I wanted the slider to be. He [the right-handed hitter] smoked it against the wall in right," the pitcher said.

"But I'll tell you something," he continued. "At that very moment, it kicked in. I mean I really understood the idea of one-pitch-at-a-time. I understood right out there what had happened to me. I was thinking way ahead of myself."

"Way ahead" is a relative term. But one pitch ahead is still enough ahead to qualify as an "x factor"—the distracting unknown and irrelevant future.

Aeschylus wrote 2,400 years ago (in "Agamemnon"), "The future / you shall know when it has come; before then, forget it." Better yet, ignore it before it needs "forgetting."

For all of us, there will not always be a future. But there will always be a present. A pitcher should devote himself to that "now" during competition. It is what he has, what he knows, and what he is responsible to be attentive to.

What the Pitcher Should Do...

- Understand that the future is beyond his recognition and control.
- Realize that his ability to effectively perform is reduced by a focus on the unknown future, rather than the manageable "now."

- Understand that "one-pitch-at-a-time" is a mantra specifically used to direct attention to his most important approach—the exclusive focus on the immediate task at hand.
- Realize that the regular tempo and flow of his game is enhanced or diminished by his ability or inability to maintain a disciplined focus on the "now."
- Monitor and evaluate this ability during and after each performance.
- Make necessary mental adjustments to his focus during competition through awareness and the use of gathering and self-coaching techniques.
- Know that the future will become the present through his actions, which always take place in the present.
- Determine, therefore, to have his mind and actions always functioning in the same time zone.

■ YESTERDAY

Yesterday can be a help or a hindrance. It is helpful to those who learn from it and then "let it go." It hinders those who dwell on it and thereby distract themselves from the needs of the present.

"Yesterday," in my use of the term with pitchers, is defined as any time before the present. What is over and completed is "yesterday." The players might say, "It's history," but I prefer "yesterday," as in "I can't get yesterday's [bad] game out of my head." A previous pitch, hit out the ballpark by the batter, can be an indelible memory—as he approaches the next pitch. "It's a more immediate and damaging yesterday," I tell pitchers. "But still a yesterday."

If "today is to be yesterday's pupil," as Thomas Fuller thought it should be, the prospect depends as much on the pupil's ability to learn as on the "teacher's" ability to instruct. My initial introduction of the subject to pitchers is to present two homilies about "yesterdays"; "Use it, or it will use you." And, "Use it, then lose it."

The past has value in that it can provide information to the pitcher, giving him the opportunity to learn and make necessary adjustments. Mistakes are vehicles for learning. Again, the lessons are there, but will the pitcher seek answers or be mired in his misery over having made mistakes? [See ADVERSITY and RESPONSE]

A pitcher is able to properly use the past if he has asked himself, "What was I trying to do? What went wrong? What do I want to do next time?" And then answers these questions. The quicker he is able to follow this process, the quicker he is able to rid himself of the past. "Lose it."

254

Dwelling on the past is as common as trying to conjure up an unknown future. Perfectionists, and there are many pitchers who proclaim themselves as such—with either false pride or dismay—tend to punish themselves with the past. Any mistake is given longer life by being dragged along into the pitcher's present. (Perfectionists tend to see "mistakes" where no realistic pitcher would, intensifying the issue of "letting it go.")

The understanding of tending to business in the "now" must gain power over past behaviors and outcomes. The pitcher who gives more power to the past does not usually learn from it. That is what is meant by, "It will use you." The past controls the pitcher's thought patterns and diminishes his ability to focus on matters of the moment. "Yesterday" is alive, though not well, in his head. A distraction, to say the least. At worst, an obsessive thought, which can lead to dysfunction.

D.H. Lawrence wished the past would "decently bury itself, instead of sitting waiting to be admired by the present." Pitchers usually agonize, rather than admire the past which, unfortunately, will always be sitting and waiting, just as Mencken's future always "sits calmly…licking its chops."

Past and future are brought into the present only as mental images and imaginings. The fact that "X" and YESTERDAY are consecutively presented in the book is helpful, in that the emphasis on the valued present can be reiterated through the juxtaposed devaluing of the before and after.

All pitchers' yesterdays should be appropriately summarized in his todays, and all his tomorrows are his to shape—as they become the "now."

"This only is denied even to God: the power to undo the past." (Aristotle) Available to all is the power to use it well.

What the Pitcher Should Do…

- Understand that the past can be useful or harmful, depending on his connection to it.
- Understand that the past provides him with the opportunity to learn from it.
- Understand that dwelling on the past is a distraction and inhibitor of present performance.
- Develop the ability to recognize what adjustments are called for during competition, through a quick assessment of what caused a past mistake.

- Develop, then, the habit of jettisoning these past mistakes from his mind.
- Focus on the moment during competition by redirecting thoughts related to past events and behaviors, using gathering and self-coaching techniques.
- Realize the choice and power to control his focus are his to make and use.

■ ZEROS

Zeros are the ultimate result goal. Their value is apparent to everyone, as is the fact that a pitcher who puts up only zeros on the scoreboard will never lose. Still, zeros are ends, not means. Because of *this* fact, a pitcher's focus on zeros during competition is not appropriate. That focus does not direct him to present task, but rather to future outcome. Desired outcome, that is. The more divided the pitcher's attention is, the less likely he will achieve that desired outcome.

Putting zeros on the scoreboard is a what-to-do. Executing one pitch at a time is the how-to-do-it. Whether the zero is desired in the first inning, the fifth inning, a shutdown inning, or a closer's save inning, the approach is the same. This has been reiterated many times in these pages. And it comes down to this final topic—the zero as ultimate result—as an opportunity to provide a final reiteration. Execute the next pitch!

The persistence with which a pitcher approaches the development of his ability to have pre-potent concentration on his immediate task will be a factor in the enhancement of his performance. It has all been said.

And it all is related to the difficulties a pitcher must understand and overcome and the philosophy and behaviors he develops. In this regard, his effective mental approach will facilitate his efforts to perform well. Clear-headed focus will help him put up an abundance of zeros. By thinking small, keeping it simple.

Chekhov wrote, "If many remedies are prescribed for an illness, you may be certain that illness has no cure." The "remedy" advocated in these pages is a singular one: stay on task by focusing on the "now"—the execution of the next pitch. The zeros will come.

What the Pitcher Should Do...

- Execute that next pitch.
- Trust that zeros will come, because of his effective approach and trust in his talent.
- Know his ABC's [See ALL PRECEDING PAGES]

■ APPENDIX A

The purpose of this page is to provide the reader with access to additional information related to topics treated in this book. Because of the nature and purpose of the book, these topics have not been presented as broadly or in the same manner here as in my previous book, *The Mental Game of Baseball*. There they have been more fully developed as chapters. The topics are listed below as they appeared in that book's Table of Contents, should the reader desire further reference to them. (They are in alphabetical order here.)

- ATTITUDES

- DEDICATION

- CONCENTRATION

- CONFIDENCE

- GOALS

- LEARNING

- MENTAL DISCIPLINE

- PREPARATION

- RELAXATION

- VISUALIZATION

Many related sub-topics are more specifically treated in the *ABC's* book. An example: COURAGE and WILL are more developed here than in *The Mental Game of Baseball*, where they are mentioned in the chapter on MENTAL DISCIPLINE.

■ APPENDIX B

Listed here are goals of behavior and attitude. They are all within the control of the pitcher. Result goals are not. A pitcher who trusts his talent and commitment will be able to devote himself regularly to the development of routines and habits that are conducive to effective performance.

The list is not to be considered all-inclusive. Pitchers will be able to think of other goals related to their individual needs. Setting these specific goals—and monitoring his attempts to reach them—allows a pitcher to be attentive to his own strengths and weaknesses. Behavior goals provide purpose and direction. Just as a pitcher should focus on executing one pitch at a time, so should he work on one goal at a time. He should establish his own list of needs and priorities and work diligently at mastery, before moving to the next goal. Establishing those priorities is an initial act.

His dedication to excellence will determine the level of behavior and achievement he will reach. Elite athletes, by definition, have exceptional habits, which are tools of an effective worker.

■ GOALS

To develop:

- an aggressive mentality (challenging hitters)
- an effective intensity level (aggressiveness under control)
- consistent focus and concentration on the target and task at hand
- a steady tempo and flow
- an ability to recognize adverse settings, thoughts and behaviors and make the necessary adjustments (gathering & self-coaching)
- poise (utilizing positive self-talk, breathing patterns, good body language, consistent behavior on the rubber, appropriate responses)
- ability to visualize effectively
- a positive and realistic attitude toward self and the game

To:

- be consistent in throwing first-pitch strikes
- get outs early in the count by forcing contact

- establish the count in my favor
- finish hitters when ahead in the count
- have good ball-strike ratio
- develop ability to effectively locate pitches (good focus on intended target)
- have a consistent preparation routine
- treat all situations consistently (focus on behavior and purpose, rather than on possible consequences)
- field position well
- hold runners effectively

A key to the pitcher's success will be his ability to be self-instructive, rather than self-critical. Making excuses for mistakes should have no place in his attitude or program. Neither should self-punishment because of mistakes or temporary inability to achieve a goal. Growth, it has been said so often, is a process. His determination to "stay with it" is critical. Will power is real power.

About the Author

Harvey A. Dorfman's background has been in education as a teacher, counselor, coach, and consultant. He has a Master's Degree in Communications/Psychology and is most knowledgeable about baseball and the factors necessary for success in the game. He was employed from 1984 through 1993 as the Oakland A's full-time instructor/counselor and from 1994 through 1997 with the Florida Marlins. He joined the Tampa Bay Devil Rays in the same capacity in 1998. In 1999 Dorfman became full-time sport psychology consultant for the Scott Boras Corporation. He lectures extensively on sports psychology, management and leadership training, and personal development. He has, as well, been a consultant to the Vancouver Canucks and the New York Islanders of the NHL, and to a number of major universities. In addition, he has experience as a newspaper columnist and freelance journalist, writing for *The New York Times*, *Boston Globe*, and *Miami Herald*, among others. In 1989, his first book, *The Mental Game of Baseball: A Guide to Peak Performance*, co-authored with Karl Kuehl, was released. Published by Diamond Communications, Inc., this bestselling book is considered to be the classic guide to developing the mental mechanics of the game.

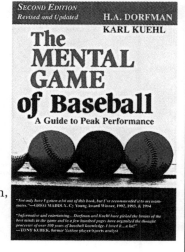